JELLY ROLL,
BIX, AND HOAGY

JELLY ROLL, BIX, AND HOAGY

Gennett Studios

AND THE

•

Birth of Recorded Jazz

Rick Kennedy

Indiana University Press Bloomington & Indianapolis

This book is a publication of

Indiana University Press
601 North Morton Street
Bloomington, IN 47404-3797 USA

http://www.indiana.edu/~iupress

Telephone orders 800-842-6796
Fax orders 812-855-7931
E-mail orders iuporder@indiana.edu

Jacket illustration by Jim Callaway
Frontispiece: Gennett Records logo on a dilapidated
Starr Piano building (*Jim Callaway*)

Library of Congress Cataloging-in-Publication Data

Kennedy, Rick, ate.
Jelly Roll, Bix, and Hoagy : Gennett Studios and the birth of
recorded jazz / Rick Kennedy.
p.   cm.
Includes bibliographical references and index.
ISBN 0-253-33136-6 (cloth : alk. paper)
1. Starr Piano Company. Gennett Record Division. 2. Sound recording
industry—United States. 3. Jazz—History and criticism.
I. Title.
ML3792.K45   1994
781.64'09772'63—dc20   93-23970
ISBN 0-253-21315-0 (paper : alk. paper)

3 4 5 6 7 04 03 02 01 00 99

CNTENTS

5.
Yet the Music Lives On   192

Illustrations

Foreword

by Steve Allen

Most books based on historical research appeal only to those who already have an interest in the basic subject matter. Rick Kennedy's study of a now-obscure Indiana record company, by way of contrast, is so inherently fascinating that even those who have heretofore evidenced no particular interest in American cultural history, and even those with no special involvement with jazz, will be stimulated by the combination of the many cultural and social threads the book weaves together.

From this remarkable account one learns not only a great deal of the origins of the now gargantuan record industry, but about our national patterns of migration, about the roots of the modern American economy, and about the U.S. contribution to the Industrial Revolution itself.

As a traveling concert entertainer, I have noted how similar many Midwestern communities are. So many factories surrounded by farms, so many nineteenth-century self-made millionaires and their surviving descendants—who still tend to dominate their local scenes, sometimes distinguishing themselves for their philanthropic contributions and interest in the arts and education.

Given that jazz itself is the only art form ever created in America, *Jelly Roll, Bix, and Hoagy* must be considered required reading for anyone with an even casual interest in the history of American popular music. Many separate audiences will find Kennedy's study of particular interest. Those who care about the background of popular music will consider it a treasure, as will those who care only about jazz.

It's also highly recommended for African Americans concerned with their special cultural history. One of the sadder aspects of the current general national ignorance is that many of today's black teenagers are unfamiliar even with such giants as Count Basie, Duke Ellington, and Louis Armstrong. The number who have never even heard of Jelly Roll Morton, about whom Kennedy provides a great deal of information, is depressing enough.

Although the Gennett Company released now historically important material by Duke Ellington, Fletcher Henderson, Louis Armstrong, and other giants, Gennett was by no means a purely jazz label. Lawrence Welk and Guy Lombardo also recorded for them, as did many other nonjazz dance bands, and the company's importance in being the first to record many pioneer country-and-western artists is also impressive.

Even though my childhood was spent largely in Chicago, which meant I was familiar with country radio station WLS, I never knew until reading *Jelly Roll, Bix, and Hoagy* that that station was owned by Sears, Roebuck and Co., which consciously catered to its millions of rural catalog customers, even though its programs originated from Chicago's very cosmopolitan Sherman Hotel. The Gennett Company provided records, in massive amounts, to Sears catalog customers.

The word *treasure* must be used for any book that surprises the reader with so many previously unknown but fascinating facts. Despite my own love of Hoagy Carmichael's immortal "Stardust," from the first moment I heard it as an impressionable teenager, I didn't know till now that it was originally conceived, performed, and recorded as an up-tempo novelty rather than a ballad. Nor did I know that the original lyric was written not by Mitchell Parish but by Carmichael himself.

Considering that Carmichael and I were personal friends

in his late years, I feel like a dunce for never having known, until reading Rick Kennedy's book, that the great composer had also been a cornet player and had recorded, as a vocalist, with the famous Paul Whiteman orchestra.

If Kennedy's account doesn't excite you, you have no serious interest in the history of American music.

Preface

I n England in 1988, I was introduced to Lord Napier's, a venerable jazz pub in the working-class neighborhood of Thornton Heath, south of London. On this particular night, the pub was packed to hear a local band play the sophisticated 1920s jazz of the immortals Louis Armstrong, Jelly Roll Morton, King Oliver, and Bix Beiderbecke. In the United States these days, you rarely hear such reverence for traditional jazz, especially in the informal surroundings of a neighborhood bar. To close their first set, the English musicians re-created, seemingly note-for-note, the original 1923 recording by Oliver's Creole Jazz Band of "Chimes Blues," a New Orleans–style classic remembered foremost for featuring Armstrong's first recorded cornet solo. During the intermission, I was eager to tell the musicians that Oliver had actually recorded "Chimes Blues" at a piano factory in the small Indiana town of Richmond, where I had once lived.

"Ah, yes, you must mean the Gennett Records studio," the piano player responded in a thick London accent. "There along the tracks, where the trains used to interrupt the recording sessions. At least, that's the legend, right? Bix recorded there as well, I'm told." Then he asked politely, "Just where in the States is this Richmond, Indiana?"

I had learned not to be surprised by such reactions. Among serious record collectors and historians of early jazz, blues, and country music, the hard-to-find, antique 78-rpm discs on the Gennett Records label have been coveted for years.

Their extreme rarity, however, says nothing of their importance. The small Indiana label, like a Rosetta stone for early 1920s jazz, released the debut recordings not only of Armstrong, Oliver, Beiderbecke, and Morton, but also of Hoagy Carmichael, Earl Hines, Muggsy Spanier, Johnny Dodds, Leon Roppolo, and other jazz pioneers. Also, the Gennett label is a lightning rod in American folk music. Hundreds of rare Gennett "old-time," sacred, and country blues recordings from the 1920s and early 1930s preserved regional songs and music styles, from Appalachia to the deep South, which were part of the early evolution of country and rock music. Simply put, few record companies in the 1920s documented America's musical grassroots as thoroughly as Gennett Records.

My introduction to Gennett Records was through the long-abandoned factory complex of Starr Piano, the record label's parent company and once a thriving manufacturer in a secluded river gorge in Richmond's oldest neighborhood. When I lived nearby in the early 1980s, "Starr Valley," as the locals called it, was an eerie industrial ghost town. The huge brick buildings stood vacant for years, victims of vandalism and decay, and were eventually demolished. The Gennett family, the owners of Starr Piano, had recorded musicians in Starr Valley, in a small, wood-frame shed along the river until 1934. Afterwards, the studio was boarded up and later torn down. But on a brick wall of a lone surviving piano assembly building, there remained a faded Gennett Records sign, a remnant of Starr Piano's immortal record label. I remember taking James Dapogny, a jazz author, musician, and professor from the University of Michigan, to Starr Valley. Like many music enthusiasts before him, he picked out a souvenir brick from the rubble, surveyed the blighted area, and still felt he was on hallowed ground.

And for good reason. Gennett jazz, blues, and country records from Richmond have been reissued dozens of times over the decades, first on other 78-rpm labels, then on vinyl album compilations and cassette tapes, and finally on digital compact discs. Some record collectors can recite certain original Gennett discs by recording date, matrix, and serial number. Music scholars continue to study them. Yet, while Gennett Records is a persistent footnote in music history, a detailed account of the record company and its owners has never been undertaken. So music aficionados tend to ask the same question: How did Italian piano manufacturers in a small Indiana town manage to stumble across and record so many of America's music innovators? How did young musicians in the 1920s make history with a most unlikely company in a most unlikely place? The story lies beyond the record liner notes.

The 1920s was an amazing era for the young recording industry. Small record labels proliferated, partly because of the Gennett family's legal triumphs over Victor Records. The courts ruled that recording techniques controlled by Victor patents were public domain. During the decade, record companies grew parallel with America's emerging jazz, blues, and country music styles. Gennett Records, in particular, embraced these new genres on the fringe of the music mainstream. In fact, Gennett was one of the first record labels to cater to both the segregated white and black record markets. The Richmond studio might record a black jazz band in the morning, and a white Appalachian string band in the afternoon.

Despite the social barriers imposed between races, a cross-pollination between white and black approaches to jazz, blues, and country music is evident on the Gennett releases. Gennett even advertised certain white jazz bands as black bands. Today, with the great attention paid to the differences between white and black cultures in America, we tend to forget that a healthy mutual respect existed between white and black musicians in the 1920s.

Gennett's ground-breaking jazz, blues, and country records sold modestly in Starr Piano's network of music stores and through department stores and mail order catalogs. It was an era when "hit" records generally sold by the thousands, not by the millions. Records were not promoted on the radio until a decade later. The Gennett artists were typically regional or small-time touring musicians who made little money on their low-fidelity discs. Then again, the label was receptive to almost anyone eager to make a disc, resulting in some recordings of great originality. With the Great Depression of the 1930s, Gennett Records, and a marvelous era in music recording, came to a crashing halt.

I began my research on Gennett Records as a reporter with the Richmond (Indiana) *Palladium-Item,* through casual chats with Gennett relatives and other elderly people who had worked at Starr Piano, which closed in 1952. In the decade since leaving Richmond, I have continued to accumulate Gennett 78-rpm discs, reissued Gennett recordings on albums and compact discs, bits of information from books and old magazines, and Starr Piano literature. A late-model Starr piano even sits in our living room. While Gennett's daily recording ledgers were miraculously preserved intact over the decades, my grasp of the day-to-day workings at Gennett Records was still sketchy. With Starr Piano and Gennett Records executives long deceased, the thought of a detailed book on the record company was still a stretch.

That changed after a record collector steered me to the John MacKenzie Collection at the Indiana Historical Society Library in Indianapolis. John MacKenzie was an avid Gennett Records collector from Portland, Oregon, who spent decades researching the label. After he died in 1982, his wife, Joyce, had the foresight to donate his research materials to the IHS Library. The real treasure trove was his detailed interviews, conducted from 1961 to 1970, with surviving Starr Piano and Gennett Records employees. From these detailed accounts, and my own interviews and materials, I was able to reconstruct the human side of the Gennett Records story.

The book leans heavily toward Gennett's jazz recordings for two reasons. First, these milestone releases from the early 1920s represent the label's most enduring legacy. Second, details from these recording sessions in Richmond are relatively well documented by first-hand accounts from Armstrong, Carmichael, Baby Dodds, and others. Fortunately, the history of early jazz was well chronicled from the beginning, by both jazz enthusiasts and music scholars. On the other hand, the early recordings of America's rural music traditions did not attract scholarly attention until later, toward the 1960s. During this period, numerous music folklorists, such as Gus Meade and Charles Wolfe, tracked down the long-forgotten, surviving blues and country musicians who recorded in the 1920s on several labels, including Gennett Records. As a result, the details surrounding Gennett's rural recordings are somewhat sketchy.

Finally, I've attempted to shed light on the little-known Gennett family of the 1920s. During my research, I encountered numerous people who were well informed about Gennett Records and eager to learn anything about Henry Gennett and his three sons—Harry, Clarence, and Fred—the operators of Starr Piano and creators of the historic record label in Richmond. The Gennett descendants provided me with invaluable insight into the family's triumphs and eventual financial setbacks those many decades ago. Yet, the later generations of Gennetts, who are no longer in Richmond, were amazed to learn that Gennett Records' contribution to music history has been so profound.

The most gratifying part of this book has been the willingness of many people to help make it happen. Special thanks go to my wife, Jane Kennedy, for her encouragement and enthusiasm; Dwight Weber, my boss at General Electric's Media Relations Department in Cincinnati, who edited the first draft during his waking hours on frequent international flights; photographer Jim Callaway, for his illustrations and suggestions; Richard Gennett, Henry Gennett Martin, and Gennett recording artists Marion McKay and Bud Dant, for their invaluable first-hand accounts; Sally Childs-Helton and Alexandria Gressett at the Indiana Historical Society Library; retired Richmond

(Indiana) *Palladium-Item* columnist Dick Reynolds, for his on-site detective work; and Frank Powers, a longtime Cincinnati musician and walking encyclopedia on traditional jazz.

Other people and organizations whose assistance is sincerely appreciated are Pete Whelan, publisher of *78 Quarterly*, Duncan Schiedt, Jean Kennedy, Chuck Kennedy, Jim Stump, James Dapogny, Harry Leavell, Sam Meier, Bill Angert, Stan Kandebo, Guy Norris, Charles Wolfe, Ivan Tribe, Paul Turk, Wayne Vincent, Robert Highland, Tom Totsi, Phil Pospychala, Ryland Jones, Loyal Jones, Linda Gennett Irmscher, the *Cincinnati Post*, the Wayne County (Indiana) Historical Museum, the Richmond (Indiana) *Palladium-Item*, and the record sleuths of the International Association of Jazz Record Collectors.

JELLY ROLL, BIX, AND HOAGY

The studio was primitive, the room wasn't soundproof, and just outside was a railroad spur with switch engines puffing away noisily. Yet this obscure recording studio in a small Indiana city saw a history-making parade of musicians. They made the name of the Hoosier Gennetts one of the greatest names in recorded music, and the gold-lettered Gennett label is one to collect.

Hoagy Carmichael

A Music Dynasty in
Victorian Indiana

T he rise of the formidable Starr Piano Company and its fabled Gennett Records label from the small Quaker town of Richmond, Indiana, smack in America's heartland, sounds improbable today, if not fantastic. Yet it wasn't unusual. Richmond was among several small towns in Indiana and Ohio that gave rise to nationally prominent manufacturing companies after the Civil War. From the late nineteenth century up to the stock market crash of 1929, a plethora of industrial innovation sprang from the communities near Richmond—the mass production of farm implements in Springfield, Ohio, the Wright brothers' revolutionary airplanes in Dayton, and the ornately crafted Duesenberg and Cord luxury automobiles in the small Indiana cities of Connersville and Auburn.

In each of these industrial towns, similar social dynamics were at work. European entrepreneurs and skilled tradesmen flocked to the Midwest, a region bolstered by untapped natural resources and growing populations. The cultural traditions of Old World craftsmanship were being meshed with America's emerging, mass-production technologies. Finished products, distinguished by hand-crafted workmanship, rolled off the assembly lines of the Midwest in large quantities. Because of the nation's newly established railroad network, products from the small industrial towns of the Midwest could reach virtually every market in America and overseas.

It was amid these social and commercial dynamics that

Richmond developed and prospered. Settled primarily by Quakers beginning in 1806, Richmond was founded along the Whitewater River in east-central Indiana. On the eastern fringe of America's grain belt, close to the Ohio border, Richmond is 68 miles east of Indianapolis and 70 miles north of Cincinnati.

Richmond's transportation channels enabled the village's industrial base to develop quickly. The Whitewater Canal along the Whitewater River helped link Richmond with the Ohio River valley. Among Richmond's first manufacturers were cotton and wool mills that utilized the river for power. During the mid-nineteenth century, the National Road (now U.S. 40) was routed through the heart of Richmond. The National Road became a primary passage for wagon trains crossing the central states to the West. By the Civil War era, the small, self-sufficient village had its own paper mills, tanneries, foundries, iron factories, and a neighborhood German brewery, as well as farm implement and carriage manufacturers.

The *History of Wayne County Indiana*, published in 1884, proclaimed that Richmond "stands without a rival in the beauty of her location, the wealth of her surroundings, the solidity of her growth, and in the refinement, culture, and hospitality of its citizens."[1] The authors attributed Richmond's low death rate to the pure air, which "gave energy to a man and elasticity to his steps," and to an absence of "stagnant pools and miasmatic bottomlands." Within a few years, however, it wasn't pure air, hospitality, and solidity of growth that gave the small community of 10,000 people a growing reputation for excellence with consumers well beyond Indiana. Rather, it was a booming piano manufacturing complex along the banks of the Whitewater River.

The Starr Piano Company

In 1872, two prominent local businessmen teamed up with an Alsatian piano maker named George M. Trayser to form a modest manufacturing company. Trayser, who had apprenticed in the piano-building trade in Germany, had traveled halfway across America to open a small factory in Indianapolis in 1849, the first piano factory west of the Allegheny Mountains. Trayser also produced pianos just after the Civil War in Ripley, Ohio, before moving his operation in 1871 to Hamilton, Ohio, about 30 miles southeast of Richmond. His little company produced quality keyboards, but Trayser needed financial backers in order to expand his enterprise.

Trayser found them in nearby Richmond in the form of Richard Jackson and James Starr. A hard-driving Irishman, Jackson had arrived in America in 1843 as a teenager. He soon moved West, and by his early 30s was operating a dry goods store in Richmond, considered the town's first to operate strictly on a cash basis. Jackson made a comfortable living and expanded his influence in the village by financing the construction of several downtown buildings.

Jackson's coterie of business peers included James Starr, a wealthy merchant and scion to one of Richmond's founding Quaker families. His father, a well-to-do importer named Charles Starr, moved from Philadelphia to Richmond early in the century, when the village population was less than 700. He purchased 240 acres in the heart of Richmond for $6,000 and soon sold off parcels at $100 per lot, on which homes and factories were built. Starr constructed the town's first hewed-log house.

In the 1830s, the Starr family established a cotton factory in Richmond and helped to develop the downtown area. The family also was instrumental in incorporating the Cincinnati, Richmond & Muncie Railroad, which was routed through Richmond, thereby giving the town further access to the region's major markets.

With Jackson and Starr's financial clout and Trayser's expertise in piano building, the Trayser Piano Company was founded in 1872, with Trayser as president and Jackson as secretary-treasurer. Trayser moved his wood-working equipment to a building that Jackson had secured on the downtown corner of North Eighth and Elm streets. Richmond was a suitable location, as the growing town included large numbers of European wood craftsmen.

By 1878, the company reorganized after the arrival of M. J. Chase, a former Trayser associate and piano manufacturer from Ripley. Details are sketchy, but previous relations with Chase apparently caused Trayser to leave the new company. Benjamin Starr, a 36-year-old Civil War hero who had sustained a near-fatal head wound, joined his older brother James as a company owner.

The piano company was renamed the Chase Piano Company, but internal turmoil continued. Jackson became seriously ill from an undiagnosed brain ailment in 1880, which "baffled the skill of some of the ablest physicians in Richmond and elsewhere."[2] He died a year later at age 54. By 1884, yet another company reorganization prompted the Starr brothers to further assert themselves. The company was renamed James Starr & Co., with James as president and Benjamin as factory general manager.

Shortly after Benjamin Starr assumed his new duties, the Starr family secured larger manufacturing quarters in Richmond. They purchased 23 acres near the center of town, along the bottom of a vast gorge formed by the Whitewater River. Starr constructed a six-story brick factory on the east bank of the river, which supplied critically needed water power. While just a stroll from Richmond's central business and residential neighborhoods, the Starr factory was isolated from view, tucked away in the gorge. As Starr Piano grew from one factory into a mammoth complex, this secluded stretch of the Whitewater gorge came to be known in Richmond as "Starr Valley." (During the 1920s era of Gennett Records, it assumed such nicknames as "Banjo Valley" and "Harmony Hollow.")

For James Starr & Co. and other American piano manufacturers, opportunity abounded in the late nineteenth century. For America's emerging middle class, the piano embodied a respectability and civility to which many people aspired. While Europe was captivated by the wilds of the American frontier, Americans, on the other hand, sought to emulate the values and cultural refinement associated with England's Victorian lifestyle. In photographs of American homes in the late nineteenth century, the piano was a central element in rooms elaborately decorated with furniture, rugs, and draperies. Before the age of phonographs and radios, the piano was a fixture in the parlors of America's middle class, a social centerpiece, particularly for women, who were expected to master the instrument out of what seemed to be a sense of duty.

A common image of courting in nineteenth-century advertising literature was the woman seated at the piano, playing sentimental classics to her anxious male caller. Certainly, the minds of these young couples were on other things besides Chopin nocturnes, but the piano stood as a moral institution. To a people who embraced a Protestant work ethic, the piano symbolized its virtues.

The Starr operation started slowly, but by the mid-1880s the factory employed about 150 workers, mostly tradesmen of German origin. From Starr Valley, hand-crafted pianos were shipped in great numbers to outlets of the Jesse French Piano & Organ Co., based in St. Louis. Founded in 1873 with a $3,000 investment, the Jesse French Co. was one of the pioneering piano retailers, with a chain of stores throughout the southern states. During the 1880s, French's retailing base expanded rapidly by selling several brands of pianos, including the respected Starr products. The tie between French and Starr Piano soon proved lucrative to both the retailer and the supplier. That relationship radically altered Starr Piano's position in the industry, after two entrepreneurs associated with the Jesse French Co., John Lumsden and his son-in-law Henry Gennett, began merger negotiations with the Starr brothers in 1892.

Born in 1852 as the eighth child in a family of nine chil-

dren, Henry Gennett was the son of a prominent Italian entrepreneur in Nashville, Tennessee, who had operated a
wholesale business in the city since 1833. Henry was four
years old when his father died. As a young adult, he joined his
brothers in the family business. At age 23, he married Alice
Lumsden, a member of a prosperous Nashville family. Her father, the England-born John Lumsden, had extensive land assets and a substantial equity interest in the coal and iron
industries.

Another of Lumsden's sons-in-law happened to be Jesse
French. Through his personal relationships with Lumsden and
French, Gennett became involved in the retail piano business.
In the 1880s, Gennett joined Lumsden in operating a chain of
retail music stores in the South. By 1891, Gennett moved his
family to St. Louis, where he became vice president of the
Jesse French Co.

Lumsden stayed in Nashville, but he maintained significant holdings in the Jesse French Co., despite his expressed
concern with French's aggressive, and potentially unsavory,
method for retail markup. In a revealing letter to Gennett in
the 1890s, Lumsden warned of price gouging in a French retail
store. "We have in the store a good stock of cheap pianos,"
Lumsden wrote. "Mozarts cost $83, Waverlys $100, Majestics
$100, so you can see we have a house full of trash. And these
pianos are priced from $250 to $350. The better grades only
come in when these can't be forced off. I want to give you the
facts so that you may see the drift of the business."[3]

By 1892, the Jesse French Co. executives sought to link up
with a piano supplier closer to its southern operations. One of
its primary suppliers, Starr Piano, had continued to build upon
its solid reputation, winning awards at the Chicago World's
Fair of 1892. Back in Richmond, Benjamin and James Starr
were eager to establish an alliance with the French executives.
Gennett and Lumsden soon began merger negotiations with
the Starr brothers.

On April 7, 1893, the new Starr Piano Co. was organized

and significantly recapitalized with a $100,000 stock issuance. Gennett and Lumsden acquired about half ownership in Starr Piano, and, along with French, joined the Starr brothers on the company's board of directors. Benjamin Starr, Lumsden, and Gennett were the newly organized company's primary officers, with Lumsden as president. French did not actively participate in Starr Piano operations, but remained a director for several years.

Initially, the Starr brothers must have felt jinxed by their new southern partners. In early 1894, a huge fire in Starr Valley nearly destroyed the entire manufacturing complex. Not long after the facilities were back up and running, they were shut down again by a Whitewater River flood in 1895, the same year Gennett and his family moved to Richmond. In 1898, Lumsden died.

Despite the setbacks, Starr Piano made strong progress in a booming industry. By the 1890s the rate of U.S. piano production was five times as fast as the nation's population growth.[4] More than a hundred companies manufactured pianos in the U.S., including the highly successful Baldwin Company in nearby Cincinnati. Many American piano manufacturers evolved into full-blown corporations fueled by high levels of capitalization and expanded distribution networks. Through its alignment with French's established retail distribution network, Starr Piano was positioned to become one of the industry's major players. The manufacturing plant in the Starr Valley rapidly expanded as the owners poured money into the company; in 1897 the capital stock of Starr Piano was doubled, to $200,000.

After Benjamin Starr's death in 1903, Gennett assumed control of the company and gradually elevated his three sons into prominent positions. In 1898, at age 21, Harry Gennett became vice president. In 1905, Henry Gennett appointed son Clarence, 26, as treasurer, and Fred, nineteen, as secretary. The Gennett family, having now lived in Richmond for a decade, fully controlled the vast piano manufacturing operations in the Whitewater gorge.

A distinctive, tan-skinned Italian with a black moustache, Henry Gennett was colorful and dynamic. Though he was short and slightly built, he more than compensated for his small physical stature with an outgoing, confident personality and a reputation among employees as a bold decision maker. Known for his impeccable attire, Henry could be seen walking through the Starr factory complex with a white Panama hat, white suit, and a fancy cane with a gold knob. In his later years, he was chauffeured around town in a black Packard; one relative laughingly said that Henry had to climb up in order to get into the back seat.

Henry was not a craftsman; he was a hard-driving, creative merchandiser. A typical example of his style was relayed to his grandson Richard Gennett by the family's long-time chauffeur, Howard Thomas. While driving Henry's twelve-cylinder Packard down Main Street in Richmond one morning, Thomas was stuck behind a slow-moving wagon loaded with corn on its way to one of the Whitewater River grain mills. Henry told Thomas to pull into the local Starr Piano Store at 10th and Main Street. He charged into the store and ordered a Starr salesman to follow the corn wagon to the mill and sell the driver a Starr piano. Henry figured that the farmer delivering the corn would soon have cash in his pocket, making him ripe for a big purchase.

With such leadership style, Henry Gennett further developed the Starr Piano Company into one of the nation's largest mass producers of pianos. By 1915, more than 250 U.S. companies were manufacturing pianos, with about 25 of them controlling 75 percent of the market. Starr Piano was among this elite group, which, in the Midwest alone, included the Continental Piano Co. in nearby New Castle, Indiana; the Baldwin Co. and the Wurlitzer Co., both in Cincinnati; and the W. W. Kimball Co., The Cable Company, and Steger Products, all of Chicago.

The highest grade Starr pianos won gold medals for excellence at various exhibitions, including the St. Louis World's Fair in 1904, the Tennessee Centennial Exposition of 1907, the Alaska-Yukon-Pacific Exposition in 1909, and the Panama-Pacific Exposition of 1915. Henry heavily promoted the Starr Minum Grand piano, one of the best-selling baby grands in the Midwest. The Starr upright pianos of the 1910s possessed a quality of tone and durability that rivaled the Steinway or Baldwin uprights. Like his competitors, Henry saw huge potential in the new player pianos, which Starr Piano produced with a vengeance beginning in 1906. The company even marketed a small player piano for apartments called "The Princess," which stood just four feet, four inches tall. But wisely, Henry was never convinced that the player piano would supersede the conventional instrument, as many in the industry had predicted.

In addition to the Starr-name pianos, the company mass-produced a wide variety of lower-cost pianos. By 1915, Starr Piano was manufacturing more than 50 styles of grand, upright, and player pianos under such brand names as Richmond, Trayser, Remington, and French. Also, pianos were stenciled with the names of retailers who bought wholesale from the Starr factory for sale in their department stores or through mail-order catalogs.

Starr Piano's indiscriminate approach to the wholesale distribution of its pianos did not sit well with all of its retailers. Wilson Taggart, a Starr salesman from 1914 to 1924, recalled the wrath of an Ohio piano retailer who stormed out of his office and announced that he wanted nothing to do "with any company that would make stuff for a mail-order house." Starr Piano also manufactured pianos under the name of A. J. Krafts of Richmond, Virginia. "He [A. J. Krafts] had the biggest and fanciest stencil you ever saw," Taggart said. "He put that on the board on top, you know. That old devil, I betcha, was getting $100 apiece for those pianos over the price of the Starr Piano."[5]

The Starr distribution network was enormous. By 1915, Starr retail stores were established in the major cities of Ohio and Indiana, as well as in Detroit, Michigan; Chicago, Illinois;

and San Diego and Los Angeles, California. Through the Jesse French chain stores, Starr pianos were sold in the cities of the South and Southwest. In addition, retail agencies essentially made Starr pianos available nationwide. Because Starr pianos were constructed for durability, by the 1910s the company even exported instruments to South America, where heat and humidity could ruin a cheaper piano.

Part of Starr Piano's aggressive merchandising strategy involved wholesaling to independent retailers on a consignment contract, which meant that Henry Gennett's team had to keep after the stores which had not paid up on their inventory. From Starr Valley, Taggart heard amusing stories from the Starr account executive in charge of hunting down unpaid accounts from independent stores around the country. "He stopped in Denver where some gal was way behind [in payments]," Taggart said. "So he made a date to see her in his hotel room. He said he had a funny feeling, so he just backed up and jerked the door open real quick. There was a fella out there listening. She was going to compromise him so that she could get out of that piano debt!"[6]

As early as 1907, enamored with the business potential of vastly unsettled California, Henry established Starr's Pacific Division in Los Angeles to handle his piano distribution in the West. Starr Piano held 70 percent of the new division, with the remaining 30 percent owned by Harry Holder, a former Richmond resident and confidant of Henry. After forming the Pacific Division, Henry increased his interest in California, where he made significant real estate acquisitions in the Los Angeles area.

By 1915, Gennett's sprawling Starr Piano Co. factory in the Whitewater gorge was a mass-production machine. Many piano companies had become assembly operations using finished parts from a growing number of specialty piano suppliers. However, the Starr Piano complex was a self-sufficient, highly departmentalized manufacturing plant. With the exception of large metal castings supplied by Swayne, Robinson &

Co., an iron works plant two hundred yards up the hill from Starr Valley, the piano factory basically produced all the essential components in a piano. The factory's massive lumber inventory was said to ensure production for five years. Starr Piano was producing 15,000 pianos annually by 1915. By then, more than 100,000 Starr pianos had been sold nationwide.

The Starr factory complex now spread over 35 acres along the river gorge. Two long rows of factory buildings, divided by a secondary railroad spur for hauling materials and finished products within the complex, covered more than 300,000 square feet. Impressed by the self-contained, modern manufacturing complex, trade magazines in the early 1900s praised the massive industrial park in Starr Valley as a model of scientific efficiency. About 750 people worked in the Richmond factory by 1915, including more than 50 women and numerous adolescents, and the Starr national sales network around the country totaled another 400 people.

Starr Piano became an industrial cornerstone of Richmond. Even though the company never had a glowing reputation for its wages and benefits, Starr Piano operated for many years without laying off workers. The guaranteed paycheck attracted the townspeople, who commonly spent their entire careers amid the sawdust in Starr Valley, an area that gets unmercifully hot and sticky in the summer. And, like the railroad and newspaper businesses, the piano business gets into the blood. The village's tradesmen and laborers, from woodworkers to piano polishers, were proud of the pianos that put Richmond on the map. "Even in the 1940s, when Starr Piano was nearing its end, there were employees still around the plant who had worked for my grandfather as far back as the turn of the century," said Henry Gennett Martin, grandson of Henry Gennett. "A typical Starr worker seemed to stay down there at the factory for the duration."[7]

The stature of Starr Piano placed the Gennett family among the elite of Richmond, now an industrial boom town that claimed to have one of the highest percentages of million-aires of any U.S. community. In 1900 along a stretch of East Main Street lined with stately Victorian homes, Henry and Alice Gennett constructed one of the most stylish mansions in town. They hired a prominent local architect, John A. Hasecoster, who designed a three-story mansion in a Greek revival, neo-Classical style. The structure's exterior was distinguished by an imported, yellow-brick facade and a white-columned portico. The front hallway, lavishly wood-paneled, led to a large stone fireplace. On the first floor there was a spacious music conservatory, where Alice Gennett organized recitals at a Starr grand piano. A billiard room for Henry and his sons adjoined the conservatory. On the third floor, in an exquisite ballroom with an enormous chandelier, Henry and Alice hosted gala dance parties for Richmond socialites. "Papa loved that house," recalled their daughter, Rose Gennett Martin. "He would stand on the lawn and just look at it."[8]

The Gennetts actively supported Richmond's vibrant cultural scene. In 1899, the family opened the 1,200-seat Gennett Theater downtown. For the grand opening on December 23, the family brought in a stage star of the day, Cornelia Otis Skinner, who performed in Henry James's play *The Liars*. In 1905, the theatre was remodeled and the family formed the Gennett Theater Company, with Alice Gennett as president. She was also an active member of the Richmond Musical Club, which sponsored recitals. Starr Piano also helped finance Richmond's annual May Festival, supported the Richmond Symphony, and underwrote the costs of bringing leading classical soloists to the city. All of this in a town of fewer than 30,000 people in rural Indiana.

"The Starr Piano Company and the cultural life of the community, in the latter's musical phases, have been inextricably interwoven from the beginning of the company's existence and are drawn closer with each succeeding year," reported the Richmond *Palladium* in 1913. "Its effect is seen also, in the large number of its employees and attaches who are among the city's leading amateurs and are included in its choral and orchestral organizations. The inter-relationship of the Starr Piano Company and the civic body in short, is one of the finest manifestations of our social life and should never be minimized in the consideration of the forces, that, welded together, give this city its individual social atmosphere."[9]

In 1915, with the Starr factory steaming along at peak production and Starr stores established nationwide, the Gennett family formally amended the company's original articles of incorporation in order to pursue "every kind of instrument, machine, device, process and material necessary and suitable in and about the production, preservation, use and control of sound vibration for musical, commercial and other economic purposes."[10]

The legal jargon did not imply that the Gennetts had lost faith in pianos. On the contrary. Their piano business continued to expand, despite growing competition from the latest American craze: the phonograph. But by 1915, forces within the tightly controlled phonograph industry were making it possible for new companies to enter the competition. The business had become fair game, and the Gennett family, through Starr Piano's amended articles of incorporation, simply declared that it wanted a piece of the action.

The Gennetts had successfully established Starr Piano nationally as a leading piano maker, while the family at home maintained a profile as philanthropists with high cultural aspirations for their quaint Indiana community. Now, they were about to enter a very different business arena in the new, brash world of records and phonographs. No one could have suspected in 1915 that, within five years, the Indiana firm, with its fledgling Gennett Records division, would lead a group of other small record companies into a series of lengthy court battles against the record industry's undisputed giant, Victor Talking Machine Co. of Camden, New Jersey. The eventual outcome of these court cases would change forever the competitive nature of the developing record industry.

Courtroom Showdown: Victor vs. Starr Piano

Few people benefited more from the genesis of America's recording industry than the patent lawyers. From Thomas Edison's cylinder phonograph of 1877 to the national craze over disc-playing phonographs four decades later, the developing industry was awash in patent litigation. Suits piled up one on top of the other as powerful entrepreneurs wrestled with a flurry of advances in sound recording.

The outcome of bitter patent lawsuits between phonograph kingpins heavily affected the fortunes of the competing firms. Such was the case in Starr Piano's landmark court victories over the Victor Talking Machine Company in 1921–22. But in order to appreciate the events surrounding the creation of Starr Piano's Gennett Records, its court battles with Victor, and its overall impact on the emerging recording industry, one must trace the tangled web of inventions, corporate wars, and legal shenanigans that shaped the phonograph and record industry before Starr Piano began pressing records during the World War I era.

Edison's phonograph in 1877 was initially treated as a scientific novelty; attendees of industrial exhibitions marveled at hearing their own voices played back to them. In fact, Edison saw little commercial promise for his cylinder machine and nearly abandoned the invention for about a decade as he concentrated on developing the light bulb. Yet until the advent of digitally recorded compact discs in the 1980s, the conventional needle and turntable record player remained faithful to Edison's original principles of sound reproduction.

Edison's first recorder consisted of a brass cylinder with a spiral groove around it and two diaphragm-and-needle units. A horn was fixed permanently, with a steel point mounted in the diaphragm. The steel point made contact with a piece of tin foil wrapped around the brass cylinder. When words were spoken into the horn, the diaphragm vibrated from the sound waves produced by the voice. In turn, the steel point, or stylus, moved vertically, producing a "hill-and-dale" pattern of indentations on the tin foil. Upon replaying the tin foil, the reproducing needle converted these indentations into sounds waves which reproduced the voice spoken into the horn.

While Edison focused full attention on the light bulb in the early 1880s, his phonograph was further advanced by Chichester A. Bell and Charles Sumner Tainter, who replaced the tin foil with a cardboard cylinder coated with wax. Their invention was patented in 1886. Bell and Tainter also experimented with flat discs for sound reproduction, but everyone stayed with the wax cylinder. When Edison returned to the cylinder phonograph in the mid-1880s, he further refined the Bell-Tainter wax-cylinder concept. By the 1890s, Edison's skillfully crafted cylinder phonographs, marketed through his North American Phonograph Company, were sold in large quantities to America's elite, while stage celebrities raced to be recorded onto Edison's wax cylinders.

At the same time, a German immigrant named Emile Berliner developed a new machine he called the gramophone, which recorded and played flat discs. In contrast to Edison's "hill-and-dale" etching method, Berliner's recording stylus etched sound vibrations in a lateral zigzag motion onto a zinc plate. From this zinc master disc, Berliner produced a copper disc matrix by means of an electroplating process. This matrix was used to stamp out playable discs made of a heat-softened shellac compound.

Though it was not apparent then, the disc player was inherently more practical than Edison's cylinder machine. Discs were more easily duplicated and were easier to store and handle than wax cylinders. Still, in the 1890s, cylinder phonographs from Edison's National Phonograph Company and the American Graphophone Co. (later known as Columbia Phonograph, the name used henceforth in this book) hit the market first and controlled the industry. Edison and Columbia's cylinders produced high-quality sound reproduction, especially of the human voice.

But Berliner persisted. In 1895, he established the United States Gramophone Company, which licensed his patents to the Berliner Gramophone Company, manufacturer of the machines. They were sold through yet another organization, National Gramophone Company. Berliner's gramophone operated with a special spring motor, supplied by Eldridge Johnson, a machinist in Camden, New Jersey. By 1897, Johnson was mass-producing spring motors by the hundreds from his small shop.

Buyers were soon attracted to the Berliner machine by the aggressive marketing of National Gramophone Company, headed by master promoter Frank Seaman. In 1898, Seaman's National Gramophone Company claimed sales of Berliner gramophones of more than $1 million. The Columbia and Edison cylinder machines were suddenly threatened by another contraption.

Columbia responded by waging war in the courts. Despite vast differences between Berliner's patent for recorded discs and the Columbia-held, Bell-Tainter patent for cylinder recording, Philip Mauro, Columbia's lawyer, concocted the "floating stylus" theory. In essence, he claimed that Berliner's recording stylus copied the manner in which Columbia's recording stylus "floated" along the grooves of the wax cylinder.

Mauro marched into court and charged Berliner with patent infringement. Amazingly, the court initially sided with Mauro in 1899; its injunction against further sales of Berliner gramophones lasted about a year. Yet even stranger things would happen. With the court injunction, the companies involved with the Berliner gramophone were in limbo, especially Johnson, the chief supplier of gramophone spring motors. Unlike Berliner, who had other business interests, Johnson had sunk almost all his money into gramophone technology. Having brushed with bankruptcy, Johnson soon realized he could not depend entirely upon the Berliner gramophone.

In the late 1890s, Johnson had developed another disc-recording method using Berliner's lateral recording technique, but with a soft-wax master disc instead of a zinc disc. From the wax master, Johnson produced a metal stamper, which was used to produce the shellac-based records. Johnson believed the scratchy sound in Berliner's shellac discs was caused by the zinc master discs. Berliner apparently never pursued wax masters, figuring they would infringe on the Bell-Tainter patent for producing wax master cylinders.

After the injunction on Berliner's gramophone was lifted, Johnson seized the opportunity to market a new gramophone, which played shellac discs derived from wax masters. The sound produced by Johnson's machine was better than Berliner's. Johnson wagered his remaining savings on a risky promotional campaign and managed to generate public enthusiasm.

The new market entrant aroused the ire of Seaman, the original sales agent for Berliner's gramophone, who was now selling another disc player not affiliated with Berliner. Seaman sued Johnson, claiming that Johnson's Consolidated Talking Machine Company was nothing more than a thinly veiled Berliner Gramophone Company.

The court did not agree. In Philadelphia in 1901, Johnson won a stunning victory. He was free to sell his improved gramophone as long as he did not use Berliner's "gramophone" name. No matter. The word soon disappeared from the American vernacular as disc-playing machines overtook cylinder machines and also became known generically as phonographs. During the court case, Johnson had stayed on good terms with Berliner and paid royalties for Berliner's patent for lateral disc recording. Johnson, however, had clearly advanced the concept by developing an improved spring motor and the wax master. Johnson merged with the Berliner organization, which acquired 40 percent of Johnson's company. Johnson now owned Berliner's original gramophone patent. He also created a new company name inspired by his "victory" in court: the Victor Talking Machine Company, which would become the dominant phonograph and record manufacturer over the next three decades.

But soon after Victor Talking Machine Company was formed, Johnson was handed the shock of his life. In December 1901, the U.S. Patent Office awarded one Joseph W. Jones a patent for the lateral engraving of wax master discs, the same basic process already being commercialized by Johnson. Johnson, like Berliner, had not originally sought to patent his method, figuring the original Bell-Tainter patent covered all types of wax recording.

This time, Johnson was outsmarted. In 1896, Jones had handled basic chores in Berliner's Washington, D.C., laboratory when Berliner experimented with wax discs. Jones took good notes. In 1897, he filed a claim for laterally engraving a groove of even depth on a wax blank master, which the U.S. Patent Office accepted four years later. Meanwhile, Johnson's nearly identical patent was filed in 1898 and accepted in 1905, years after his machine hit the market. Jones had no phonograph for sale, just a legal document from the U.S. Patent Office that caused Johnson headaches for years.

Enter once again Columbia attorney Mauro, still fuming from his failure to stop the Berliner gramophone. With Victor Talking Machines overtaking the original cylinder machines, Columbia desperately wanted to produce its own disc player. Mauro snatched up the Jones patent for $25,000, and in 1902 Columbia began selling the Columbia Disc Graphophone.

Johnson was livid. But as Victor prepared to battle Columbia in the courts for patent infringement, cooler heads prevailed, and the two companies agreed to pool their patents in 1902. Collectively, Victor and Columbia now owned all key aspects of manufacturing disc machines and lateral-cut records. Victor and Columbia had essentially monopolized the disc recording industry.

Victor, maker of the Red Seal Record, moved to take the market for classical music discs by signing exclusive contracts with the opera giants, most notably the tenor Enrico Caruso. In 1908 Columbia introduced the first double-sided discs and signed up a slew of opera singers and stage entertainers. Despite Columbia's headway, Victor maintained the industry lead. Besides, the Victor-Columbia lock on America's booming disc phonograph market allowed both companies to reap fortunes. By 1912, Columbia's disc business was firmly established as its cylinder business waned. Columbia soon dropped its cylinder machine, thus leaving Edison the last industrial titan committed to his original invention.

Yet even Edison's people weakened. In 1910, they began secretly exploring a disc-playing phonograph. Two years later, Edison introduced his Diamond Disc Phonograph. Where Columbia and Victor phonographs played only lateral-cut discs, Edison's phonograph played only vertical, "hill-and-dale," Edison-brand discs. The vertical-cut disc employed the original engraving technology developed by Edison decades before for his cylinder machines.

By 1915, the stage was set for new competitors in the phonograph industry. For one thing, several basic patents related to the manufacture of phonograph machines had expired. And even though Victor and Columbia's lateral-cut records and companion phonograph machines dominated the market, Edison's vertical-cut discs and Diamond Disc Phonographs created a commercial opportunity for a second method for recording discs that was less safeguarded by patents. Finally, with both lateral-cut and vertical-cut records now on the market, enterprising companies saw potential for developing phonographs with tone arms that could play both types of records.

Enter Henry Gennett's Starr Piano. With an army of skilled wood craftsmen in Richmond and an established chain of music stores, Starr Piano was a natural for the phonograph business. Tooling in the Richmond factory was well suited for producing wooden phonograph cabinets and the necessary metal fabrications. By 1916, Starr Piano was manufacturing and retailing in the company's stores a "Starr" brand phonograph that played both vertical- and lateral-cut discs simply by changing the needle's position.

Starr Piano was not alone. Six new companies entered the phonograph business in 1914. A year later, another half-dozen or so threw their hats into the ring. By 1916, there were close to 50 phonograph makers. Yet, this increased competition did not discount Victor; its assets grew from $13.9 million in 1913 to $21.6 million in 1915. By 1916, more than 500,000 phonographs were being sold across the country, a number that would quadruple in three years.[11]

Starr Piano Co. also established a record division to produce discs for the Starr phonographs. Ever the deal maker, Henry Gennett bought into the recording business after acquiring recording equipment and a stack of vertical-cut masters from a bankrupt Boston company. He set up a primitive recording studio in Starr Piano's new office at 9–11 East 37th Street in New York City. The company began recording discs, using the vertical-cut technology developed by Edison. The records bore either green or blue Starr labels and were sold with the phonographs in the Starr retail stores.

Initially, Starr records were pressed by a custom pressing outfit, most likely the Scranton Button Works in Scranton, Pennsylvania, which offered record pressing as early as 1915. By 1917, Starr Piano had constructed a six-story phonograph-manufacturing and record-pressing facility in Starr Valley in Richmond. Starr Piano's Manhattan recording studio, with access to the city's marching bands, orchestras, and stage entertainers, produced the bulk of master discs that were used to press records on the Starr label at the Richmond facility. The Gennett family then established a second recording studio in Starr Valley in a single-story shed along a row of Starr factory buildings.

Despite the plethora of new phonograph companies, the dominance by Victor and Columbia remained virtually invincible. New phonograph and record manufacturing firms, thrown together by eager investors between 1915 and 1920, often shut down as quickly as they opened. First of all, Victor threatened to slap lawsuits on anyone who attempted to produce records using the more popular lateral-cut method. Equally hard to crack was consumer loyalty to the superior Columbia, Victor, and Edison products, not to mention their established network of retail outlets and exclusive distributorships.

The smaller phonograph and record companies that did survive in this environment were generally divisions of large manufacturers of furniture products with established retail access. By the 1910s, the conspicuous tin horns on the first phonographs were hidden inside stylish cabinets. Phonographs, right along with the piano, were increasingly regarded as desirable pieces of furniture. The early phonographs and their companion records were sold together in furniture and department stores, as well as in music stores. For example, the department stores carrying Edison Diamond Needle Phonographs sold them right along with the Edison discs, and the same approach applied to Columbia and Victor.

Starr Piano's network of stores, for example, sold Starr phonographs along with an undistinguished selection of popular and classical records on the Starr label at prices ranging from $.65 to $1.00. The Aeolian Company, a leading manufacturer of pianos and organs, produced the Aeolian-Vocalion phonograph and vertical-cut Vocalion records. Wisconsin Chair Company built phonograph cabinets for Edison before it began selling its own phonographs as a sideline in 1915. Within two years, Wisconsin Chair introduced its Paramount record label. The General Phonograph Company, financed by a mighty German firm, the Lindstrom Company, issued the OKeh record label. Brunswick-Balke-Collender, known for billiard and bowling equipment, also produced phonographs and records.

These leading manufacturers entered the phonograph and record business just as manufacturers began riding the 1917–

18 industrial boom created by American involvement in World War I. Companies with advanced mass-production capabilities soon became part of the American war machine. Edison's factories, for example, were engaged in the mass production of wooden rifle parts. Starr Piano took advantage of its 40-mile proximity to Dayton, Ohio, where warplanes were being built near the Wright brothers' historic airplane factory. The Gennett family secured major government contracts for the production of propellers, flaps, rudders, and wooden supports for aircraft wings, as well as accessories for hot-air balloons. The war created a peculiar situation for the many German craftsmen at Starr Piano, who were now producing parts for a war against their old homeland. (While government contracts were a financial boon for Starr Piano, U.S. aircraft contributed little to the Allied war effort. American aviation had advanced marginally beyond the original Wright Flyers of the 1900s, and American-made aircraft were not involved in the legendary dogfights over Europe.)

When the armistice ended World War I in 1918, Starr Piano was near its industrial peak. Starr pianos continued to sell in huge quantities, while Starr phonographs rode the general wave of popularity for the newest gadget in home entertainment. But the Gennett family was forced to reassess the Starr record label, which faced hurdles beyond the Victor-Edison-Columbia lock on the market.

For one, Starr records were only sold with Starr phonographs in the Starr stores. Independent dealers hesitated selling records with a name so strongly associated with Starr pianos. For retailers carrying other brands of pianos, Starr records presented a potential conflict of interest. Worse, Starr records were vertical-cut. These records were a losing proposition because they could not be played on the ubiquitous Victor and Columbia phonographs, which played only lateral-cut records. Of the vertical-cut discs, only the Edison discs made respectable market inroads.

So Henry Gennett and his sons took bold measures. On

the urging of his youngest son, Fred, the label's name was changed to "Gennett," thereby minimizing the association with the piano company in order to widen the label's distribution base. The Gennett family now could more easily strike deals with independent distributors. The Starr Piano name only appeared in fine print at the bottom of the record label. The first records issued under the new ornately lettered Gennett label were a series of classical discs.

But Gennett's second move was more fortuitous. In mid-1919, Gennett Records introduced lateral-cut discs for $.85 apiece, without paying a licensing fee to Victor for the patented recording technology. It was a direct and dangerous assault by little Gennett Records on the recording titan. In 1919 issues of *Talking Machine World*, a leading phonograph trade magazine, Starr Piano advertised that its Gennett records could improve the tone of all phonographs. The not-so-subtle message was that Gennett's new lateral-cut discs could be played on the prominent Victor and Columbia phonographs.

As expected, in 1919 Victor Talking Machine sued Starr Piano in the United States District Court for the Southern District of New York, charging infringement of Johnson's patent. In addition, Victor sought a temporary injunction against Starr Piano to cease production of the Gennett lateral-cut records until the case was settled. On the surface, the confrontation resembled the battle between David and Goliath. Besides its enormous financial resources and a file cabinet full of U.S. patents for recording technology, Victor had a long and impressive track record in winning patent infringement suits. Victor's Eldridge Johnson had successfully defended his 1905 patent for the lateral-cut recording process in several cases, including a 1911 court decision in which Johnson's patent was ruled valid over the nearly identical Jones patent of 1901!

The Gennett family, on the other hand, had no patents to wave back in Victor's face. Their defense was lack of invention on the part of Johnson's patent. In other words, they argued that the general concept of lateral-cut recording belonged in the public domain and should not be protected by a series of confusing and often contradictory patent rulings. Once and for all, the Gennetts were determined to break the monopoly.

The Gennett family had another factor in its favor. In similar cases, the courts often rendered decisions totally inconsistent with previous rulings. In the early days of the record business, any outcome was possible when phonograph-related patents were at issue. And while Gennett Records was a tiny player in a business ruled by Victor, the Richmond parent company of Starr Piano had the financial clout to handle protracted litigation with just about anyone.

Starr Piano also received enthusiastic support from other small record companies—General Phonograph (OKeh), Aeolian Company (Vocalion), and Canadian Compo Company—which joined Starr Piano in the suit. None of them had made substantial inroads with vertical-cut records, and all stood to gain enormously from free access to the lateral-cut recording technology. Starr Piano hired a veteran patent lawyer, Drury W. Copper, to defend the case, one that would break forever the cozy Victor-Columbia lock on the lateral-cut recording industry.

In early 1920, Victor suffered its first setback when the temporary injunction was denied by both the U.S. District Court and the U.S. Circuit Court of Appeals. When a patent in question has been held valid in an earlier ruling, as was the case with the Johnson patent, a temporary injunction is usually granted. But not this time. Starr Piano's attorneys effectively attacked the validity of Johnson's patent in view of the earlier 1901 Jones patent. Even though Johnson's patent had been successfully defended in court in the past, Starr Piano cited rulings surrounding the Johnson patent that appeared contradictory.

In refusing to issue a temporary injunction against Starr Piano, the Circuit Court of Appeals in January 1920 noted that possibly "Jones had a prior patent and was a prior inventor. If so, it then became incumbent upon Johnson, in order to succeed, to prove beyond a reasonable doubt that he was, in fact, the inventor."[12] The court added that because of the questionable correctness of previous cases, the case should be moved for an early trial. Starr Piano's opening-round victory enabled the company to continue pressing lateral-cut discs, knowing that final settlement of Victor's impending patent infringement suit would be held up in court for months, possibly years.

U.S. District Court Judge Learned Hand, a future U.S. Supreme Court justice, presided over *Victor Talking Machine* v. *Starr Piano*, which began in 1920 and dragged on several months into early 1921. During the testimony, Starr Piano's attorneys hauled motion picture equipment into the courtroom for close-up observation of the Gennett recording stylus and the grooves it cut into wax master discs. After months of technical badgering, Starr Piano's original defense, which had buried Victor's temporary injunction, proved convincing to Judge Hand. In a 2,500-word decree issued on February 11, 1921, Judge Hand concluded that Victor's attorneys could not prove that Johnson had invented the concept of lateral-cut recording on a wax master disc.

Hand acknowledged that certain tools and methods relating to lateral-cut recording had been developed and legitimately patented by Victor. But the general concept, he concluded, existed years before Johnson's patent. Judge Hand also ruled that Victor had legally "abandoned" Johnson's patent, because the lateral-cut recording process had been in commercial use several years before the patent was awarded.

The final crushing blow in the dispute was handed down on April 4, 1922 in the U.S. Circuit Court of Appeals, where Judge Augustus Hand (a cousin of Learned Hand) massacred the once-intimidating Johnson patent. He agreed that Johnson's keeping his patent secret for several years constituted abandonment. Then, after assessing numerous recording patents leading up to Johnson's own, Judge Hand affirmed that previous inventors were already familiar with the concept of lateral-cut recording: "The most that can be said of the Johnson patent in suit is that it disclosed a method of cutting out a lateral undulatory groove of substantially constant depth by an improved form of stylus. Everything except the improved tool which his specification discloses seems to have been old, and the improved tool was apparently a matter of workmanship, and at any rate is not an element in the claims in suit."[13]

Augustus Hand ruled that Johnson's patent for lateral-cut recording was directly foreshadowed by Jones's patent, and even earlier by Bell and Tainter's nineteenth-century patent for recording with a soft wax cylinder! "Nothing remained but work for skilled artisans in order to fabricate a satisfactory sound record," Hand wrote. "Nothing was achieved worthy of a patent in producing the Johnson matrix. It seems evident that Johnson invented nothing new in the way of a matrix laterally cut out of wax, and that he did not think that he had done so. He, at most, by more experienced workmanship, produced better results through methods that were undoubtedly older than had formerly been secured."[14]

After two years of court battles, Starr Piano soundly defeated mighty Victor. The decision attracted little attention. After all, it did nothing immediately to affect Victor's dominant position in the recording market. Victor's sales of phonographs and records by the end of 1921 had reached an astounding $50 million. But Starr Piano and its Gennett Records helped to set the stage for dramatic change in the competitive nature of the recording business. The court decisions opened the floodgates. With lateral-cut recording technology securely in the public domain, smaller recording labels switched to this process. New labels were formed. The heightened competition between labels in the 1920s promoted improvements in recording processes, reduced record prices, and generated more recording activity than could have been imagined before the advent of Gennett Records.

The informal alliance between Starr Piano's Gennett Records Division and the other small competitors did not end with the Starr court victory. Through the 1920s, the Gennett family maintained loose business ties with these other record companies, as hundreds of Gennett master discs were pressed for several different labels. With the onset of the Roaring Twenties, the Gennett family's small, Indiana-based record company had earned a respectable place in the rapidly evolving recording industry.

Halcyon Days in Starr Valley

Starr Piano entered the 1920s in the right business. While the radical industrial shift to a peace-time economy after World War I caused a national recession, the nation was poised for years of unprecedented consumerism. U.S. troops returned from European battlefields seeking domestic stability. Within a short time, the public appetite for household goods, such as pianos and phonographs, was stronger than ever. Meanwhile, competition between a growing number of new record labels, abetted by Starr Piano's winning its legal battle with Victor Records, sparked a proliferation in the sheer number of new record releases available to phonograph owners.

Times were good in Richmond's Starr Valley. By 1920, the company was annually producing about 15,000 pianos, 3,000 phonographs, and 3,000,000 records.[15] With the switch to lateral-cut records in the early 1920s, the Gennett label prospered, with a sizable catalog offering classical, sacred, popular, and military band music, as well as specialty foreign-language and instructional discs.

While Gennett Records was now among the nation's largest record companies, it was still dwarfed by the East Coast's recording giants. Victor and Columbia secured exclusive contracts with most of the era's leading classical and pop artists. Whenever Gennett produced hits by promising entertainers, Victor and Columbia seemed to snatch them away with a lucrative contract. Also, their records had better sound quality than the Gennett discs, which were recorded in both the New York and the Richmond studios but were all pressed in the Richmond plant.

But the competitors' dominance did not keep the frugal Gennett Records division from churning out thousands of new releases, which sold by the millions through Starr Piano stores and independent distributors, known in the business as "jobbers." In fact, most Gennett discs that surface today in antique stores, old record shops, or garage sales are the blue-labeled, acoustically recorded discs of the early 1920s.

By 1922, Gennett's Richmond recording studio, hidden back in the Starr Piano factory complex, was busily recording musicians at a pace comparable to the company's Manhattan studio. Before the decade was over, the Richmond studio had produced what are now regarded as seminal jazz, blues, and country music recordings. Yet it was certainly one of the most improbable settings for the recording of landmark American music.

The single-story, gray wooden studio was situated along a row of factory and warehouse buildings on a concrete flood-wall against the Whitewater River. Next to the studio was the factory's flood pumphouse. In the spring, the small river's active waters moved swiftly past the back of the studio. A secondary railroad spur ran along the buildings, about three feet from the studio's front door, for slow-moving cars hauling freight through the crowded Starr factory. The trains could generate enough commotion to interrupt recording sessions, so the studio was generally aware of their schedule. In later years, a red light outside the studio alerted the entire factory that recording sessions were under way.

Over the decades, musicians have described how train noise interrupted sessions or completely ruined recordings at the Richmond studio. The culprits were thundering steam locomotives of the main Chesapeake & Ohio railroad line routed through downtown Richmond, which passed above Starr Piano along the high eastern ridge of the Whitewater gorge. From the C&O railroad line, one has a bird's-eye view of the entire Starr Valley below. This main railroad line, situated about 50 yards from the recording studio, produced noise and vibration at the most unpredictable times. In fact, some collectors of vintage records are convinced that a couple of Gennett discs contain the faint sound of churning trains in the background. "It could be a nuisance with the railroad tracks down there, but you didn't think a lot about it and went on," said Marion McKay, a 1920s bandleader who recorded numerous times at the Richmond studio.[16]

The Richmond studio, about 125 x 30 feet, adjoined a control room where the engineer oversaw the recording session through a double pane of glass. Sawdust between the interior and exterior walls was a feeble attempt at soundproofing. This being before the era of acoustic wall tiles, the studio was "deadened" by monk's cloth draperies from ceiling to floor. On one wall hung a large Mohawk rug, which had once been on a floor in Harry Gennett's home.[17] The Richmond studio could end up so dead that people standing twenty feet apart practically had to yell at each other to be heard. On occasion, Gennett staffers faced the wrath of musicians of large orchestras who complained they couldn't hear each other's instruments. In such cases, the Gennett technicians tried to improve the room's resonance by simply pulling back the drapes.

Before the advent of electronic recording in 1926, recording companies engaged in "acoustic" recording. The process required musicians to gather around and play into a couple of large megaphone-like horns, one to two feet in diameter. The horns transferred the sound, via a crystal, to the recording stylus, which engraved the sound vibrations onto a polished, soft-wax master disc. Consistent with industry practice, the Gennett studios experimented with horns of various sizes, depending upon the type of instruments or voices to be reproduced. In the Richmond studio, the horns, affixed to a multi-pronged pipe, protruded from a small opening in the wall. Just behind the horns, through the opening in the wall, was the large recording machine. In order to avoid picking up excess noise during recording, the horns were enclosed by a curtain at the opening in the wall.

The Gennett turntable on the recording machine operated by a cable and pulley system, much like a grandfather clock. The center pin on the turntable was attached to one end of the cable, which had a large weight on the other end. When the weight was lowered down a shaft, the turntable spun. If the studio had been extremely cold overnight, the grease on the turntable's gear would gum up by morning, and recording would have to be delayed until the room was heated. The pulley system occasionally gave the turntable an inconsistent rotation speed. Thus, while a 78-rpm disc should be recorded while rotating 78 times per minute, some early Gennett discs were cut at uneven speeds or entirely at speeds slightly faster than 78 rpm. Because early phonographs were spring-wound, the discrepancy was not very noticeable to record buyers. But some Gennett discs played on an electronic phonograph seem to slide in and out of tune.

The cutting stylus on the recording machine, which etched sound vibrations from the recording horns onto the polished wax master, could be made of glass, mica, diamond, or, most often, sapphire. The Gennett staffers brushed powdered graphite into the grooves of the wax master to ensure smooth etching by the stylus. Recordings were made on a blank wax disc, consisting primarily of the carnauba wax commonly used in candles. The blank disc, about 13 inches in diameter and 1.5 inches thick, was first polished to a mirror-like finish on two large machines, called the "shaver" and the "polisher." Preparing the wax discs could be tedious. The shaving machine was not always reliable, recalled Gennett staffer Rena Clark, and hard impurities in the wax discs could damage the machine's delicate sapphire shaver.[18]

With the Richmond studio situated in the hinterlands, its business depended on signing bands passing through town. Thus, the company's front office would frequently book recording time for artists without giving the studio staff much advance notice. A band might show up at the studio, and only a couple of wax discs would be polished and ready for recording. Clark would scramble to polish the rough wax discs on the sensitive machinery while the band stood around waiting.

Before actual recording began, Ezra Wickemeyer, the Richmond studio's chief engineer in the early 1920s, established the sound balance by placing the performers at various distances from the horns. Balancing took place only after numerous wax test records of the performers were made and played back through the horns. Certain musicians, such as banjo players, sat on high stools in front of the horns. Naturally, louder brass players were positioned in back. If necessary, Wickemeyer would make dozens of wax takes until he felt the sound balance was correct. Judging from the bizarre instrument balance on some Gennett discs, it's a wonder he bothered.

In addition to establishing sound balance, the test pressings played back through the acoustic horns exposed some musicians as simply incompetent. Wickemeyer would politely send them on their way. Other, more diplomatic sound engineers pretended to record them, knowing full well nothing would be released.

Once Wickemeyer settled on the proper placement of musicians, actual recording could begin. During the recording, the engineer would flick on a red light in the studio to alert the musicians that two minutes and 30 seconds had passed and that the song should end soon. Generally, the Gennett policy was to produce three master discs of each song attempted by the musicians. Each song was given a master number, which was inscribed in the inner circle of the wax disc. If the first take of a song was designated No. 6543, for example, then the second and third takes were designated 6543–A and 6543–B, and so on.

The Richmond studio's location in the bottom of a humid river gorge made recording during the summer months unpleasant enough. But in order to keep the wax discs soft during recording, the unventilated studio had to be kept uncomfortably hot throughout the year. In recalling his recording sessions in Starr Valley, McKay remembered first and foremost the horrendous climate in the studio: "The temperature was always way up. It could be in February and still 80 to 85 degrees in there."[19] The small fans placed to each side of the recording horns offered little relief. In photographs taken in the Richmond studio, the musicians appear as if they had performed in a sauna.

What with the studio temperature, the need for numerous test recordings, and the company's desire to process as many songs as possible in a one-day session, the musicians were put through an exhausting exercise. "Wickemeyer was a good guy to work with, pretty reasonable," said McKay. "They [the Gennett staff] didn't give you any problems; they had plenty of their own problems getting the right sound and balance. You had to be pretty patient sitting through all the playbacks. But nobody minded since recording was such a new thing to everybody. We didn't know any different."[20]

In fact, the musicians who recorded in the Starr factory almost universally held a nostalgic affection for those long, tedious recording sessions by the railroad tracks. "How could you forget it?" asked Bud Dant, a horn player with Hoagy Carmichael's 1928 pickup band for a late-night session in Starr Valley. "When I think of all the places where I've recorded music, that spot in the old piano factory in Richmond had to be one of the most unusual."[21]

After a recording session concluded and the musicians went on their way, the studio staffers took the fragile wax master discs, which were gently packed in cloth-lined boxes, to the plating department in another building in the Starr factory. Copper-plated master discs were then made from the wax masters. Because the studio used powdered graphite in cutting the original wax master disc, rough spots could appear on the copper plating. The staffers very carefully scraped away the rough spots with the help of magnifying glasses, dentist chisels, and engraving tools. If they failed, the copper master was melted down and used again. For example, master discs from a historic Bix Beiderbecke recording session in Richmond were destroyed for this very reason.

From the copper master a few test pressings and a "mother" disc were produced. The mother disc, from which final record pressings were derived, was made from very highly durable shellac-based materials. It was sent to the matrix department for storage. Meanwhile, the test pressings went to the Starr Piano administrative building, where Gennett family members, company managers, studio engineers, or whoever was available, played them on a phonograph to determine which selections would be pressed into finished records.

When the best takes were selected, the matrix department pulled the corresponding mother discs, from which they produced metal "stampers." The stampers were used to press the shellac-based records sold to the public. After about 500 records, the stamper would wear out. New metal stampers were then duplicated from the mother disc, and the pressing would continue.

Rarely were the musicians themselves involved in deciding which selections would be released. Such decisions fell almost exclusively to the small Gennett staff in Richmond, which also evaluated the metal master discs shipped in by railroad from the Manhattan studio. In fact, the control the Richmond staff exercised over the selections was a regular source of consternation at the New York studio, where the staff regularly complained about the quality of discs that Wickemeyer recorded in Richmond.

No recording artist ever got rich from the releases selected by the Gennett staff. Many musicians were paid a basic flat fee, anywhere from $15 to $50 per recording session. Many of the black artists received even less. Most of Gennett's more popular artists signed a royalty contract that guaranteed quarterly payments of one penny for each copy of each side sold. (Later, the royalty payment was one-half cent per release when selections were issued on the many Gennett subsidiary labels.)

A breakage allowance of up to ten percent of these minuscule royalties could be deducted to cover the costs of records broken during shipping. Occasionally, Gennett provided its recording artists with a stack of personal discs to be used for promotional purposes. One must remember that most entertainers in the 1920s viewed their record releases as vehicles for promoting their live shows, not as primary sources of income. The obvious exceptions were the leading artists on the Victor and Columbia labels, such as crooner Rudy Vallee or bandleader Paul Whiteman.

Gennett's meager payment to artists, combined with an efficient plating and pressing organization employing fewer than a hundred people in the Starr Valley, enabled Gennett Records to churn out millions of records profitably in the early 1920s. As America became the melting pot of nationalities, the Gennett Records catalogs during the period reflected wildly diverse musical tastes: the National Marimba Orchestra, Greer Brothers Xylophone Orchestra, Gonzalez's Mexican Band, Lieutenant Matt's 106th Infantry Band, the Knights of Columbus Band, the Orpheus Trio, the Italian Degli Arditi Orchestra, the Hawaiian Guitars, and the Heidelberg Quartet. Gennett also pressed records in German, Italian, Spanish, Swedish, Hungarian, and Czechoslovakian, which were popular with the wave of immigrants pouring into New York.

For many of Gennett's classical releases, the New York studio organized a group of area musicians for its "Gennett Symphony Orchestra." The studio recorded classical soloists, such as violinist Scipione Guidi and pianist Herman Ostheimer. The Richmond studio also pressed records by classical music ensembles in the Midwest, including the nearby Cincinnati Symphony Orchestra.

During the early 1920s, the Gennett studios also recorded such popular singers as Arthur Hall, Sam Ash, George Wilton Ballard, Henry Burr, Al Bernard, Arthur Fields, Harry "Singing Sam" Frankel, Harry McClaskey, and Ernest Hare, a popular New York entertainer who sang in blackface in New York. However, because Gennett Records did not bind these artists to long-term contracts, the company lost many of them to competing labels.

Such was the case with Wendell Hall, a folk singer who performed in hillbilly garb. In 1922, Starr Piano chartered a Pullman car and brought Pittsburgh piano dealers to Richmond for a factory tour and party. A huge buffet luncheon, with a stuffed pig as the centerpiece, was set up in the administration building. As dealers were gathering, a shabbily dressed, red-haired Hall arrived, wanting to make a few records. Hall eventually found his way to the buffet line and later pulled out his ukelele and entertained the amused audience with his collection of original hillbilly songs. "He looked like a tramp," said Taggart, whose job at the luncheon was to hobnob with dealers. "He and his darned old ukelele, there was just something about him."[22] With typical Gennett Records spontaneity, Wickemeyer took Hall down to the recording studio the same afternoon, where Hall knocked out one song after another.

Hall's "It Ain't Gonna Rain No Mo" and "Red Headed Music Maker," back-to-back on a blue-labeled Gennett disc, were an instant success. But Hall wasn't as dumb as his image suggested. At the afternoon recording session in Richmond, the Gennett staff gave him a souvenir test pressing, a common courtesy extended to the studio's recording artists. Hall promptly presented the test record to Victor Records as part of his bid to record for America's dominant label. Within a few months, he was recording for Victor.

Comedy records were easy money for the record labels, as consumers were eager to buy anything new on disc, and Gennett recorded several. Still found in antique stores is the odd "Gennett Laughing Record," which finds a group of people laughing hysterically at a series of muffed violin solos. Such a disc met the fundamental Gennett Records objective of making profit by selling enough records to exceed the low production costs. Hardly art, but great business.

Gennett's Physical Culture exercise package, a three-record set of twelve exercises set to music, featured enthusiastic instructions from one Clarence Nichols, dubbed the "New York Physical Director." The Physical Culture record sleeve showed a hefty woman in a slip working out next to her Gennett phonograph. The Gennett exercise collection promised an invigorating workout for the body without dieting, gym grind, or long hours of training.

In addition to countless discs by local hotel dance orchestras, Gennett Records produced thousands of sacred music records, mostly by the Criterion Male Quartette and by gospel baritone Homer Rodeheaver. White gospel records were enormously popular in the 1920s, as a Christian evangelical revival swept across the Heartland. Gennett's Richmond studio, with ready access to the tent gospel groups touring the Midwest, became a leading supplier of sacred discs. The Richmond pressing plant also custom-pressed thousands of discs for the singing Rodeheaver family's personal Rainbow record label.

William Jennings Bryan, the famous orator, statesman, and three-time U.S. presidential candidate, traveled to Richmond in 1923 to record the "Cross of Gold" speech, his famous oration from the 1896 Democratic presidential convention. The studio also recorded Bryan gently reciting the 23rd Psalm, backed by a string accompaniment of "Rock of Ages." Gennett sold the Bryan records during Christmas on a seasonal red label. Long after Gennett Records closed down, Fred Gennett expressed particular pride in the discs by Bryan and other dignitaries, as opposed to the musical releases.[23]

Gennett Records also profited from the radical political winds blowing through Indiana. In the early 1920s, membership in Indiana's KKK chapters exceeded 250,000, representing the largest Klan contingent of any state in the nation. Part of the attraction was David Curtis Stephenson, who headed a Klan region covering 23 states from his office in Indianapolis. A forceful speaker, Stephenson wielded tremendous political clout in the Indiana capital before his imprisonment in 1925. (He was found guilty of second-degree murder in the highly publicized suicide death of Madge Oberholtzer, who poisoned herself after having been molested by Stephenson.) White-water Klan 60, the Richmond-based klavern that met in the Pythias Building downtown, was several thousand members strong. Not a group of outcasts, it was a cross section of Richmond's middle class and included doctors, lawyers, ministers, and city councilmen.

Gennett's Richmond studio recorded specialty discs and pressed thousands of copies for klaverns in the Indiana cities of Richmond, Muncie, and Indianapolis, while its New York studio also made Klan records. These discs, pressed with red labels and gold lettering, were typically vocal numbers with piano accompaniment. The KKK would take old hymns and politicize them with new lyrics, such as "The Bright Fiery Cross" (based on "The Old Rugged Cross"), "Cross in the Wildwood" ("Church in the Wildwood"), or "Onward Christian Klansman" ("Onward Christian Soldiers"). Other KKK records recorded and custom-pressed by Gennett, and distributed solely by the Klan, included "The Pope's Warning," "There'll Be a Hot Time, Klansman," "You're Going to Leave the Old Home, Jim," and "Johnny Join the Klan, Come to the Cross." Several Starr Piano employees were active Klan members and posted Klan literature in Starr factory buildings. While the Gennett family employed blacks in their homes, the Starr factories never employed blacks in the 1920s.

One morning in the early 1920s, C. A. Rhinehart and W. R. Rhinehart, two Klan members who drove an ice truck in nearby Muncie, entered the administration office near the entrance of the Starr factory and laid $400 on the table with the idea of making 1,000 records. Clayton Jackson, assistant sales manager for Gennett Records, received their request. He pointed the Rhineharts in the direction of the recording studio and then telephoned studio engineer Ezra Wickemeyer. "Ezra was quite a Catholic. I told him to cut two numbers and get them the hell out of there before lunch, and that I'd take care of the details," Jackson said. "He wouldn't have to do anything except just number them [the master discs] and I'd give them the labeling dope after lunch so he could fill in his books. I had these boys' $400 in my pocket. Ezra quit. Ezra said he was going up the hill, going home, and to hell with it."[24]

Harry Gennett, Henry's eldest son, became incensed with Jackson upon learning of the incident. "Harry's face got red and he said to me, 'Are you ever going to grow up? Send Ku Kluxers down to that Catholic to record?' I didn't know that much about the KKK then," Jackson said. "We made a helluva lot of records for them. We used to load them passenger inter-urban cars [commuter trains] and take them [records] to Indianapolis."[25] By the way, Wickemeyer never permanently quit Gennett Records because of the Klan records.

In another incident, Taggart recalled Clarence Gennett objecting to a Klan test record he heard playing on a phonograph in the Starr front office. After Gennett ordered the discs destroyed, Taggart quietly instructed a staffer to "send the wax down to the electroplating room so we each got a copy of it before we destroyed everything. Clarence never knew that." Taggart added that "some of the Catholics took up the fact that they [Gennett Records] were making records for the KKK."[26]

Though Klan literature was circulated in the factory, the Gennetts did not publicly support the organization, according to former employees and family members. The company pressed Klan records simply because it was a guaranteed cash business. "I sat on the front lawn of my grandfather's house [Henry Gennett's estate] on Main Street and watched the Klan parade down the street," said Richard Gennett, son of Fred Gennett. "The Klan was a big thing in Richmond back then. But the Gennetts weren't a part of that. The Gennett studio did all kinds of custom pressing because you got paid up front. That was good business."[27]

Specialty pressing for private individuals was a profitable sideline for Gennett Records. Numerous personal recordings by Gennett have been prized by collectors over the years, such as a rare 1922 disc by bandleader Joe Kayser. However, the primary revenues for the company were always derived from the standard Gennett releases in the Gennett Records catalog. These discs were sold in a Gennett record sleeve with an emblem depicting three girls in dresses dancing gleefully below the slogan, "The Difference is in the Tone."

The Gennett releases were shipped by railroad car or truck to the numerous Starr Piano stores, which had large Gennett Records displays set up near the Starr phonograph retail area. Gennett discs in the early 1920s sold for $.85 to $1.10 each, a range comparable to competing labels. Jackson said Gennett Records considered the break-even point for a particular release to be 18,000 to 20,000 copies, though many Gennett releases later in the decade never approached such sales figures.

The independent dealers purchased the Gennett records wholesale, directly from the Starr plant, at 55 percent off the retail price. Small department stores and variety stores around the nation could obtain Gennett records through independent jobbers, who purchased large quantities of records at a discount from a Starr Piano store. They drove around the countryside with the discs piled up in their cars and called on small retailers.

"When we had a hit on the East Coast, we'd ship records to beat hell to New York," Jackson said. "We had two dual-wheel trucks and we'd send loads of records on those two trucks. We'd send them trucks to New York, and they'd bring records back through Philadelphia and Pittsburgh. We kept cycling them back this way."[28]

Starr Piano salesmen commonly promoted Gennett Records during sales calls for the piano company. While Starr Piano employees were paid paltry salaries, the salesmen loved to travel for the company, because the Gennett family demanded that they stay in the best hotels in order to enhance the company's image. Once, when Taggart stopped in Iowa for the piano company, he met with one of Starr's independent jobbers in order to promote the Criterion Quartette's new release of "Iowa Corn Song" on the Gennett label. "I had more fun than a barrel of monkeys on that trip,'' said Taggart. "This old man [the jobber] would always hunt up a cheap hotel; I'd always stay at the best. In those days, they had listening booths in the record stores. So I'd go into a music store, slip into one of those booths, and put this 'Iowa Corn Song' on, and the people would stack up trying to hear it.''[29]

The early 1920s were the halcyon days for Gennett Records. Back in Richmond, Taggart would encounter Henry Gennett making the rounds of the Starr Piano factory when the division's record business was booming. "He used to come around in the morning, rubbing his hands together, round and round," Taggart said. "This was when the record business was pretty good. He'd ask 'How are the checks coming in today?' I'd tell him what we got in our end of it. He said, 'Well, you're holding up the piano business right now.' "[30]

Clearly, Henry Gennett, who turned 65 in 1918, had provided the vision behind Starr Piano. But in the years leading up to 1922, he had essentially turned over day-to-day management to his sons, while he and his wife, Alice, took long trips to exotic spots around the world. Henry also maintained a close connection with Starr Piano's thriving Pacific Division in California. He enjoyed long stays along the Santa Barbara coast. California had also become a second home to Henry and Alice's only daughter, Rose.

During these prosperous years, the Gennett sons—Clarence, Fred, and Harry—were raising families in stately homes, all within a couple of blocks of their parents' mansion on Main Street in Richmond. The eldest son, Harry, helped his father manage the piano manufacturing operations. Like his father, Harry was a short man, but more robust. Probably the best liked of the Gennett sons at Starr Piano, Harry was known for his humor, infectious laugh, and private philanthropy. He took an interest in the welfare of Starr employees and personally secured work permits for Richmond boys under the legal working age who sought employment at the piano factory.

Clarence, the company's treasurer, was more removed

from the manufacturing operations in the Starr Valley. In 1915, he and his wife purchased a vacation home in Nantucket, Massachusetts, where the family spent much of the summer. More of a social lion and small-town aristocrat, Clarence was actively involved in numerous social and civic organizations, including the Richmond Country Club. Like his father, he served on the boards of local companies. He was active in the local Presbyterian Church and even found time to moonlight as a sheriff's deputy.

Some Starr employees found Clarence aloof. "He was a stiff-shirt; he thought he was top-stuff," said Harold Soule, former recording engineer at the Richmond studio. "He used to drive down the street in his electric car. He wouldn't even spit on you, let alone look at you."[31] Clarence's niece Florence Gennett offered a more gentle assessment, noting that he "tried to be well-mannered. He wasn't very down to earth. I used to see him downtown, I'd say 'Hi Uncle Clarence!' He would nod his head slightly and say, 'How do you do, Florence.' No smile. Nothing else. He'd just go on his way."[32]

The youngest son, Fred, supervised Starr Piano sales accounts and the Gennett Records division. A thin man of medium height, with receding black hair and horn-rimmed glasses, Fred resembled a scholar more than a Midwestern businessman engaged in the pioneer recording industry. Personable and unassuming, Fred was the prototypically conservative Indiana executive. Like his brothers, he went to work in the family piano business right out of high school. He married Hazel Reid, a member of a prominent local family who spearheaded the construction of Richmond's Reid Memorial Hospital. A true blueblood, Hazel held local offices in the Daughters of the American Revolution and the Daughters of American Colonists.

Fred and Hazel and their four children lived comfortably, employing a maid and a grounds keeper, in a spacious mansion some twenty blocks from Starr Valley. Fred routinely walked to work each morning, and neighborhood women would say that they could set their clocks by his passing. Fred's house was filled with music. On their Starr phonograph, Fred and the children cranked up test pressings or new Gennett releases. When they grew tired of the discs, they simply returned them to the Starr factory to be melted down. Richard Gennett said that his father fancied himself a good pianist, though his skills were limited. Hazel, on the other hand, was an accomplished violinist and pianist and sang in the church choir.

Unlike brother Clarence, Fred was a bit more private. He did not attend church, and he had a particular aversion to Catholicism. Neither was he active in the local country club. He spent many free hours around the house, working in the yard or planting a garden. Richard said that his father didn't drink or smoke, at least around the kids, and eschewed crude language. "Whenever I would cuss, Pop would stare down at me and say 'You should be ashamed of yourself.' "[33]

Fred shared his father's fascination with California and spent weeks at a time with his father on the West Coast. He was actively involved in the development of the Pacific Division and once expressed the desire to move the company's piano manufacturing operations to the West Coast. But, as with many projects Fred envisioned or initiated, he did not follow through. He was easily bored with details, a personality trait that cost the company money in later years.

In April 1922, while Henry Gennett was conducting business at Starr's Pacific Division in Los Angeles, he became ill. He promptly returned to Richmond, where his health continued to deteriorate for about a month. On a Friday night, June 2, 1922, he died at Miami Valley Hospital in nearby Dayton, Ohio, with his wife and son Harry at his side. Henry was 69 years old.

His body was laid out for viewing the next day at his home. That evening, hundreds of his employees assembled at the downtown Starr Piano store and walked as a group to the Gennett mansion, where hundreds of other local friends paid respects. On Sunday morning, members of the local Elks lodge assembled to attend the funeral in the open area of the mansion's main floor, with the casket positioned in front of the huge fireplace. The room was packed. Richard Gennett remembered that a Starr employee service pin, awarded to company workers, was attached to his grandfather's coat lapel but was removed by someone just before the casket was closed. Henry's body was cremated in Cincinnati, and the ashes were sent to California, the state he loved.

Henry died at the financial peak of Starr Piano and Gennett Records. Shortly after his death, a letter from the company's accountants arrived in Starr Valley. Taggart accidentally opened it and learned that the estimated net worth of Starr Piano was $7 million. From the viewpoint of many Starr Piano employees, including Taggart, Henry's hard-driving demeanor had been key to the company's national prominence. "One time we had sent down a whole mess of records that were to go to Los Angeles," Taggart said. "When we would get them ready, we would take them down to the packing room and then they were supposed to go in with a carload of pianos. We got a telegram back one day saying there were no records in that car. Right away, old Henry jumped on me. I got the books out which showed where the packing room had receipted for them when we took them down [to the train car]. Henry gathered together Harry, Clarence, Fred, myself, and the packing room boss. He said, 'Well now, I'll tell you boys, whoever is to blame for this foul up, I want him fired right now. Let's clean it up.' He never fired the packing room boss or anybody. He would make decisions though. The old man had the reputation that when orders for pianos and records would slow up, he'd go out himself and get some orders. None of those boys would."[34]

Harry became company president upon his father's death. He regularly sought business counsel for years from his mother, Alice, who served as company vice president and a director and often visited the plant. In fact, the three sons frequently met with their mother at noon at the Gennett estate to brief her on company activities.

The gradual financial slide of Starr Piano and its record division began with Henry's death. Certainly, the company soon faced enormous challenges beyond the control of the sons. By 1923, the arrival of the cheap home radio seriously affected the piano, phonograph, and recording industries. The annual production of pianos in the U.S. declined by more than half between 1923 and 1929, with the production of player pianos falling some 86 percent in the same period.[35] Another deadly blow was the onset of the Great Depression in late 1929. In the 1930s, the surviving Gennett family members were locked in bitter disputes over the direction of Starr Piano and its confusing web of subsidiaries. Family friction only contributed to the company's steady losses, leading to the sale of the company in 1952 at a fraction of the financial worth it had attained during Henry Gennett's life.

Fortunately for music history, the Gennett family kept their record label in operation throughout the 1920s. Had Gennett Records closed down at its financial peak in the early part of the decade, the label would be long forgotten, a faded memory surviving only in the dusty piles of 78-rpm records in antique stores. But when home radio began to impact on the sale of pop and classical records, Gennett Records and its competitors responded aggressively, pursuing previously neglected market segments, such as urban black and rural white customers.

A leader in pursuing these market segments, the small Gennett label was among the first companies to record America's indigenous music genres: jazz, blues, and old time music, the precursor to country music. As Henry's ashes were being sprinkled into the Pacific Ocean in mid-1922, a new American music was evolving in noisy dance halls on the south side of Chicago. His youngest son, Fred, was unknowingly about to secure for the small Indiana record label a permanent place in the annals of American recorded music.

A New Wind Is Blowing through Chicago

I n mid-1922, Fred Wiggins was managing Starr Piano's music showroom on South Wabash Avenue in downtown Chicago when he caught wind of a white dance band creating a stir at the Friars Inn, a basement club just a few blocks down the street. Young white musicians from New Orleans fronted the band, which played the syncopated, malign music captivating American youth: jazz.

The scene was increasingly common in Prohibition Chicago. An influx of black and white jazz musicians from New Orleans appeared on Chicago bandstands, a phenomenon driven largely by the mass movement of Southern blacks into Chicago's south side. Dixieland jazz imported from New Orleans, birthplace of the controversial music, was doing big business in boomtown Chicago's theatres and dance halls. And despite all the excitement, the New Orleans jazz players now based in Chicago were virtually untapped by the nation's record companies.

Gennett Records' Manhattan studio, in keeping up with its larger competitors, had begun to produce jazz-flavored, commercial dance discs by white New York studio bands organized for the purpose of recording. Many of them played a homogenized jazz that was showcased more as a novelty, while Chicago's soulful jazz was rooted in the New Orleans tradition and undiluted by commercialization.

Always scouting for new talent to record at Gennett's Richmond studio, Wiggins contacted his boss and close friend,

Fred Gennett, at the Starr factory and urged him to hear for himself the house band at the Friars Inn. After his father's death, 36-year-old Fred Gennett took over full management of Gennett Records, though he lacked his father's business acumen. "Pop was one smart fella, but money never meant anything to him," Richard Gennett said about his father. "He'd rather do a million dollars worth of business and lose money, than do a little business and make a few bucks."[1]

Fred was more a dreamer, always open to a new gimmick or potential fad. The brash, new jazz music flourished in a world light years away from his comfortable, small-town environment. He had no personal interest in jazz, but it represented a business opportunity. Fred saw the wisdom in pursuing black record buyers, and the jazz musicians in nearby Chicago offered real potential for that audience, as well as for the enthusiastic white record buyers. As Gennett technician Harold Soule observed, "When it came to the recording end, it was Fred who dreamed up many of the ideas. In fact, any time something new came up, Fred was the one who tried it out. Fred would always hear you out. He was way ahead of his time."[2]

Fred also respected the opinions of Wiggins, his lifelong friend and confidant. They essentially grew up together in the Starr Piano business. A descendant of one of Richmond's founding Quaker families, Wiggins, 41 years old in 1922, had worked up through the Starr Piano ranks, starting in the shipping department in 1906. Before Henry Gennett's death, the Gennett family assigned Wiggins to manage Starr Piano's Chicago store, one of the company's largest retail centers. A tall, thin man with a squeaky voice and a passion for Wheeling stogies, Wiggins was astute and confident, if not overly opinionated. Associates said Wiggins couldn't carry a tune, but possessed, at least for a short period of time, a reliable knack for knowing which musicians would sell on records.

Predictably, Fred listened when Wiggins spoke enthusiastically about the band at the Friars Inn. He soon took the five-hour train ride to Chicago to join Wiggins at one of the small tables near the bandstand. At the corner of Wabash and Van Buren in the Chicago Loop, the Friars Inn was a hopping joint that attracted Chicago's rich and infamous, such as mobsters Al Capone and Dion O'Bannion. The new eight-piece house band, known in the club as the New Orleans Rhythm Kings, was fronted by clarinetist Leon Roppolo, with cornetist Paul Mares and trombonist George Brunies, all from New Orleans, along with five Midwestern jazz converts in the rhythm section.

It was an eccentric group. While Brunies and Roppolo were notable soloists, only pianist Elmer Schoebel could adequately read music. Roppolo might play while leaning against a post near the bandstand or play in a corner with his back to the audience—a full half-century before jazz giant Miles Davis adopted the same iconoclastic demeanor on stage. As is common with young musicians, the boys were notorious practical jokers, guilty of such antics as putting mustard oil on each other's chairs.

The crowd's reaction to the band's charisma was undeniable. Wiggins viewed the group as commercially viable, a worthy entry into the Chicago jazz scene for Gennett's Richmond studio, one that could give the label a leg up on the competition. Fred agreed and signed the young band to its first record contract. A recording date was set for August 29, 1922, in the Richmond studio. "We were so anxious to record that we took the first offer to come along and beat all the rest of the bands," cornetist Mares said. "We could have made a fortune with that band if we had played our cards right, but we didn't. We rushed into everything like we did that recording deal."[3]

The story went that Starr Piano employees, many of them skilled German artisans who looked down their noses on the shenanigans at the so-called Gennett Recording Laboratory, were amused when a dusty car from Chicago, packed with eight sweaty musicians and their instruments, pulled down the narrow lane through the industrial complex in Starr Valley. No one suspected it then, but it marked the beginning of a remarkable era for Gennett's modest recording shed, and for the recorded history of early jazz.

Over the next two years, Gennett Records introduced American record buyers to an authentic, Chicago-based jazz from New Orleans originals and their Midwestern followers. A new breeze of jazz was blowing in the Windy City in the early 1920s, and Gennett Records became its aural diary. Behind the deal making of Fred Gennett and Wiggins, Gennett Records produced the first discs by the New Orleans Rhythm Kings and, more important, debuted on record the King Oliver Creole Jazz Band, with immortal New Orleans cornetists Joe Oliver and Louis Armstrong, clarinetist Johnny Dodds, and drummer Baby Dodds.

New Orleans Creole Jelly Roll Morton, the first major jazz composer, was based in Chicago in 1923–24. In Richmond he made a series of brilliant solo piano recordings, and also collaborated on some disks with the New Orleans Rhythm Kings. Pioneer cornetist Freddie Keppard, one of the New Orleans jazz stars, recorded on Gennett sides with Cook's Dreamland Orchestra of Chicago. Earl "Fatha" Hines, a father of modern jazz piano and longtime Chicago bandleader, debuted on record in Richmond in 1923 with Lois Deppe's orchestra. Among the leading white disciples of the jazz cornet who first appeared on Gennett were Muggsy Spanier and the legendary Bix Beiderbecke.

More than 75 sides of influential jazz music from Chicago-area musicians were waxed in Richmond by mid-1924. Despite its location in rural Indiana, the Richmond studio produced some of the first significant jazz recordings and exerted an impact on the music scene that was immediate, widespread, and lasting. Although Gennett's New York studio was no match for the Richmond studio in producing innovative jazz, it also contributed to the early recorded jazz scene. Between the two studios, Gennett Records played a central role in the early pollination of the new music genre in the 1920s, a decade soon pegged as the Jazz Age.

Despite the parallel emergence of sound reproduction and jazz in the late nineteenth century, the infant recording industry had largely ignored the music before the arrival of Gennett Records. Thomas Edison was perfecting sound reproduction while jazz was evolving in the black South from an amalgamation of African rhythms, ragtime, Southern blues, spirituals, folk music, and marches. By 1900, jazz came into greater focus with the publishing of ragtime piano music and the emergence of a distinct jazz march style in New Orleans. Early in the twentieth century, ragtime sheet music by Scott Joplin and others influenced commercial dance music and popular songs. By 1915, several ragtime songs had been recorded, but, since the piano was barely audible on acoustic recording equipment, ragtime was more often scored for small brass ensembles. Even famed concert band composer John Philip Sousa incorporated rag styles into his arrangements. Player pianos were popular, and Harlem "stride" ragtime pianists, such as Eubie Blake and James P. Johnson, supplemented their incomes by producing ragtime piano rolls.

In 1916, the Johnny Stein Band, led by white New Orleans jazz musicians, set up in a Chicago club and developed a large following. The cornetist, Nick LaRocca, soon quit and formed a new jazz ensemble with the nucleus of the Stein band. When the new group, which called itself the Original Dixieland Jazz Band, played the radical new music for patrons in New York's Reisenweber's Restaurant in January 1917, it immediately attracted Columbia Records.

The band recorded "Darktown Strutters' Ball" and "Indiana," but Columbia was hesitant to release the records. So, in late February, rival Victor Records, also observing the excitement at Reisenweber's, recorded the band playing "Livery Stable Blues" and "Dixie Jass Band One-Step." Victor didn't waste a moment and had the 78-rpm discs for sale by

March. The first official jazz release sold more than a million copies.

By 1920, the Original Dixieland Jazz Band had recorded a string of hits that provided white bands for years with a stock of jazz tunes such as "Tiger Rag" and "Sensation." During 1919-20, the band sold out shows in England, where some listeners fueled a preposterous myth that jazz was created by white New Orleans musicians and performed by black "imitators." (Reaction to this initial undermining of jazz's black origins later contributed to a politicization of jazz scholarship, which still exists today. In an attempt to correct early historical distortions, important contributions by white players to early jazz are often denied.)

Despite the rage over the Original Dixieland Jazz Band, record labels were generally lukewarm to white jazz bands and essentially ignored the black jazz ensembles. Even though the phonograph blossomed into a $150 million industry by 1920 behind a growing dance craze, record labels underestimated the sales potential among black people who could afford to buy them.

Except for discs of the Original Dixieland Jazz Band, the jazz recorded by white bands in New York in 1918–20 was rather limited. Gennett's New York studio jumped on the bandwagon as early as 1919, recording a white ensemble called the New Orleans Jazz Band. Jimmy Durante, later to become a popular entertainer, made the rounds of the New York studios in 1919–20 as a jazz pianist, recording for Gennett and for General Phonograph Corporation's OKeh label.

A key milestone in jazz recording was the birth of "race records" in 1921, sparked by Harlem blues singer Mamie Smith's hits on OKeh Records. Perry Bradford, a southern black entrepreneur and composer, could not interest Victor and Columbia in his songs, but he attracted OKeh with Mamie Smith as his vocalist. OKeh's second disc by Smith in late 1920, Bradford's "Crazy Blues" and "It's Right Here For You," sold more than a million copies by early 1921.

The concept of race records involved recording and marketing blues, jazz, gospel, and spirituals specifically for black consumers. The labels gradually maintained long lists of race records, often packaged in separate catalogs. The concept stayed with the recording industry well into the 1940s. The term "race" was a preferred term in 1920s black culture and was used in black newspapers to denote black entertainers. In the North, race records were advertised primarily in the black media, such as Chicago's *Defender* newspaper.

With Mamie Smith's success in 1921, OKeh marketed a series of race recordings by black female vaudeville singers. Paramount Records, a subsidiary of the Wisconsin Chair Company of Port Washington, Wisconsin, began its race series in mid-1922 with recordings from its New York Recording Laboratories by Alberta Hunter and others. Columbia's powerhouse race catalog was launched in late 1923 with Bessie Smith and Clara Smith. About the same time, Gennett Records issued its Gennett Colored Artists Records catalog, touting black composer Richard Jones and Chicago theatre vocalist Callie Vassar, both of whom recorded in the Richmond studio, and singers Viola McCoy, Mandy Lee, and Edna Hicks, each of whom recorded in the New York studio. Gennett's advertisements described these artists as famous in musical comedy and vaudeville.

Female singers dominated race recordings in the early 1920s. While their repertoires mostly consisted of standard tunes, the singers were backed by skilled jazz instrumentalists, primarily cornetists. The fascination with female blues singers soon led the music publishers to include the word "blues" in the titles of countless blues, jazz, and popular songs of the era. As the 1920s progressed and discount records came into fashion, Gennett Records and other competing labels pressed race records for mail-order record catalogs circulated by Sears, Roebuck & Co. and Montgomery Ward.

While the record labels focused on black female blues singers for the race market in the 1921–23 period, white

America experienced a dance craze with white studio bands in New York recording commercial dance tunes with a jazz feel. By late 1921, Gennett's New York studio actively produced commercial dance music by two related white studio session groups, Ladd's Black Aces and Bailey's Lucky Seven. Ladd's Black Aces, organized by cornetist Phil Napoleon, was a pseudonym on Gennett for the prolific Original Memphis Five, probably New York's best white studio jazz band in the early 1920s. The band had no connection with Memphis or the South, but the misleading name enabled Gennett to include Ladd's Black Aces in its Colored Artists catalog.

Bailey's Lucky Seven, organized by New York promoter Sam Lanin, included members of Ladd's Black Aces. Combined, the two groups recorded more than a hundred sides for Gennett. In view of the availability today of the original 78-rpms, these ensembles were obviously big sellers for Gennett. In fact, French composer Darius Milhaud, who visited New York in 1922, returned to Paris with the Ladd's Black Aces recording of "Aunt Hagar's Children's Blues." Milhaud was among several serious European composers captivated by America's newly commercialized jazz music. With a little imagination, you can hear strains of "Aunt Hagar's Children's Blues" in Milhaud's 1923 composition *La Création du Monde*.

The competent Ladd's Black Aces and Bailey's Lucky Seven ensembles produced well-polished recordings in the spirit of the Original Dixieland Jazz Band. Though unfairly dismissed by some critics, these recordings feature several capable instrumentalists, including clarinetists Doc Behrendson and Jimmy Lytell and trombonist Miff Mole. Most often cited is Lytell's solo on "Hopeless Blues," recorded by Ladd's Black Aces at Gennett on May 25, 1922. Mole, a New York native, was possibly the best improvising trombonist in Manhattan in the early 1920s. He recorded prolifically with Gennett and other labels, and later became one of New York's most imitated trombonists. Fortunately, the clarinet and trombone could be clearly picked up by Gennett's crude acoustic recording equipment. (The Ladd's Black Aces recordings, which have been reissued in recent years, have remained especially popular in England.)

While record labels promoted white jazz bands, such as Ladd's Black Aces on Gennett, authentic New Orleans black bands were yet to be documented in any meaningful way. Black New Orleans trombonist Kid Ory was recorded in 1922 on the obscure Sunshine label in Los Angeles, but other instances were few and far between. That would change soon after Fred Gennett's all-important record contract in mid-1922 with the New Orleans Rhythm Kings. It was a white band, but the record companies could no longer bypass Chicago's vibrant scene, which included some of the most original black as well as white jazz artists in America. The race by the record companies to record jazz was just over the horizon.

The New Orleans Rhythm Kings

New Orleans jazz had thrived in Chicago's clubs and dance halls several years before the Gennett label stumbled across the New Orleans Rhythm Kings. As the Midwest's industrial giant, Chicago attracted waves of southern blacks in the early twentieth century, which peaked with the manufacturing boom created by World War I. Mayor "Big Bill" Thompson's Chicago, with a blind eye to Prohibition and mobster organizations, housed more than 200,000 blacks by 1920, a black population three times that of New York. Chicago's large black community supported a well-established black entertainment industry, with dance clubs and theatres such as the Royal Garden Cafe, the Vendome Theatre, and the Dreamland Cafe on Chicago's famed South State Street. Chicago's blacks were far from wealthy, but they had more disposable income than they had ever enjoyed down South.

Many New Orleans jazz musicians working the Mississippi River steamboats began to settle in Chicago. But the real migration began in 1917, when the infamous New Orleans Storyville red light district was shut down, and the jazz players who worked the district were forced to seek work in the North. New Orleans cornetist Freddie Keppard settled in Chicago in 1917, along with fellow musicians Roy Palmer and Ed Garland. The best New Orleans jazz cornetist, Joe "King" Oliver, arrived a year later and was featured in Bill Johnson's Original Creole Orchestra at the Royal Garden Cafe.

It is often assumed, because of institutionalized segregation, that early black musicians played jazz solely for black audiences. But, as was evident in Chicago during 1916–22, black jazz players attracted a substantial number of white listeners as well. At the same time, white musicians in New Orleans, particularly in the Italian neighborhoods, incorporated the black jazz style into their own playing long before much of black America had been exposed to New Orleans jazz. The Original Dixieland Jazz Band is the most obvious example. As white jazz musicians from New Orleans also settled in Chicago, they actively recruited white players from their old neighborhoods; likewise, New Orleans black musicians in Chicago engaged in talent searches back home.

In 1920, Abbie Brunies, a young white cornetist working in New Orleans, was offered a job with a Chicago-based Dixieland band. He passed the invitation to a neighbor, twenty-year-old cornetist Paul Mares, who jumped at the offer to work in Chicago. Abbie Brunies' eighteen-year-old brother, trombonist George Brunies, soon joined Mares. George Brunies and Mares naturally associated with Chicago's white jazz players, including pianist Elmer Schoebel, saxophonist Jack Pettis, and banjoist Louis Black. Mares and Brunies then hooked up near Chicago with a childhood friend, Leon Roppolo, a virtuoso clarinetist who had been performing professionally since he was fourteen. The scion of a classically trained New Orleans family, Roppolo had already played riverboats and toured as a sideman throughout the Midwest.

A Chicago band organizer and promoter named Husk

O'Hare, whose own commercial dance orchestra recorded at Gennett's Richmond studio in early 1922, began booking the ensemble of Mares, Roppolo, Brunies, Schoebel, and friends at several Chicago venues in 1921–22, leading to a booking in the downtown Friars Inn. Here, the saga of the New Orleans Rhythm Kings began.

We do not know how Starr Piano's Wiggins learned of the new house band at Friars Inn. O'Hare obviously was acquainted with Wiggins and Fred Gennett. Also, Lester and Walter Melrose, two white men from the South, claimed that they suggested the New Orleans Rhythm Kings to Gennett. (Their Melrose Brothers Music Co. store on Chicago's State Street prospered in the 1920s by selling stock arrangements of Chicago jazz and blues.) What matters is that the subsequent collaboration between Gennett Records and the New Orleans Rhythm Kings documents the first important link between New Orleans and Midwestern jazz musicians. Gennett produced an incredible 31 sides during three visits by the band to Richmond in 1922–23; these include multiple versions of a couple of the songs.

At the first session in August 1922, the eight-piece band arrived with a mix of original songs, standards from the Original Dixieland Jazz Band, and commercial dance tunes from their play list at the Friars Inn. Gennett's Wickemeyer cut more than twenty takes on the primitive acoustic equipment, with the usual technical annoyances. Brunies, for example, recalled playing the trombone too close to the recording horn, causing the stylus to bounce, and forcing recording to stop. The Gennett studio showed exceptional faith in the untried band after the first recording date, releasing seven sides on the Gennett label under the name Friar's Society Orchestra. Though the overall quality of the songs is uneven, it is easy to understand why the record pressing plant in Richmond issued so many releases.

While employing varying tempos, the New Orleans Rhythm Kings played in a pleasant, legato style. It was an interesting departure from the hyperactive, choppy jazz of the Original Dixieland Jazz Band, the primary model for all white jazz in 1922. The rhythmic ease of the New Orleans Rhythm Kings reflected their admiration for, and understanding of, the black New Orleans jazz, which was not yet recorded. As a consequence, Gennett debuted a band that drew inspiration from both the black and the white worlds of jazz emerging in Chicago.

Mares patterned his cornet playing after Joe "King" Oliver, the most original jazz cornetist from New Orleans based in Chicago. Oliver's influence on these Gennett releases is omnipresent. On the band's first batch of sides, such as "Eccentric" and "Farewell Blues," the twenty-year-old Mares adopts Oliver's muted cornet technique at every opportunity, while capably improvising in his own right on "Bugle Call Blues," an original by the band.

Most revealing from the band's first recordings are the stunning passages by twenty-year-old clarinetist Roppolo, arguably the first great jazz soloist ever recorded. Behind Roppolo's blues-driven virtuosity, the band takes "Tiger Rag," an Original Dixieland Jazz Band standard, to a high emotional level. The subtlety and rich fluidity in his solos confirm Roppolo's total grasp of the developing jazz tradition. Few jazz clarinetists in the early 1920s could match the great Roppolo, an eccentric Sicilian who was exposed to black New Orleans jazz as a boy. If only for Roppolo's clarinet solos, the New Orleans Rhythm Kings releases are of historical value as examples of early jazz improvisation.

Gennett distributed seven songs using the name Friar's Society Orchestra to exploit the band's association with the well-known Chicago club. The impact was instant. The band's originals, "Farewell Blues" and "Bugle Call Blues," were soon covered by numerous white jazz bands. When a popular jazz band called the Georgians recorded "Farewell Blues" in 1923, they copied Roppolo's solo from the Gennett release note-for-note. "Bugle Call Blues" was covered in the late 1920s by the famed New York cornetist Red Nichols, and by The Whoopee Makers, a pickup studio band featuring clarinetist Benny Goodman and trombonist Jack Teagarden. But possibly the New Orleans Rhythm Kings' most ardent followers were the white jazz enthusiasts from Chicago's Austin High School. Jazz history would later immortalize them as the Austin Gang: Jimmy McPartland on cornet, Bud Freeman on saxophone, and Frank Teschemacher on clarinet. These classmates were the leading torchbearers of the Dixieland jazz revival in the 1940s.

But back in 1923, McPartland and his buddies were high school students hanging out after class at an ice cream parlor called the Spoon and Straw, where they listened to records on a Victrola. One afternoon, the blue-labeled Gennett releases by the Friar's Society Orchestra were stacked on the table. "I believe the first tune we played was 'Farewell Blues,' " McPartland recalled years later. "Boy, when we heard that, I'll tell you we went out of our minds. Everybody flipped. It was wonderful. So we put the others on. We stayed there from about three in the afternoon until eight at night, just listening to those records one after another, over and over again. Right then and there we decided we would get a band and try to play like these guys."[4]

After McPartland, Freeman, and the others picked up musical instruments, they wore out the Gennett discs, memorizing the New Orleans Rhythm Kings numbers a few bars at a time. After about a month, the band had memorized "Farewell Blues" in its entirety. They even called themselves the Blue Friars. "We were too young to get into the Friars Inn, so the only way we could hear the Rhythm Kings was to go down and stand in the doorway and listen," McPartland said. "It was great when someone opened the door, and we could hear it louder."[5]

With Chicago jazz listeners buzzing over the Rhythm Kings' first batch of releases, the band returned to Richmond on March 12, 1923 as a quintet. Pianist Mel Stitzel replaced Schoebel, who worked as an arranger/transcriber for the Melrose Brothers Music Co., which had begun publishing the band's compositions. The band's drummer, Frank Snyder, was replaced by a young Ben Pollack. (In the 1930s, Pollack led bands featuring trombonist Glenn Miller and clarinetist Benny Goodman.)

Pared down to a front line of clarinet, cornet, and trombone, which was the standard Dixieland ensemble mix, soloists Roppolo, Brunies, and Mares were liberated from the musical traffic of the eight-piece group and masterfully wove their lines together with greater clarity. While the August 1922 recordings contained some forgettable commercial numbers, the band's repertoire at the March 1923 session was steeped in New Orleans jazz tradition with the influence of the still-unrecorded King Oliver Creole Jazz Band strongly evident.

Whereas the Original Dixieland Jazz Band had denied the influence of black New Orleans jazz music, Mares in later years went so far as to say that the New Orleans Rhythm Kings tried to copy black musicians. This public reverence for black jazz, though well received by the jazz cognoscenti, contributed to a long-standing perception of the New Orleans Rhythm Kings as mere imitators of jazz, and not genuine innovators. Fortunately, that attitude is being re-evaluated. A careful listening of the March 1923 sessions confirms that Brunies, and especially Roppolo, had mastered individualistic approaches toward jazz improvisation, which inspired a generation of imitators.

The band recorded eight songs for Gennett in March 1923, with multiple takes preserved of "Sweet Lovin' Man," "Wolverine Blues," and the classic "Tin Roof Blues." Other songs were "That's a Plenty," "Shimmeshawable," "That Da Da Strain," and the old ragtime tunes "Weary Blues" and "Maple Leaf Rag."

Three versions exist today of the lazy "Tin Roof Blues," which the Melrose Brothers published with the entire band credited as the composers. The song was clearly inspired, however, by "Jazzin' Baby Blues," written by black composer Richard M. Jones, who recorded the song as a piano solo for Gennett in 1923. The takes are memorable for the crying blues solos by Brunies and Roppolo, whose deeply expressive lines are still copied note-for-note today by clarinetists in the traditional Dixieland field. Roppolo's solos on "Sweet Lovin' Man," from the King Oliver play list, and "That's a Plenty" are equally dramatic.

The New Orleans Rhythm Kings' cuts of "Wolverine Blues" were essentially a preview to memorable events just ahead in the Richmond studio. "Wolverine Blues," popularized at Chicago's Lincoln Gardens by Oliver's band, was composed by pianist Jelly Roll Morton, who returned to Chicago in early 1923 from California and began composing prolifically for the Melrose brothers. Morton and the New Orleans Rhythm Kings would collectively make history in Richmond later that summer. But not before Wiggins and Fred Gennett booked studio time in the spring of 1923 at the piano factory complex for the giant among Chicago jazz bandleaders. Joe "King" Oliver was about to be immortalized.

King Oliver and His Legendary Creole Jazz Band

On April 6, 1923, Joe "King" Oliver's Creole Jazz Band boarded a train on Chicago's south side, traveled across Indiana's vast rural landscape, and arrived at Richmond's downtown train station near the Starr Piano factory. Pulling into Starr Valley, Oliver and his band mates probably felt a long way from Chicago, as the only black people amid hundreds of German workers in the secluded factory complex. Crowded around the acoustic horns in the Gennett studio along the river, Chicago's most popular black jazz band recorded more than two dozen takes in one perspiration-filled session before catching the train back to Chicago.

It was a landmark day in jazz, though no one knew it then. While six years had passed since the Original Dixieland Jazz Band produced the first jazz records in history, King Oliver's discs on the Gennett label are universally regarded as the first genuine masterpieces in jazz recording. Although many jazz and ragtime players had recorded before Oliver, his debut in Richmond's Gennett studio was the most notable recording date in jazz to that point.

In the early 1920s, Oliver led a talented young band that adhered to his strict approach to New Orleans jazz. King Oliver's Creole Jazz Band reigned over black jazz in Chicago's south side, inspiring scores of black and white admirers. After being ignored by record companies for years, Oliver signed his first contract with Fred Gennett in 1923 and opened up a whole new world. Over a nine-month period beginning with the Gennett debut, Oliver's band recorded some 40 sides for four labels. The battle between the Gennett, OKeh, Columbia, and Paramount labels to record Chicago's black jazz went into full swing.

The magic of Oliver's first recording date was in its timing. After two years as the headliner at Chicago's Lincoln Gardens, his disciplined band arrived in Richmond in peak form, with a well-rehearsed play list of original songs tailored to the band's strengths. In addition to Oliver, the Gennett sessions contain the first recorded solos by his second cornetist, Louis Armstrong, soon to become the most influential soloist in jazz, as well as solos by another New Orleans giant, clarinetist Johnny Dodds.

The avuncular Oliver, with an imposing physical stature, demanded rigid unity within his band of much younger players. Contrary to the loose, free-wheeling approach to ensemble playing associated with jazz, Oliver's arrangements were highly polyphonic and studiously orchestrated, with the collective sound taking precedence over solo improvisations. A sort of Japanese corporate approach to a jazz band.

The nine Oliver sides released by Gennett from the April 1923 session were the first authentic records by an established black New Orleans jazz ensemble. Because the 1923 Oliver Creole Jazz Band, unquestionably Oliver's greatest collection of talent, broke up within a year of the Richmond debut, the Gennett discs are rare snapshots of a refined, classic jazz style that developed in New Orleans over many years.

Oliver had clearly contributed to its evolution. Born in New Orleans in 1885, he grew up near the Storyville red light district, a breeding ground for jazz. By 1900, Oliver, under the care of a half-sister, played in local brass bands and picked up on the emerging jazz sounds. He later doubled as a house butler for a white family by day and a cornetist by night. When the U.S. Navy shut down the Storyville district in 1917, Oliver was one of the district's leading jazz players, a clever cornetist who used cups, glasses, and mutes to achieve a distinctive sound. When work dried up in New Orleans, he joined the migration to Chicago.

Bill Johnson, a popular New Orleans jazz string player in Chicago, first approached Oliver about work. Johnson had managed a touring band called the Original Creole Orchestra in the 1910s, fronted by Freddie Keppard. After Johnson settled in Chicago in 1918, he hired Oliver as lead cornetist at the Royal Gardens. Oliver also took a job as second cornetist with New Orleans clarinetist Lawrence Duhe's band at the Dreamland Cafe. Oliver soon assumed leadership of the Duhe ensemble, renaming it the Creole Jazz Band. By 1921, the band included Johnny Dodds, trombonist Honoré Dutrey, and the attractive pianist Lillian Hardin (who later married Louis Armstrong). After a stint in California, during which drummer Baby Dodds (Johnny's brother) joined the band, Oliver's Creole Jazz Band returned to Chicago in mid-1922 to headline the old Royal Gardens, now called the Lincoln Gardens.

For reasons never clearly explained, Oliver, 37 years old in 1922, wanted a second cornet. He wired New Orleans for Armstrong, a shy, backward 22-year-old with a big reputation from engagements in theatres and Mississippi riverboats. Behind the dueling cornets of Oliver and his amazing upstart from New Orleans, the Creole Jazz Band was the talk of Chicago's south side. During 1922–23, the band packed the Lincoln Gardens. Because the club opened one night a week for whites only, both black and white musicians, including the New Orleans Rhythm Kings, learned from Oliver's band. The

Lincoln Gardens audience on the "whites only" night included the Melrose brothers, future publishers of Oliver and
Armstrong compositions, and acquaintances of Fred Gennett
and Wiggins.

By early 1923, the record industry was more receptive to
race recordings, after releases by black female blues singers
had developed a substantial following among black listeners.
Gennett's New York studio was producing a series of records
by blues singer Viola McCoy. That same year, New York's Columbia Records obtained far greater success with a series of
race records by the legendary Bessie Smith. But Chicago was
essentially virgin recording territory for black jazz ensembles
when Fred Gennett signed up Oliver. Richard Jones, the com-
poser/pianist who supplied tunes for Gennett's female blues
singers, was a key contact between Oliver and the record labels. Jones may have brought Oliver to Wiggins's attention.
Baby Dodds recalled the Gennett contract being secured
through someone who heard the band at the Lincoln Gardens.

Riding the successful sales of the New Orleans Rhythm
Kings, Wiggins was eager to sign up other Chicago jazz musicians. Because the Gennett label had already catered to the
race market with black blues singers and pianist Richard
Jones, the progression to Chicago's best black jazz band was
only logical. Fred Gennett recalled meeting Oliver in Chicago,
through Wiggins, and signing him immediately to the first contract. In 1953, seemingly indifferent to the jazz musicians on
the Gennett label, Fred Gennett's only recollection of Oliver
was that he possessed "the biggest lips I ever saw on a human
being."[6]

With no lodging secured in Richmond, the seven-piece
Oliver band fit its first recording session at Gennett between
train rides to Richmond and back, Dodds recalled. Even
though Oliver's play list for the session was polished from
countless sets at the Lincoln Gardens, the steamy purgatory of
the Richmond studio put the band on edge. "It was something
none of us had experienced and we were all very nervous,"

Baby Dodds recalled. "We were all working hard and perspiration as big as a thumb dropped off us. Even Joe Oliver was nervous; Joe was no different from any of the rest. The only really smooth-working person there was Lil Armstrong. She was very unconcerned and much at ease."[7] Dodds settled his nerves at an intermission with sips from his bottle of alcoholic spirits. He had a relatively stress-free day. Except when he smacked his sticks on the rim of his drums or used wood blocks, he was essentially inaudible on Gennett's acoustic recording system.

Under Wickemeyer's direction, the Oliver band waxed no fewer than 27 takes, from which the Gennett staff pressed nine songs for release. The eighteen alternate takes were never released, and the copper-plated masters were soon destroyed, a horrific thought to generations of traditional jazz enthusiasts worldwide.

As expected, Gennett's hollow sound reproduction washes out much of the band's dynamics on the recordings. No bassist can be picked up on the April 6 sessions, leaving us to wonder if one was present. Armstrong's countermelodies, played to Oliver's lead, are sometimes lost or barely audible. In fact, the solo cornet lines of both Oliver and Armstrong are sometimes muffled on the Gennett sides because they often used mutes. The overpowering sound of their cornets was a constant threat to the ensemble's sound balance, not to mention a threat to the delicate Gennett equipment. As always, Wickemeyer solved the problem by carefully placing the band members at varying distances from the recording horns. Wickemeyer's system for balancing the sound levels of Oliver and Armstrong led to one of the great stories in jazz.

"We all had to blow in this great big horn, the old style," said Lillian Hardin Armstrong. "And in trying to get the balance, Joe and Louis stood right next to each other as they always had, and you couldn't hear a note that Joe was playing, only could hear Louis. So they said, 'Well, gotta do something,' and they put Louis about fifteen feet over in the corner, looking all sad . . . he thought it was bad for him to have to be separated from the band. I looked at him and smiled to reassure him that he was all right. And then I said to myself, 'Now if they have to put him that far away in order to hear Joe, he's got to be better.' Then I was convinced."[8]

Armstrong at one time laid claim to the same story, saying he played his cornet from near the door of the Gennett studio. In later years, he modified it somewhat, saying he was a few steps behind Oliver. Baby Dodds, whose recollections of his days with the Oliver band have proven to be quite reliable, did not confirm Lillian Armstrong's story. However, he did say Oliver and the rhythm section crowded close to the acoustic horns, while Johnny Dodds, Armstrong, and Dutrey stood farther back. But the more romantic and enduring image will always be of a shy, still undiscovered Armstrong, cast off to a far corner of Gennett's stark studio, blowing his horn with Herculean power while the other band members crowded around the acoustic horns.

Primitive sound preservation aside, Oliver's first Gennett sides were a fabulous sampling of the rhythmic, laid-back atmosphere of authentic New Orleans jazz. Well-rehearsed lines by Dodds, Oliver, and Armstrong beautifully blended ragtime and blues. The Gennett sides especially pleased Baby Dodds in later years, because they reminded him of how the band sounded during its heyday at the Lincoln Gardens.

Of great significance was the Oliver repertoire at the first Gennett session. While New York studio bands recorded jazz adaptations of pop songs, Oliver recorded original numbers in the New Orleans tradition, including certain tunes created especially for the recording date. "When he started making records, he started being a writer," Armstrong told Ralph Gleason. "We'd rehearse it on the job and when we got to the studio, all we had to do was cut it up and time it. Was no trouble at all to make them records. We'd just make one after the other."[9]

Oliver's band introduced several future jazz classics on

Gennett: "Canal Street Blues" and "Dippermouth Blues," by Oliver and Armstrong; "Chimes Blues," "Just Gone," and "Snake Rag," all by Oliver; and "Weather Bird Rag" by Armstrong. Also selected by Oliver for the April session were "Froggie Moore" by Jelly Roll Morton and "Mandy Lee Blues," written by Marty Bloom and Walter Melrose. On subsequent recording sessions with Oliver's brilliant band of 1923, the repertoire was diluted with more commercial stock arrangements.

The Gennett discs teach listeners today that the traditional approach to New Orleans jazz was not grounded in the long solo improvisations that characterize contemporary jazz. Oliver's "Just Gone" is entirely an ensemble effort, while several other numbers leave room for only brief, rehearsed solo breaks as opposed to spontaneous expression. The rhythm section, especially the piano, seems to clank along, following Oliver's directive simply to keep the beat and not to interfere with the lead horns.

Oliver's band achieved a powerful ensemble sound. With such numbers as "Canal Street Blues," Oliver's strong lead cornet, Armstrong's countermelodies, Johnny Dodds' leaping clarinet lines, and Dutrey's gliding trombone all mesh with almost telepathic precision. Johnny Dodds is afforded the most freedom to solo, which he uses to good effect. His 24-bar solo on "Canal Street Blues" crescendos with a long, sustained blues line to banjo and drum accompaniment, before the band jumps in for the finale.

On the songs "Mandy Lee Blues," "Snake Rag," and "Weather Bird Rag," Oliver and Armstrong's duet breaks are in perfect step. Their duets at the Lincoln Gardens were famous, and these acoustically recorded discs show why. The beauty of these recordings is hearing the young Armstrong, for all his unlimited technical powers, in a supporting role. His brilliant countermelodies always complement but never distract from Oliver's lead melodies. The Gennett session froze in time a brief period when Oliver, still near the height of his expressive powers, collaborates with his successor as king of the jazz cornet. Horn duet breaks of such precision and originality were rarely accomplished in early jazz, or, for that matter, any time after 1923.

Oliver's most memorable moment from the April session was his muted "wah-wah" solo on "Dippermouth Blues." It isn't just the melody that is fascinating, but the entire approach: the timing and tone applied to his notes. This solo, with all its subtleties, would be repeated by generations of horn players, including Armstrong, who acknowledged few musical influences beyond Oliver.

As a side note, the Gennett recording of "Dippermouth Blues" inspired one of the venerable expressions in jazz when Baby Dodds, alcohol breath and all, forgot a very brief solo part planned for him. Reacting to the lapse, banjoist Bill Johnson screamed "Play that thing!" and the rest is history. "The technician [most likely Wickemeyer] asked us if that was supposed to be there and we said no," Dodds recalled. "However, he wanted to keep it anyway, and, ever since then, every outfit uses that same trick, all because I forgot my part."[10]

Oliver permitted Armstrong to solo at the first Gennett session on "Chimes Blues" and "Froggie Moore." Even though the Oliver band left little room for expansive solos, Armstrong provided listeners with a wonderful glimpse into the level of playing he would exhibit in ensuing years.

"Chimes Blues," unlike Oliver's other songs, is essentially built on a series of organized solos. After a piano chord sequence by Hardin creating the sound of chimes, Armstrong steps to the front and repeats a bold one-bar melody that shifts along the scale to suit the changing chords. His solo was obviously prepared beforehand. Most obvious is Armstrong's sharp, full-bodied tone and rhythmic style, picked up with great clarity by Gennett's acoustic equipment. Fortunately, Armstrong's solo is accompanied only by the rhythm section and does not compete with other lead horns. When Melrose Brothers Music Co. published "Chimes Blues" as a stock arrangement, Armstrong's cornet solo from the Gennett recording was transcribed note-for-note.

His "Froggie Moore" solo is even more enlightening. One hears Armstrong's trademark cornet tremolo, slower and more deliberate than Oliver's, and Armstrong's consistent use of accented notes and shifting volume. His innovative method of playing notes on irregular beats on the "Froggie Moore" solo was a vehicle Armstrong would use throughout his life. Even though his solos soon advanced well beyond his recording debut as second horn to Oliver, the Gennett releases provided clear indications to the growing cult of jazz record buyers that a major innovator was on the scene.

Gennett's bold foray into black jazz with Oliver's first releases was apparently well received by black listeners, as shown by the original Gennett copies still existing from the April 1923 session. As was the system for distributing Gennett's race records, independent wholesalers loaded up their cars in Richmond with the freshly pressed Gennett discs and covered all the department stores and groceries catering to black consumers. In stores with predominately white customers, race records were often kept out of sight in crates behind the counter and pulled out when black people requested the latest releases. Despite the limited distribution of Gennett discs, the Oliver sides reached enough record buyers, particularly in the Chicago area, to make a major impact on the spreading jazz movement.

By mid-1923, the label's misleading race catalog, billed as Snappy Dance Hits on Gennett Records by Exclusive Gennett Colored Artists, was formidable: releases by Ladd's Black Aces, the proficient white band featuring white singers using stereotypical pseudonyms like "Mandy Lee" and "Shufflin' Phil"; the New Orleans Rhythm Kings; and Oliver's Creole Jazz Band, the one black group honestly represented in the promotional catalog.

The extensive New Orleans Rhythm Kings and the Oliver Creole Jazz Band material recorded on Gennett exhibited the wide variety of expression available within jazz. Despite the dubious "colored artists" marketing ploy used for its talented white bands, Gennett Records was producing the most innovative jazz in America in the first few months of 1923. Compared with the Oliver and the New Orleans Rhythm Kings discs, the more commercially successful jazz recorded by New York studio bands during the same period sound curiously stiff and out-of-step. For informed jazz lovers, who could make the musical distinction between Oliver's pure brand of New Orleans jazz and the approach taken by the commercial dance bands, the Oliver discs on Gennett became classics.

Just as his recordings on Gennett were being released, Oliver was actively shopping for other labels. The Gennett organization did not seek exclusive contracts with musicians, and Oliver was certainly no exception. His band was free to record with anyone, and in June 1923, it produced seven sides at OKeh's recording facility in Chicago.

The Oliver takes for OKeh included clearer remakes of "Snake Rag" and "Dippermouth Blues," as well as "Sweet Lovin' Man," a Melrose-Hardin tune recorded by the New Orleans Rhythm Kings, and "Jazzin' Baby Blues," the Richard Jones number. From a fidelity standpoint, the OKeh sides are better than the hollow Gennett discs, especially for hearing Armstrong's playing. On OKeh's "Dippermouth Blues," a clearer distinction can be made between Armstrong's and Oliver's lines. As a result, the OKeh sides appear more frequently in jazz record anthologies. (When the Smithsonian Collection of Recordings revised its *Classic Jazz* anthology in 1987, the OKeh "Dippermouth Blues" was replaced with the Gennett take.) Oliver's famous solos on the Gennett and OKeh releases of "Dippermouth Blues" are very similar, further confirming that Oliver preferred rehearsed solos to improvisation.

The Oliver band severed its relationship with Gennett after a disappointing second and final session in Richmond on October 5, 1923. Only "Alligator Hop," "Zulu's Ball," "Workingman Blues," and "Krooked Blues" were released. A take of

"That Sweet Something Dear" was mastered and pressed, but apparently it was never put into circulation. Oblivious to the history contained within Oliver's masters, the Gennett staff destroyed the takes of "When You Leave Me Alone to Pine," "If You Want My Heart," and "Someday Sweetheart," the one song which Baby Dodds said allowed him a short drum solo. ("Someday Sweetheart" became Oliver's big seller for the Vocalion label in 1926.)

At the October 1923 session, Oliver added a C-melody saxophone to the group, which sounds awkward today against the Creole Jazz Band's classic instrument mix. The saxophone was growing in popularity in the early 1920s and may have been suggested by the Gennett organization for the recording date. The slumbering "Krooked Blues" was the most memorable side from Oliver's last Gennett session, which includes bluesy solos by Dutrey and Armstrong, and a strong crying lead by Oliver.

But this second batch of Gennett releases was afforded very limited distribution. Today, they are among the rarest treasures among jazz record collectors. In fact, only one original copy of Gennett's back-to-back release of "Zulu's Ball" and "Workingman Blues" is known to exist today. As the story goes, in the 1930s a New York journalist named Dick Reiber found a copy of *Talking Machine World* from December 1923, in which Gennett's upcoming release of "Zulu's Ball" and "Workingman Blues" was announced. Reiber revealed this to *Jazz Information* magazine in 1940, at the beginning of a national revival in traditional jazz. A hunt ensued by jazz buffs in search of the long-lost Gennett disc.

About a year later, Monte Ballou, a West Coast musician and an avid jazz record collector, discovered an original, but worn copy. As far as the recording industry is concerned, it remains the only "Zulu's Ball"/"Workingman Blues" disc to have turned up. Over the years this extraordinarily rare disc has changed hands for thousands of dollars. It was last reported in the hands of a collector in Holland!

The limited distribution of Oliver's second batch of Gennett releases, including "Zulu's Ball," may have stemmed from the fact that OKeh, Paramount, and Columbia also recorded Oliver's band in late 1923. Gennett may have feared that Oliver was over-exposed. From a sales standpoint, Oliver's band was not in a league with the Original Dixieland Jazz Band, and the release of dozens of Oliver sides within a few short months, despite their value to serious jazz musicians, was probably more than the market could bear.

The Gennett Records ledgers show only the April and October 1923 dates with Oliver's Creole Jazz Band. But in their research for their 1958 biography, *King Joe Oliver*, Walter Allen and Brian Rust found several musicians outside of Oliver's 1923 band who claimed to have recorded with the cornetist in Richmond. Two white musicians, Sam Carr and Howard Emerson, said that they sat in with Oliver's band on the same day they cut discs in Richmond with Art Landry's orchestra. Junie Cobb, who joined Oliver in 1924 when the band toured Indiana, claimed to have recorded at Gennett, but could not identify himself on Oliver's Gennett sides.

Oliver's Gennett releases have always been held in such high esteem that it is understandable that musicians who had rubbed elbows with Oliver tried to be associated with those legendary recordings. In collecting oral histories, the jazz historian can encounter mythology at every turn. However, given the informal manner in which recording dates were arranged in Richmond, other recording sessions with Oliver were possible. Under Gennett's contractual agreements, the company was not obligated to press discs, even if wax masters were recorded in the studio. On many occasions, bands were recorded, but the masters were destroyed because the music was deemed poor or technical problems resulted in unacceptable recordings. By surveying the detailed reports in the Gennett ledgers, one would assume the company kept tabs on the musicians they recorded, whether or not discs were pressed or released. However, other musicians over the years claimed to have visited the Gennett studio, even though no proof exists in the ledgers. Was this the case with Oliver? Recording for Gennett was always an adventure.

Oliver's legendary Creole Jazz Band broke up shortly after its October 1923 recording date in Richmond, as band members questioned Oliver's distribution of royalty checks. "The royalties on the records we made for the Gennett company got smaller and smaller," Dodds said. "Nobody saw the royalty checks but Oliver. They were in his name and had to be cashed by him. We had an argument when some of us wanted to see the checks. Joe Oliver wouldn't come up with the checks. In our minds that showed guilt although we didn't know for sure what the real story was."[11] The real story may have been that the royalty checks from Fred Gennett were very meager to start with, especially for the October session.

For whatever reason, Oliver did not land another recording contract until the spring of 1926. He formed a new band and moved to New York, which had become the center of the jazz universe. Former Oliver employees Armstrong, his wife, Lillian, and Johnny Dodds soon moved jazz to greater levels of personal expression in 1925–27 with Armstrong's Hot Five and Hot Seven recordings.

While they are less significant to jazz historians, Oliver's bands in the late 1920s actually sold far more records than the pioneering 1923 outfit. By then, Oliver had somewhat abandoned his rigid New Orleans style and tried to adapt to a rapidly evolving jazz style forged by the youngsters Armstrong, Fletcher Henderson, Duke Ellington, and others.

By 1938, Oliver was broke, had serious health problems, and was stranded without a band in the South. He died that year while employed as a janitor. Tragically, he did not live to enjoy the worldwide revival of traditional jazz, which began in the early 1940s. His original Gennett discs, which were later reissued on different labels throughout the world, continued to exert a great influence on musicians, particularly the aspiring traditional jazz players in Europe. "Dippermouth Blues" would be recorded by numerous bands during the 1930s and 1940s, including groups led by Henderson and Armstrong.

As the twenty-first century approaches, the recordings of Oliver's Creole Jazz Band on Gennett, produced between long train rides to and from Richmond in 1923, are still available on record albums or compact discs in virtually every major city on the planet.

The Music of Jelly Roll Morton

Gennett Records and the Melrose Brothers Music Co., working in tandem in the early 1920s, were catalysts in disseminating the local Chicago jazz scene to the nation. Lester and Walter Melrose claimed to have introduced the Gennett organization to the New Orleans Rhythm Kings in 1922. Afterwards, the public's enthusiastic reception of the band's first releases on the Indiana label encouraged the Melrose brothers to begin publishing jazz songs composed by white and black musicians based in Chicago. Jazz became the brothers' niche in music publishing.

In 1923, a pattern had emerged in which ground-breaking jazz releases on Gennett were soon published by the Melrose brothers as stock arrangements or in sheet music form, including such memorable songs as "Tin Roof Blues" by the New Orleans Rhythm Kings and "Chimes Blues" by King Oliver's Creole Jazz Band. Some of the stock arrangements published by Melrose suggested listening to the corresponding Gennett discs in order to pick up the subtleties of jazz playing which cannot be transcribed onto paper. Compared to the New York music publishers and record companies, Gennett Records and the Melrose brothers were small-time operators. However, in 1923, they stood at the forefront of the new jazz movement.

In the spring of that year, a flamboyant New Orleans Creole named Ferdinand "Jelly Roll" Morton, sporting a red bandanna, a cowboy hat, and a diamond in his front tooth, arrived at the Melrose brothers' modest store. Morton, 33, had been a pimp, hustler, pool shark, and club operator, but he was known in jazz circles as a dazzling ragtime pianist and a pretty fair songwriter.

The Melrose brothers hired Morton to write piano music to sell in the store. It is fairly certain that the association between the Melrose company and Gennett Records led Morton to the piano factory. For recording sessions in Richmond on July 17–18, 1923, the Gennett studio organized what have been called the first interracial recording dates in jazz history, when Morton teamed up with the New Orleans Rhythm Kings. It proved to be a stroke of genius. However, on the same two days, Gennett also recorded Morton as a solo pianist, allowing him to draw from an amazing repertoire he had composed over a twenty-year span. Gennett Records soon released the first substantial body of recorded piano solos by jazz music's first great composer, not to mention the music's self-proclaimed inventor. Morton's complex, multi-thematic compositions, recorded by Gennett and published soon after by the Melrose brothers, represent an important musical bridge between nineteenth-century ragtime forms and the emerging twentieth-century jazz styles.

The reason that the New Orleans Rhythm Kings and Morton collaborated in July 1923 has been long speculated. Frank Snyder, former New Orleans Rhythm Kings drummer, said in a 1963 interview in the Richmond *Palladium-Item* that he invited Morton to join the band on the trip to Indiana, and that resulted in Gennett's organizing the solo piano sessions. Such happenstance is highly unlikely. Surely, the New Orleans Rhythm Kings greatly admired Morton, but Gennett's ace talent scout, Wiggins, was also well aware of Morton's talent. Both the New Orleans Rhythm Kings and Oliver's band recorded Morton songs for Gennett Records in the spring of 1923, and the Melrose brothers had published compositions by Morton before he ever set foot in Richmond. Whatever the circumstances, therefore, one must assume that his arrival at the Gennett studio with the New Orleans Rhythm Kings was no accident.

It did not, however, assure Morton a warm welcome in Richmond. For years, George Brunies told fellow musicians that the Rhythm Kings secured a hotel room in downtown Richmond for Morton during mid-1923 only by claiming he was Latin American and not an American Negro, as Morton was generally considered. Brunies' story, which is entirely believable, in view of race relations in Richmond in the 1920s, was a sad irony, for the complex issues surrounding Morton's racial heritage may have contributed to his often difficult, self-loathing personality.

New Orleans Creoles, such as Morton, derived from a mixture of African, French, and Spanish ancestors. In nineteenth-century New Orleans, the wealthier Creoles commonly aspired to an elegant lifestyle influenced by Mediterranean culture. Many Creoles were landowners. And they often exhibited prejudice against New Orleans blacks of pure African origins. In fact, there existed a sort of self-imposed segregation between the two groups. By 1885, Louisiana state laws ruled that all "people of color" were subject to institutionalized segregation from white people. The complex relationship between Creoles and pure African descendants, coupled with white attitudes toward both groups, affected Morton's people. During his lifetime, Morton not only battled racism from whites but, on rare occasions, also exhibited his own bias against blacks.

While Morton touted his heritage, his early years did not reflect the comfort and stability commonly associated with New Orleans Creole life. Sorting out his early life requires a difficult separation of fact and his boastful claims. He was born Ferdinand J. Lamothe in 1890 and was raised as a Roman Catholic. When he was a teenager, his mother died, and his father left the home. Morton was raised by an aunt, an uncle, and a great-grandmother. His godmother exposed him to the voodoo practiced by older Creoles, which troubled Morton during his life and forced him into some bizarre decisions.

An early twentieth-century postcard of the Starr Piano Factory in Richmond, Indiana. Situated in a glacial gorge along the Whitewater River, the bustling complex was known locally as Starr Valley.

Men, women, and adolescents working in the keyboard construction area of Starr Piano, ca. 1900. (*Wayne County Museum.*)

The Gennett family in 1897. Seated (from left): Rose, Alice, Henry, and Fred; standing (from left): Harry and Clarence. (*Henry Gennett Martin collection.*)

An employee pig roast at Starr Piano, ca. 1905. Henry Gennett is seated on the left, second from the front. (*Richard Gennett collection.*)

The original Gennett Recording studio in Richmond, Indiana, as it appeared in 1957, decades after it had been shut down. Still visible are the tracks along which trains passed, disturbing many a recording session. (*Phil Pospychala.*)

Fred Gennett, the innovative
manager of the Gennett Records
division, with his sons, Robert and
Richard. Though Fred had no
personal interest in jazz, he became
a key figure in its early
documentation. (*Richard Gennett
collection.*)

The New Orleans Rhythm Kings, 1923. From left: George Brunies, Paul Mares, Ben Pollack, Leon Roppolo, Mel Stitzel, Volly De Faut, Lewis Black, and Steve Brown. (*Duncan Schiedt collection.*)

Above: King Oliver's Creole Jazz Band, 1923. From left: Baby Dodds, Honoré Dutrey, Joe "King" Oliver, Louis Armstrong, Bill Johnson, Johnny Dodds, and Lillian Hardin Armstrong. (*Duncan Schiedt collection.*)

Opposite top: "Wolverine Blues," recorded in 1923 by the New Orleans Rhythm Kings. This title was the inspiration for the name of Bix Beiderbecke's first professional band, the Wolverine Orchestra.

Opposite: The Wolverines' first recording session, Richmond, Indiana, February 18, 1924. From left: Min Leibrook, Jimmy Hartwell, George Johnson, Bob Gillette, Vic Moore, Dick Voynow, Bix Beiderbecke, and Al Gandee. (*Duncan Schiedt collection.*)

Above: Jelly Roll Morton, ca. 1920. His piano solos of 1923–24 on the Gennett label represent his first significant body of recorded music.

Opposite top: Marion McKay's controversial recording of "Doo Wacka Doo." Did Bix play the cornet solo?

Opposite: Bix Beiderbecke and the Rhythm Jugglers, Richmond, Indiana, 1925. From left: Don Murray, Howdy Quicksell, Tom Gargano, Paul Mertz, Bix Beiderbecke, and Tommy Dorsey. (*Duncan Schiedt collection.*)

Curtis Hitch's Happy Harmonists
recording Hoagy Carmichael's
"Washboard Blues," Richmond,
Indiana, 1925. From left: Haskell
Simpson, Maurice May, Harry
Wright, Early "Buddy" McDowell,
Arnold Habbe, Hoagy Carmichael,
Curtis Hitch, and Fred Rollison.
(*Duncan Schiedt collection.*)

Bradley Kincaid, the "Kentucky
Mountain Boy," a Gennett artist
from 1927 to 1929. He was one of
the first national radio singing stars.
(*Appalachian Center, Berea College.*)

Gene Autry, a Gennett ''hillbilly'' artist of the late 1920s and early 1930s. This photo was taken in 1956, after he had become a singing cowboy superstar.

The legendary Sissieretta Jones, a.k.a. Black Patti, the inspiration for Fred Gennett's short-lived Black Patti record label.

Examples of the Gennett, Champion, Electrobeam, and Sound Effects labels.

Ryland Jones with Gennett's sound effects catalog, ca. 1938. (*Ryland Jones.*)

Henry Gennett's sons in later years. From top: Fred, ca. 1964; Harry, ca. 1950; and Clarence, ca. 1950. (*Richmond* Palladium-Item.)

The Gennett mansion on Main Street, Richmond, constructed in 1900. After being vacated by the Gennetts in the 1930s, it became an apartment complex. In the 1980s it was restored and placed on the National Register. (*Jim Callaway.*)

Music was key to his early life, and he learned to play piano, guitar, and banjo. In 1938 interviews with Alan Lomax for the Library of Congress, Morton fondly recalled the New Orleans parades and the French opera. As a teenager, he was the pianist in sporting houses in the Storyville district. Between 1907 and 1917, Morton led a vagabond existence, traveling through Chicago, St. Louis, and Memphis, while composing ragtime tunes of great sophistication. During 1917–23, he worked in the Los Angeles area as a minstrel singer, pianist, and bandleader. He also ran a hotel with long-time companion Anita Johnson Gonzales, sister of jazz banjoist Bill Johnson. When Morton returned to Chicago in 1923, the New Orleans jazz scene was coming to full blossom in the Windy City.

But, unlike his contemporaries, Morton envisioned jazz from a compositional perspective, and he shunned Chicago's jazz jam sessions as noisy and low-brow. He considered himself above that. Actually, Morton never held a steady job as a bandleader in Chicago, even though he is now considered one of the great jazz orchestral arrangers. Instead, he focused on music publishing and recording, while maintaining a composing style that drew from diverse musical sources, from Missouri ragtime to Dixieland to Spanish tango.

Morton's first recording session was actually for Paramount in June 1923, with a pickup band playing his original numbers "Big Foot Ham" and "Muddy Water Blues." But a month later, his recording career hit full swing with his debut at Gennett, both as solo pianist and as a guest pianist with the New Orleans Rhythm Kings. Gennett pressed ten sides by the band during the July sessions, including six outstanding sides with Morton sitting in as pianist.

Much has been written about the way Morton transformed the New Orleans Rhythm Kings into a swinging ensemble. Roppolo, Mares, and Brunies were already capable improvisers, but Morton raised the group to a higher level with his contagious rhythmic style. Equally important, the band recorded two of Morton's better compositions: "London Blues" and "Mr. Jelly Lord," a clever, easy-going tune with a strong lead melody. Gennett also produced "Milenberg Joys," billed as a Roppolo-Mares-Morton collaboration.

On "Mr. Jelly Lord," the two-bar breaks by Mares and Roppolo really swing. The rapport between Morton and his young admirers is marvelous on "Milenberg Joys" and "Clarinet Marmalade," an Original Dixieland Jazz Band march-style tune. Predictably, Roppolo rises to Morton's level. His clarinet solo on "Milenberg Joys" was later scored for three clarinets by McKinney's Cotton Pickers for their 1928 recording of the same song. Unfortunately, without Morton, the New Orleans Rhythm Kings' cuts of "Mad," "Angry," "Marguerite," and "Sobbin' Blues" are noticeably stiffer and congested by the addition of two saxophones for the session. (Similarly, it is unfortunate that Morton did not have the services of Roppolo, Mares, and Brunies on his small ensemble recordings released by Paramount a year later.)

By the time Gennett issued its third batch of New Orleans Rhythm Kings recordings, the band had been offered jobs in New York, but chose (or was forced) to remain the head attraction at Chicago's mob-controlled Friars Inn. Because they never had a manager, the young musicians did not parlay their many Gennett releases into a commercial success. When the Friars Inn opted for a different stage show, the New Orleans Rhythm Kings disbanded. Brunies joined Ted Lewis's touring band; Roppolo and Mares returned to New Orleans. The band reorganized and cut several sides in New Orleans in 1925. But America's best white jazz band of 1922–23 soon disbanded again, this time into oblivion.

For the most part, the New Orleans Rhythm Kings' recordings were ignored for decades, their memory kept alive by dedicated record collectors and enthusiasts. Then, in the 1960s, Riverside Records reissued the band's original Gennett sides, which were followed, a decade later, by another reissue album from Milestone Records. In the early 1990s,

Milestone released the band's Gennett sides on digital compact disc.

While the New Orleans Rhythm Kings' rightful place in jazz history may be disputed, Roppolo, with his fluid and soulful solo lines, was one of the most original jazz improvisors in the early 1920s, and the Gennett discs confirm his genius. Two years after the Richmond dates, he was confined to a mental institution, where he died in 1941. While historians have called his ailment a marijuana-alcohol–induced mental illness, Brunies offered a more plausible explanation, that his band mate suffered from advanced syphilis. Any documentation of the early evolution of jazz improvisation should include Roppolo's solos on "Tiger Rag" and "Tin Roof Blues." Far from an imitator, Roppolo was an innovator years ahead of the pack.

While the July 1923 session marked the high point in Roppolo's brief career, Morton's output at Gennett was just beginning. In addition to his sides with the New Orleans Rhythm Kings, Morton recorded piano solos of six original compositions: "King Porter Stomp," "New Orleans Joys," "Grandpa's Spells," "Kansas City Stomps," "Wolverine Blues," and "The Pearls." During two days in the steamy studio in Richmond, Morton's musical life flashed before his eyes as he played original compositions dating back to his teenage years. He soon showed record buyers that ragtime piano could be a springboard for a more diverse, sophisticated approach to jazz.

It is worth noting that Gennett issued so many sides by Morton on solo piano. In the early 1920s, few discs by solo ragtime or jazz pianists were produced on other labels because the sound reproduction of pianos on acoustic recording equipment was consistently bad. But that did not stop Gennett Records, a division of a piano company, which regularly issued classical piano solo recordings.

Despite the poor fidelity, Morton's solo recordings captured his clean, studious technique and relaxed tempos. Morton took an orchestral approach to piano composition, as he imagined instruments playing the various voicings. His well-calculated solos made use of the limited time available on a three-minute, 78-rpm disc, with careful attention paid to harmonies and dynamics. Most of his original sides on Gennett have been standards in traditional jazz ever since.

Gennett's release of Morton's solo treatment of "King Porter Stomp," his most familiar composition, amazed record buyers for its sheer virtuosity and elasticity toward ragtime playing. Morton composed "King Porter Stomp" as a teenager, but he recorded it when his technical powers on the piano were at a peak. Soon after Gennett released the recording, the Melrose brothers published the song as a stock arrangement and in sheet music form. The song was recorded dozens of times over the next twenty years, including hit versions by Benny Goodman and Harry James.

Another of Morton's recorded piano solos, "New Orleans Joys," also one of his earliest compositions, is a mixture of blues and ragtime, with a tango rhythm in the left hand. In "Kansas City Stomps," named for a bar in Tijuana, Morton sounds like a ragtime player at some moments, but at other times, he veers off into his own special brand of jazz. "Wolverine Blues," also an early composition, was first published when Morton lived in California in 1922. After the New Orleans Rhythm Kings recorded the song for Gennett in March 1923, the Melrose brothers published the sheet music for the second time. The Gennett recording of the solo rendition, made in July 1923, sounds as if Morton were playing an orchestral score, given the wide-ranging voicings.

Morton described "The Pearls," dedicated to a waitress at the Kansas City Bar in Tijuana, as one of his most technically difficult songs for the piano. It packs several compositional themes, tricky counterpoint, and lightning runs into the three-minute format. Gennett pressed "The Pearls" as the "B" side of a disc featuring Chicago dance-band leader Sol Wagner on side "A." Existing copies of this blue-labeled disc suggest that "The Pearls" received wide distribution, probably on the strength of Wagner's popularity. However, Morton's solos must have sold well enough for Fred Gennett, because the pianist returned to Richmond the following year for another round of solo recordings.

During a marathon session on June 9, 1924, the Gennett studio mastered eleven piano solos by Morton, of which nine were released. While these compositions may be considered inferior to his classics, recorded the year before, the second batch of Gennett solos shows Morton in his typically flamboyant mood. The humbly titled "Perfect Rag" is a bold technical achievement, with a wild, stomping finish. The fast-paced "Shreveport Stomp" is wonderfully reckless. The experience must have been a refreshing change for Gennett engineer Wickemeyer, who spent most days in the stuffy studio warming up the wax for forgettable dance bands, fledgling pop singers, and classical music scored for small ensembles.

Morton also played "Jelly Roll Blues," another modestly titled song showcasing a gorgeous melody and the pianist's sensitive touch. It was first published in 1915, one of the very first jazz compositions ever published. Other songs recorded in the single-day session were the Spanish style "Mamanita" and "Tia Juana," as well as "Tom Cat Blues," "Big Foot Ham," "Stratford Hunch," and "Bucktown Blues." Gennett rejected Morton's solo takes of "Milenberg Joys," recorded the previous year with the New Orleans Rhythm Kings, and "Froggie Moore," recorded by King Oliver's 1923 outfit.

During 1924, Morton was also recording less-notable discs in Chicago for Paramount and other labels, both as solo pianist and with pickup bands. His affiliation with competing labels may have caused friction with the Gennett organization, which never recorded him again as a solo pianist. Years later, Morton told Alan Lomax that his Gennett recordings were very popular and made plenty of money for the label. That is questionable. Morton also said Gennett Records wanted to sign him up for ten years, an outrageous claim, since the company allowed marketable musicians to come and go with regularity.

"I didn't want to work for a salary, and I didn't want to be tied down," Morton said. "You see before that [Gennett Records] contract was up, I was recording for just about everybody else under different pseudonyms. Those days I used to call myself almost anything for a disguise and go on in and make the records. Naturally, Gennett didn't like this too well."[12]

His last visit to the Richmond studio was in early 1926, while Morton was touring with a small band. He recorded "Mr. Jelly Lord," which Gennett issued under the name of Jelly Roll Morton's Incomparables. Played from a basic stock arrangement, "Mr. Jelly Lord" is an amusing, original performance. In the context of Morton's total recorded output, this rendition seems to parody his upcoming Red Hot Peppers ensemble recordings for Victor Records. Morton's 1926–27 recording sessions by his Red Hot Peppers ensemble, which was organized by the Melrose brothers, are regarded as the high point in his career as a bandleader and arranger. Gennett's "Mr. Jelly Lord" release has always interested historians as the forerunner of those historic ensemble records for Victor. If nothing else, Morton's last Gennett date shows the jazz maestro exhibiting light-hearted showmanship—the offbeat Richmond studio managed to bring out the most eccentric qualities in musicians.

But Gennett's immortal association with Morton are the fifteen solo piano recordings of 1923–24. They represent his first significant body of recordings and one of only three major series of recordings he ever produced. The other collected works are the Red Hot Peppers recordings for Victor and the solo piano recordings and interviews that Alan Lomax produced for the Library of Congress in 1938, near the end of Morton's life.

Morton's compositions seem to grow in stature with each passing decade. Thus, the Gennett recordings, despite their muffled, hollow fidelity, have a life of their own. Perhaps no one is more familiar with the Gennett piano solos than Professor James Dapogny, of the University of Michigan School of Music, who produced the first complete piano transcriptions of Morton's compositions for the Smithsonian Institution Press in 1982. After listening countless times to these discs, Dapogny considers them among the most important jazz piano solos ever recorded: "The Gennett recordings put the music world on notice that it was dealing with a composer of major significance. No other records before Morton's Gennett sides give us such a glimpse into the future possibilities for jazz piano. Because the Gennett piano solos preceded Morton's classic ensemble sides with Victor, they help us to understand the thought process that went into his remarkable arrangements on the Red Hot Peppers recordings. When Morton was in Chicago, there was a new breeze blowing through jazz and it's there in the grooves of those old, scratchy Gennett records."[13]

Just Passing Through: Other Jazz Debuts in Richmond, 1923–25

Lois Deppe's Serenaders, a Pittsburgh-based black orchestra, was scratching out a living in 1923 playing for dance halls around western Pennsylvania, West Virginia, and central Ohio. It was often a tough road, but Deppe, the handsome lead vocalist and occasional C-melody saxophonist, figured a record release might boost the band's visibility. Deppe scheduled recording dates that fall with the Gennett label, now established among black record buyers for its many race recordings.

On tour in central Ohio, the band crossed into Indiana on the National Highway, and dropped off in Richmond. Deppe's skinny, teenage pianist never forgot the studio by the railroad tracks, with acoustic horns that failed to pick up all the instruments and odd-looking drapes hanging from the rafters to deaden the room's resonance. The studio was so hot and steamy that Deppe's perspiring band members pulled off their shirts. They spent hours in the room, knocking out one song after another.

Ultimately, Gennett mastered and later pressed six tunes by Deppe's band. When the blue-labeled discs were distributed in Pittsburgh's black community, the extra exposure helped Deppe's Serenaders land additional work. For a few fleeting moments, Deppe was a bona fide recording artist. Soon after, his teenage pianist fought with band members and quit, and Deppe faded back into obscurity. We remember Deppe's 1923 Gennett recordings these many decades later because his cocky, baby-faced pianist was Earl Hines, soon to be known as Earl "Fatha" Hines, an architect of modern jazz piano, long-time bandleader, and one of jazz's most beloved figures for half a century.

While Gennett's place in jazz history is firmly rooted in the recordings of Oliver, Beiderbecke, Carmichael, Morton, and the New Orleans Rhythm Kings, other jazz pioneers, like Hines, found their way to Gennett's Richmond studio during the label's acoustic era, which ended in 1926 with the advent of electronic recording. More often than not, these players passed through virtually unnoticed at the time, working as young sidemen with territory bands that found room on the Gennett recording schedule. Because engagements could be arranged at a moment's notice, jazz bands touring the Midwest could arrange for a quick, one-day session, sign a contract for a flat payment or royalty agreement, and be on their way. Now that jazz has been recognized as a significant American art form, many once-forgotten Gennett discs are proving useful in piecing together the music's early evolution.

At Deppe's recording session, for example, the band recorded one of Hines's first compositions, a little-known number called "Congaine." The band sounds awful on the disc. The banjo player was placed too close to the recording horns and practically drowns out the band. But the 32-bar piano solo by the nineteen-year-old Hines reveals an amazing technical prowess. No wonder Deppe personally sought permission from Hines's father to allow his son to join the band. Hines also backs Deppe's lead vocals and takes sixteen-bar piano solos on "Dear Old Southland," "For the Last Time Call Me Sweetheart," and Lucky Roberts' "Isabel."

Given the Serenaders' limited talents and schmaltzy arrangements, Hines's ragtime-based piano style, with a strong, lightning-fast right hand, overshadows everyone else. During his brief tenure with Deppe, Hines began playing lead melodies with the right hand in octaves. There was no particular genius behind this; Hines simply wanted to be heard over the horns and Deppe, who sang into a megaphone. But the octave runs were no simple task, as is evident from these recordings.

Within a few years, Hines was a fixture in Chicago as a jazz pianist and bandleader. He made history in 1928 by recording with Louis Armstrong. Hines was never again subjected to the sweaty Richmond studio.

On January 21, 1924, Doc Cook and his Dreamland Orchestra, a popular black Chicago band, arrived in Richmond for a lone session. Cook's eleven-piece band, based out of Paddy Harmon's Dreamland Cafe on Chicago's south side, knocked out six numbers. Again, the main interest resides in the sidemen, cornetist Freddie Keppard and reed player Jimmy Noone.

Keppard, born in New Orleans in 1890, was a contemporary of King Oliver and a top cornetist. After moving to Chicago, he was featured in Bill Johnson's Original Creole Orchestra. By 1924, however, Keppard had been drinking heavily for several years, and he was certainly not at the height of his powers for the Gennett date with organist and director Doc Cook. However, behind Cook's basic stock arrangements, Keppard's strong cornet is heard distinctly on the tunes "Scissor-grinder Joe," "Memphis Maybe Man," and "Moanful Man." Keppard also shares a brief solo duet with Noone on "The One I Love." Noone, born in 1895 and another Louisiana immigrant to Chicago, does not play a major role on these

Gennett sides. But they are the beginnings of Noone's rich discography as a leading Chicago bandleader.

In February 1924, the Richmond studio recorded two of the Midwest's great white jazz bands. Bix Beiderbecke's Wolverine Orchestra, a band comprising primarily Chicago-area musicians, debuted on record on February 18. (Beiderbecke's recordings on Gennett are discussed in the next chapter.) A week later, another enthusiastic group of white jazz players from Chicago, known as the Bucktown Five, debuted on wax at Gennett. The lasting value of this band's seven sides, pressed from a February 25 session, rests on the expressive solos of an eighteen-year-old Chicago cornetist, Muggsy Spanier, later to become one of jazz's leading traditionalists.

The band, directed by pianist Mel Stitzel, formerly of the New Orleans Rhythm Kings, patterned its driving, tightly arranged approach to jazz after the Original Dixieland Jazz Band. For the cuts "Steady Roll Blues" and "Hot Mittens," Spanier's solos reflect Armstrong's and Oliver's influence. His muted cornet solo on "Mobile Blues" demonstrates the impact Oliver had on Chicago's aspiring white horn players. The Bucktown Five sides are not overwhelming in their originality, but they show how New Orleans jazz was being adapted by young bands in the Midwest.

A couple of weeks later, a Canadian vaudeville-style dance band passed through Richmond during a Midwest tour. The rare Gennett sides from Guy Lombardo and His Royal Canadians, soon to be among the most saccharine orchestras of the Swing Era, are avidly sought today by record collectors. The selections for Gennett, "Cotton Pickers Ball," "Mama's Gone," "Goodbye," and "Cry," capture a young Guy Lombardo on violin, and his brothers Carmen on saxophone and Lebert on cornet. Lombardo said that his band began to mesh that winter, as well as dress and behave like professionals. In their Gennett studio portrait, the nine members of the band are impeccably clad in white shirts, vests, and ties. The session, however, did not make a lasting impression. In his 1975 autobiography, Lombardo never mentions it, and a cut-line under a Gennett studio portrait of the band incorrectly refers to a first recording date in Indianapolis.

As Lombardo's band became established in Chicago and Cleveland in 1925, a jazz band from Cincinnati, the Chubb-Steinberg Orchestra, featuring cornetist "Wild" Bill Davison, also recorded in Richmond. The band was named after the Chubb-Steinberg Music Store in downtown Cincinnati, which sponsored the band as a promotional gimmick.

The outfit made four visits to the Richmond studio in 1925, with such sides as "Because They All Love You" and "Mandy Make Up Your Mind" pressed by Gennett and sold in the Chubb-Steinberg store. Also that year, the Chubb-Steinberg orchestra and Gennett technicians held a public record-ing session at Cincinnati's Music Hall to give patrons a first-hand glimpse of "modern" recording technology.

The rare Chubb-Steinberg sides are sought after by collec-tors simply because they capture the 21-year-old Davison. These recordings of standard stock arrangements actually swing a bit. Years later, Davison fondly recalled the Gennett dates as a period when he began developing as a jazz musician. Davison, along with Spanier, McPartland, and Brunies, all very young men at the time of their recording debuts for Gennett, would be at the forefront of the 1940s Dixieland revival that swept the United States and Europe. Like McPartland, Davi-son's professional career spanned six decades.

Louis Armstrong and the Red Onion Jazz Babies

By embracing the Chicago jazz movement, Gennett's re-cording studio in Indiana managed to overshadow its Manhat-tan studio in producing the label's most enduring music. However, the output from Gennett's Manhattan studio in the early 1920s was more viable from a financial standpoint. The dozens of Bailey's Lucky Seven discs originating there outsold any jazz recorded in Richmond. Gennett's military and symphonic bands, pop music, and foreign language discs from the Manhattan studio were pressed in great quantities. Yet, by virtue of operating in New York in 1924, Gennett's Manhattan studio also brushed with jazz immortality.

That September, the Manhattan studio recorded "Battleship Kate" by Wilber Sweatman and His Acme Syncopators, an area black jazz orchestra that included a young pianist from Washington, D.C., named Duke Ellington. A month later, cornetist Bix Beiderbecke's territory band from the Midwest, the Wolverine Orchestra, arrived in New York and recorded several sides at Gennett. But in November and December of 1924, the most memorable jazz discs ever waxed by Gennett's Manhattan studio stemmed from a couple of carefree sessions with a pickup band of black musicians billed as the Red Onion Jazz Babies. The band's cornetist happened to be a new arrival from Chicago, Louis Armstrong.

After leaving King Oliver's band, Armstrong headed for New York in late 1924 for a spot in Fletcher Henderson's New York–based dance orchestra. At the time, female blues singers were extremely popular with the New York record labels, and Armstrong picked up extra work in the neighborhood studios backing several singers, including the great Bessie Smith. Not only did these free-lance recording dates bring Armstrong a little extra money, but the freer, slow-moving blues format perfectly suited his expressive cornet playing. The kid from New Orleans who created excitement in Chicago now had New York talking.

Armstrong was contacted by Clarence Williams, a black pianist and composer originally from the New Orleans area. The versatile Williams was a brilliant promoter in the vein of black songwriter Perry Bradford. In conjunction with his music publishing company near New York's Times Square, Williams organized powerhouse recording sessions with hand-picked jazz instrumentalists and singers covering tunes for which he

owned the rights. The result was some of the best jazz recorded in the early 1920s.

In November 1924, Williams organized recording dates
for two related bands—Clarence Williams' Blues Five and the
Red Onion Jazz Babies, a name derived from the Red Onion
bar in New Orleans. Armstrong played in both bands, each of
which covered many of the same tunes from Williams's publishing catalog. OKeh Records pressed sixteen sides by the
Blues Five during Armstrong's year-long stay in New York.
During November and December 1924, Gennett's New York
studio also recorded the Red Onion Jazz Babies, producing
seven sides for the Gennett label.

To accompany New York blues singer Alberta Hunter (under the pseudonym of her sister, Josephine Beatty) on the
Gennett sides, Williams hired two of the finest New Orleans
jazz players—Armstrong and soprano saxophonist Sidney
Bechet. Other members of the band were Armstrong's wife,
Lillian Hardin Armstrong, on piano, Buster Bailey on clarinet,
Buddy Christian on banjo, and Aaron Thompson on trombone. Clarence Williams, who played piano on the Blues Five
sides for OKeh, did not appear on the Gennett dates, apparently for contractual reasons.

The band first recorded at Gennett in early November,
choosing a blues number, "A Texas Moaner Blues," and a pop
tune, "Of All the Wrongs You've Done to Me." Armstrong's
muted cornet solo on the latter song is unusual, in terms of
both its drastic syncopation and its paucity of notes. Armstrong plays a broken outline of a solo melody against stop-
time breaks. He had never been recorded playing in this manner before, though it is reminiscent of his scat vocal solos recorded later in the decade. The slow-rolling "A Texas Moaner
Blues" showcases Hunter in a vocal style popularized by Bessie
Smith, with Armstrong playing a minor role.

Later that month, the Red Onion Jazz Babies returned to
the Gennett studio to produce "Santa Claus Blues" and "Terrible Blues." Armstrong is the session's undisputed leader, par-

ticularly on "Terrible Blues," a Williams composition that is reminiscent of the early King Oliver recordings. Armstrong delivers a masterfully constructed solo consisting of syncopated variations built on two simple musical themes. Even though the songs celebrate the New Orleans tradition, Armstrong had already branched out with his own approach to improvisation.

In late December 1924, the Red Onion Jazz Babies recorded three more sides with Hunter on lead vocals and Bechet on lead clarinet and soprano saxophone. A New Orleans Creole born in 1897, Bechet was known internationally by 1924, after playing in London with the Will Marion Cook Orchestra. He took up soprano saxophone after finding one in a London junk shop. Even though Bechet was at the forefront of jazz improvisation, his long tenure in Europe during the 1920s prevented him from being a fixture in the Chicago and New York clubs.

On the vocal numbers "Early Every Morn" and "Nobody Knows," Bechet steals most of the few solo breaks, while Armstrong has a very minor role. But on the most memorable song of the session, "Cake Walking Babies from Home," Armstrong and Bechet are in a friendly showdown as they blast away nonstop through almost the entire song. Because Gennett's equipment picks up the soprano clarinet with greater clarity than the cornet, the aggressive Bechet has the upper hand. His two brief solo breaks are brilliant. Combined with the precise interplay between Armstrong, Bechet, and trombonist Charlie Irvis, "Cake Walking Babies" became an example of New Orleans–inspired jazz that was advancing beyond the musical boundaries established by Oliver, Keppard, and their early-century contemporaries.

Predictably, OKeh's Blues Five sides are easier on the ear than the low-fidelity Gennett sides. Gennett discs were habitually unbalanced, with the banjo often overwhelming the ensemble. But since the Red Onion Jazz Babies sides have been more readily available over the years on various reissue anthologies, the Gennett cuts seem to have benefited from a far more prominent role in the recorded history of jazz than have the Blues Five recordings. The professional comeback in the 1980s of Alberta Hunter attracted new attention to her early records, including these fascinating Gennett sides.

It should be noted that Gennett's significant jazz activity in New York did not end with the Red Onion Jazz Babies. In 1926, Duke Ellington's band recorded four sides, including "Animal Crackers" and "Li'l Farina." The studio also produced discs by Fats Waller, Red Nichols, and Fletcher Henderson, who recorded "Honeybunch" and "When Spring Comes Peeping Through" in 1926. During the late 1920s, Gennett's New York studio was used to produce numerous jazz records for the QRS label, most notably sides by studio bands organized by Williams, such as Clarence Williams and His Orchestra and his Barrel House Five. But as New York's leading labels snatched up the jazz headliners in the late 1920s, the jazz discs from Gennett's New York recording studio, which was moved to Long Island in 1928, gradually slowed to a quiet trickle.

Jazz Hysteria in the Hoosier State

The success of Fred Wiggins in acquiring for Gennett Chicago's major jazz talents soon led him back to his native Richmond, where Fred Gennett promoted him in 1924 to oversee the day-to-day operations of Gennett Records. Wiggins was now in charge of signing up musicians of his choosing, and he dictated, often arbitrarily, which master discs from the Richmond and New York studios would be pressed for public release.

Musically, Indiana had changed during the years Wiggins spent in Chicago. He soon found that the seeds of jazz, spread in part by Gennett releases, were firmly planted in his home state. In fact, young people in the Hoosier State had eagerly embraced jazz in the early 1920s, ahead of most of the Midwest. The colleges, particularly Indiana University in Bloomington, the dance halls, the roadhouses, and the summer resorts in the northern part of the state, such as Lake Wawasee and Hudson Lake, were now booking young dance bands modeled after the New Orleans–style bands. Indianapolis, the state capital, with one of the Midwest's largest black populations outside of Chicago, was home base in the early 1920s to several professional black and white jazz bands.

As the only record label based in the rural Midwest, Gennett Records capitalized on the influx of popular Indiana and Ohio jazz bands barnstorming the region. Territory bands, such as Curtis Hitch's Happy Harmonists in southern Indiana or the Marion McKay Orchestra in Ohio, signed up with Wiggins and recorded on a royalty basis or for a one-time payment of a few dollars. The bands did not get rich, but nobody seemed to care. Dance bands in the heartland were actually making 78-rpm records, a luxury normally limited to performers working out of the major cities, such as Chicago or New York.

Amid this fertile musical landscape in Indiana, two of the Jazz Age's most enduring icons, composer Hoagy Carmichael and cornetist Bix Beiderbecke, became spiritual brothers. They fueled the jazz craze in Indiana and helped define an era. By producing the first body of recordings by Beiderbecke and Carmichael, two colorful young men who led separate territory bands, Gennett's Richmond studio again was in a unique position to affect the course of jazz.

Gennett's 1924 recordings by Beiderbecke's Wolverine Orchestra (better known as the Wolverines), like the King Oliver and New Orleans Rhythm Kings discs, were snatched up by enthusiastic musicians around the country. Within a few years of his alcohol-related death in 1931 at age 28, Beiderbecke, never well known by the general public during his life, was immortalized by musicians and journalists as a tragic F. Scott Fitzgerald Jazz Age figure: the sensitive, musical genius who drank himself to death before the world could fully recognize his command of a misunderstood art form.

Carmichael's destiny proved quite different. Building upon the reputation he established with musicians through his Gennett recordings from 1925–28, Carmichael emerged as one of America's most commercially successful Tin Pan Alley song writers in the 1930s. His immortal composition "Star Dust" was required playing for dance bands of the 1930s and 1940s. A caricature of the chain-smoking honky-tonk pianist and singer in 1940s motion pictures such as *To Have and Have Not,* the maudlin Carmichael lived comfortably to the ripe old age of 82. His sentimental autobiographical books, *Stardust Road* and *Sometimes I Wonder,* romanticize Indiana's 1920s jazz movement, which was so thoroughly preserved by the Richmond recording studio.

Throughout his life, Carmichael was the most loyal torch-bearer of the Beiderbecke legend. Hearing Beiderbecke's first recordings on Gennett as the musical director and lead soloist of the rambunctious Wolverines helps us understand why. They remain powerful testimony to one of the most imitated cornetists of his generation.

Of the musicians who recorded extensively for Gennett, none are more revered worldwide today than Carmichael and Beiderbecke. Whereas many musical giants on the Gennett label were recorded in fleeting moments almost by happenstance, Carmichael and Beiderbecke were familiar faces in the Richmond studio, and their musical progress can be followed on one Gennett recording after another. Gennett Records gave these two young men the necessary encouragement and sufficient public exposure to keep them in the music profession long enough to make a lasting contribution. Their early association with the Indiana label is a major reason Gennett Records is revered today.

Bix and the Wolverines

Bix Beiderbecke was among the first generation of musicians to learn the jazz craft with instruction from the phonograph. Born in 1903, Beiderbecke was a teenager when the first 78-rpm releases by the Original Dixieland Jazz Band reached his hometown of Davenport, Iowa. He spent hours recreating the solos by the band's cornetist, Nick LaRocca, by pushing the turntable speed on the family's spring-wound phonograph to the slowest level, to where he could pick up LaRocca's improvisations on the piano note by note.

In the Beiderbecke household, however, jazz was musically unacceptable. Bix was born to an educated middle-class German immigrant family in the lumber business. Several relatives played musical instruments, and his mother was an accomplished pianist. Classical music was the proper discipline for a proper Victorian-age family, and it was an inherent part of his upbringing. By age five, he could pick out simple children's songs on the piano. Yet, throughout his youth, Beiderbecke resisted formal musical instruction, and as a young teenager, he began dabbling with the cornet, emulating the rebellious jazz musicians.

Without formal lessons, he did not adhere to conventional rules for cornet playing. He developed a unique embouchure and his own system for fingering the cornet's valves, thus becoming one of a long line of self-taught musicians who subconsciously influenced musical phrasing with experimental techniques. Just as the self-taught, left-handed guitarist Jimi Hendrix used unusual fingering with his right hand to help shape the sound of rock guitar playing in the late 1960s, Beiderbecke's unconventional approach to using the cornet's valves contributed to his special style of musical expression.

During his high school years, Beiderbecke soaked up all the new jazz available to him and entertained high school friends on both the piano and the cornet. Jazz musicians working the Mississippi riverboats that docked in Davenport gave Beiderbecke first-hand exposure to New Orleans jazz rhythms. When he was sixteen, the stern-wheeler *Capital* from New Orleans pulled into Davenport; it featured a band that included future Gennett recording artists Baby Dodds and Louis Armstrong.

Beiderbecke first heard Leon Roppolo in 1921, when Roppolo backed singer Bee Palmer at one of Davenport's downtown theatres. Beiderbecke was also influenced by a New Orleans riverboat cornetist named Emmett Louis Hardy, who died at age 22, in 1925, of tuberculosis. In late 1921, just as Beiderbecke was landing paying jobs with area bands, his parents enrolled him into Lake Forest Academy, a strict boarding school about an hour's drive north of Chicago. Beiderbecke soon took advantage of the proximity and frequented Chicago's dance halls in search of the jazz pioneers. His school work was circumvented by his insatiable desire to model his jazz playing after what he heard in Chicago.

During his trips to the city, Beiderbecke associated with other white students under the jazz spell, including clarinetist Jimmy Hartwell, tenor saxophonist George Johnson, and drummer Vic Moore. They often listened to the New Orleans Rhythm Kings at the Friars Inn in Chicago, where Johnson introduced Beiderbecke to his Indiana University friend and budding jazz pianist, Hoagy Carmichael. By mid-1922, Beiderbecke was expelled from Lake Forest Academy. He stoically packed his bags and moved to Chicago, where he found work with various pickup bands, playing for theatres, country clubs, and dance halls.

Beiderbecke found inspiration throughout Chicago, whether it was with Roppolo at the Friars Inn, or Armstrong, Oliver, Keppard, and the Dodds brothers along Chicago's State Street. After having finished a band job in Syracuse, New York, the nineteen-year-old Beiderbecke caught the train to New York City to hear the Original Dixieland Jazz Band and the Original Memphis Five (the latter recorded for Gennett as Ladd's Black Aces). The band's cornetist, Phil Napoleon, shared pointers with Beiderbecke, who dropped by to watch the Memphis Five record in the Gennett studio.

Over several months, as Beiderbecke plugged into a growing network of young white jazz musicians in Chicago, his reputation grew. In late 1923, a new jazz band, consisting mainly of young Chicago musicians, was organized for an extended job at the Stockton Club in Hamilton, Ohio. This seemingly insignificant roadhouse in rural southern Ohio, hundreds of miles from Chicago, was about to change the direction of Beiderbecke's life. The new Stockton Club house band included the young Chicago clarinetist Jimmy Hartwell, who had admired Beiderbecke's playing in Chicago for more than a year. No sooner than the Stockton house band was formed, the group's personnel changed. Hartwell wired to Chicago for his buddies—Beiderbecke, banjoist Bob Gillette, and tenor saxophonist George Johnson. The story goes that because their limited repertoire included the popular Jelly Roll Morton song "Wolverine Blues," the group became known as the Wolverine Orchestra.

The short-lived Stockton Club was a prototype of the classic Midwestern Prohibition-era roadhouse. Set on an isolated strip of U.S. Highway 4, which led to Cincinnati, the club was about eight miles south of Hamilton, a small industrial town that resembled nearby Richmond, Indiana.

The roadhouse's patrons had a penchant for bootleg whiskey, gambling, women, and jazz rhythms. The Wolverines played wild, extended choruses in order to fill the long sets each night. Beiderbecke became the unofficial music director and taught the band new songs by giving out notes on the cornet, four bars at a time. Only pianist Dud Mecum could read music proficiently, but he quit the band. Hartwell replaced Mecum with Dick Voynow, who had played previously with Johnson and Hartwell.

The Wolverines' engagement at the Stockton Club lasted until New Year's Eve, when a riot between mob factions from Cincinnati and Hamilton nearly destroyed the place. With the club closed temporarily, the band found work in January 1924 in downtown Cincinnati at Doyle's Dance Academy. Vic Moore, another Chicago-area friend, joined the band on drums. The Wolverines needed the regular work, and the long hours of nightly playing made the band technically cohesive. White jazz bands still copied the Original Dixieland Jazz Band. But whereas they tended to play in a hectic, jerky manner, with choppy solos, the Wolverines opted for a smoother sound, along the lines of the Gennett recordings by the New Orleans Rhythm Kings.

At this stage of their maturation, the Wolverines wrapped up a long evening at Doyle's on February 18, packed up their Phaeton, with instruments hanging over the sides, and took U.S. Highway 27 north about 75 miles to the Gennett studio in Richmond for their first recording date.

By now, Gennett's Richmond studio was a recognized hotbed for the Chicago jazz musicians. Many of Beiderbecke's heroes had recently recorded on the Gennett label, including Oliver, Armstrong, the Original Memphis Five, and the New Orleans Rhythm Kings. The Wolverines scheduled a one-day session in Richmond. George Johnson later recalled the Wolverines spending the early morning pondering how they would sound and reaching no conclusion. For obvious commercial reasons (or likely under Wiggins's orders), the Wolverines attempted four standards from the popular Original Dixieland Jazz Band song book: "Fidgety Feet," "Lazy Daddy," "Sensation Rag," and "Jazz Me Blues."

Whereas Gennett released several numbers by Oliver's band and the New Orleans Rhythm Kings from their first recording dates in Richmond, only two sides from the Wolverines' first session were issued. Despite several attempts by the Wolverines at "Lazy Daddy" and "Sensation Rag," the Gennett studio threw out the takes. "Jazz Me Blues" and "Fidgety Feet," on the other hand, were pressed and distributed back-to-back on the blue Gennett label. Because the disc represents Beiderbecke's first recording, it has been scrutinized and analyzed for decades.

Obviously, the first release did not reflect the Wolverines' live performances, as solos were limited to a few bars, a sharp contrast from the long choruses at the Stockton Club. The young Wolverines were probably nervous and tired from the non-stop hours of playing and traveling. A picture taken by a local photographer shows the band crowded into the gloomy studio, still in their performing outfits, with shirt collars open against the heat in the non-ventilated room. Despite the difficult circumstances for a recording debut, the two Wolverines sides pressed by Gennett provide an intimate glimpse into the band and its twenty-year-old cornet player.

"Fidgety Feet" finds the Wolverines, though not as polished as the New Orleans Rhythm Kings, rather well integrated, an obvious by-product of the steady work in Ohio.

Hartwell's clarinet, Johnson's tenor saxophone, Al Gande's trombone, and Beiderbecke's cornet blend and support each other throughout the melody with an ease not common on jazz recordings from early 1924. Beiderbecke's cornet is heavy on the vibrato, possibly a sign of simple jitters. He was, in fact, very young.

The easy-going "Jazz Me Blues" tells a much different story. Hartwell's fluid clarinet runs strongly resemble the work of Original Dixieland Jazz Band clarinetist Larry Shields. Beiderbecke clearly demonstrates a rhythmic ease, great originality, and a subtle bending of notes. His solos on this number are interspersed with accented eighth notes and triplets, and his rhythmic foundation is well established. While Beiderbecke's amazing capacity for improvisation expanded with every recording, his trademark rolling triplets on "Jazz Me Blues" would turn up time and time again throughout his playing career.

Beiderbecke's well-rounded tone, often compared to the ringing of a bell, is clearly audible on his first record date. While most cornet players by 1924 strived for the horn's upper register in the spirit of Armstrong, Beiderbecke rarely wandered outside the comfort zone of its middle register. He focused on melody and tone. Just as jazz immortal Miles Davis considered his trumpet an extension of his voice, Beiderbecke's solos give the impression of his singing into his instrument. His approach to improvisation, evident on the first Gennett disc, shows a cohesiveness, with choruses on "Jazz Me Blues" built one upon the other. Beiderbecke possessed Armstrong's and Oliver's ability to produce original choruses within a song, with each maintaining a basic correlation.

The first Gennett recording by Beiderbecke, made on a winter morning in Indiana, confirms the lasting impact he was said to have on his contemporaries, even at the onset of his professional life. Without documentation from Gennett, his early musical exploits, romanticized for years by his former band mates, would have been supported only by their potentially augmented, firsthand accounts.

The distinctive cornet styles of both Beiderbecke and Armstrong are immediately recognizable on their very first recorded solos. It was an era when young men grew up fast. The older Keppard and Oliver aside, none of the cornetists recorded by 1924 possessed the level of creativity exhibited by Beiderbecke and Armstrong on their Gennett recordings. Though products of vastly different cultures, the two men greatly admired each other's cornet playing. Beiderbecke's discs with the Wolverines and Armstrong's sides with Oliver and the Red Onion Jazz Babies show the two cornetists heading down different paths in their overall approach to horn playing, reflecting their contrasting personalities. Though few people recognized it then, the Gennett sides by Armstrong and Beiderbecke capture the origins of modern jazz trumpet playing.

Behind Beiderbecke's lead horn, the Wolverines were clearly onto something. George Johnson recalled the band hearing its first playbacks in the Gennett studio: "I honestly believe that at that moment, and not at any time before, was born in each of us the idea that as a unit, we had something different in the music line. I doubt that any of us realized until that moment how different in style and how dissimilar in effect our results were from the music of the Friars' band [New Orleans Rhythm Kings] that had knocked us out, and not long before. Coming at us out of that horn, it sounded like the music of another band, not at all like it sounded on the job."[1]

The Gennett session rekindled their spirits. Looking for playing opportunities outside of Cincinnati, the Wolverines were led to the heart of Indiana. In order to free themselves of either a debt or a long-term contract with Doyle's, the band sneaked out late one night, carefully sliding their "bonded" instruments out a side window. In the spring of 1924, the Wolverines teamed up with Indiana bandleader Charlie Davis for gigs at Butler College and at the Luna Lite Theatre in Marion, Indiana.

They also made contact with Carmichael, a law student at nearby Indiana University in Bloomington, where he headed his own campus jazz band. Carmichael and others in Hoosier college circles considered the Wolverines one of the nation's best jazz bands and proud successors to the Original Dixieland Jazz Band and the New Orleans Rhythm Kings. Said Carmichael: "Their playing sort of took the style away from the Rhythm Kings, rode it a bit higher in quality and arrangements and, I thought, developed the most drive of any band in the world of that time."[2]

Carmichael not only booked the Wolverines for several weekends that spring at IU's Greek houses, but also became their most ardent promoter. He also organized student road trips to hear the Wolverines throughout central Indiana. Carmichael approached jazz with a religious fanaticism. "In those days and the days to follow, jazz maniacs were being born and I was one of them," he said. "There were leaping legions of them from New Orleans to Chicago and Bloomington was right in the middle."[3] With one Gennett record set for distribution and the charismatic Carmichael as their faithful promoter, in the spring of 1924 the Wolverines entered the most exuberant season of their short but storied history, culminating with two landmark recording sessions in Richmond.

Hoagy and Bix: Soulmates in Jazz

As a popular student and musician on the IU campus in 1924, Hoagy Carmichael in many ways was living out the dreams of his youth. He had been born in 1899 in Bloomington, near the IU campus, into a working-class family. Four years later, they moved about 45 miles north to Indianapolis. The family settled into a second-floor apartment near downtown, at East and Lockerbie streets, a few houses from the stately residence of Indiana poet James Whitcomb Riley. Carmichael's mother played piano and had a special knack for ragtime. Carmichael was exposed to both New Orleans Dixieland music and some of the earliest ragtime piano rolls and records. During those early years, he was befriended by a black ragtime piano player named Reggie Duval, who dazzled the young Carmichael with his technique. Friendship with Duval made a tremendous impact on him. At a time when Indiana responded to the rallying cry of the Ku Klux Klan, Carmichael grew increasingly fascinated with the music of black America.

As a teenager, Carmichael was occupied with thoughts of jazz music and returning to Bloomington. He was unhappy in Indianapolis, and felt terribly lonely and shy. One of his sisters, Joanne, died in 1918, a tragedy that scarred the family, particularly Carmichael's father. The college town of Bloomington, surrounded by rolling hills and steep stone quarries, and the beauties of nearby Brown County held grand illusions for him. Carmichael felt bonded to his birthplace and hoped to raise enough money to return there for high school. He figured two years of high school could get him into college. He viewed IU as his ticket out of despair. These dreams helped him accept the menial jobs he was forced to take in Indianapolis.

By age nineteen, Carmichael had scraped together enough money to return to Bloomington, where he took a room in his grandmother's house and entered the local high school. Not a standout student, he gravitated toward the piano. Like many of his post–World War I contemporaries, he sought out the new jazz and worked tirelessly to apply its unorthodox musical principles and rhythms to his piano technique. Unlike most of America's music establishment, Carmichael viewed jazz as a unique skill. "The totality of feeling that came out of a brass horn was amazing," he said. "Maybe, I thought, it was because jazz carried no long words, culture, or phony intellectuals' patter in the playing, so that, like all primitive sound, it was an emotion in most ways beyond taking apart and examining."[4]

During his senior year in high school, Carmichael frequented the Book Nook on Indiana Avenue, a spacious, popular hangout for IU students. On a lark one afternoon, he entertained students on the piano. The positive response led him to form a band, and paying jobs soon followed. Carmichael's musical talent was rivaled only by his knack for self-promotion. Behind his personal charm, the five-piece group built up a loyal following around the Bloomington campus. The bookings helped Carmichael support himself and pay school expenses.

By mid-1920, it was a foregone conclusion that Carmichael would enroll at IU and move into the Kappa Sigma house. He gravitated to students of similar disposition: poetic dreamers, filled with jazz and always on the lookout for a good jug of kerosene-scented bootleg whiskey. Carmichael took every opportunity to hear New Orleans–style bands. He was particularly taken by the live jazz of a black band from Louisville led by Louie Jordan, who played at local dances and often performed at Sunday afternoon sessions in the Book Nook.

During 1922–23, Carmichael took his college band on the road, playing for dances in central Indiana. He spent summers listening to jazz bands at northern Indiana resorts, or in Indianapolis or Chicago. At the Friars Inn, in the Chicago Loop, Carmichael first heard the new rage on the Gennett label, the New Orleans Rhythm Kings, and met the future members of the Wolverines. For a short period, the Friars Inn was a breeding ground for many important white jazz artists who eventually recorded in Richmond.

"At the Friars Inn, I found George Johnson and Vic Moore at a table," Carmichael said. "I was in a panic of anticipation by the time I had checked my hat. The clarinet player [Leon Roppolo] was wiggling in his seat. He started in on 'Sensation Rag'! It was the doodle-style George had taught me. Then the cornet player picked it up and blasted his notes jerkily, with penetrating brassy tones. The notes smacked me at unexpected times and in unexpected places. They went right down through my gizzard and made my feet jump."[5]

Through Johnson, Carmichael kept close tabs on the exploits of the newly formed Wolverines. After learning of their first recording date at Gennett and hearing the band live in the early spring of 1924, Carmichael booked the Wolverines for dances at the IU Booster Club's spring event and at the Sigma Alpha Epsilon fraternity. These engagements, during the last week of April 1924, coincided with the release of the Wolverines' disc of "Fidgety Feet" and "Jazz Me Blues," which was distributed through the Starr Piano stores in the Midwest. With one lone recording out there, the Wolverines basically set up shop for the next two months at Indiana University, through bookings arranged by Carmichael. The Wolverines' engagements at Carmichael's Kappa Sigma house were particularly eventful, as Carmichael carefully laid the groundwork for wild receptions, topped with bootleg whiskey.

Carmichael and Beiderbecke became spiritual brothers in the pursuit of musical understanding. Behind the cheery backdrop of college youth and stomping jazz music, Carmichael still sensed a certain, unexplainable despair deep within the cornetist. The irony was that Beiderbecke's music represented pure joy for Carmichael. One drunken Sunday morning in the Kappa Sigma house led to an important moment in jazz. Of all his meetings with Beiderbecke, this encounter in the fraternity house was the clearest in Carmichael's mind. As the two listened to Igor Stravinsky's *Firebird* on the phonograph and passed the jug, Carmichael confessed he wanted to be a composer. Beiderbecke, whom Carmichael practically worshipped, provided some necessary, if somewhat incoherent, encouragement before he passed out. A couple of days later, Carmichael went to the Book Nook to face the keys of the house piano.

The Wolverines were returning for weekend engagements at the Sigma Chi house and Kappa Sigma house, and Carmichael, having shared with Beiderbecke his private desire to take composition beyond his random doodling on the piano, wanted to compose a bona fide song for the group. Carmichael repeatedly hammered out the same musical lines on pianos at the Book Nook and the Kappa Sigma house, driving students out of both locations. When the shouting was over, Carmichael had carved out his first composition, called "Free Wheeling."

When the Wolverines pulled into Bloomington for the weekend engagements, he gathered them around the piano for his
composition's first public hearing.

To Carmichael's surprise, one of the Wolverines suggested
they record it at an upcoming Gennett recording date, just a
few days away. The Wolverines pulled out their instruments,
and in their own informal way, quickly memorized the tune.
On May 6, they packed the car and drove across central Indiana back to the Gennett studio.

Things were going well for the Wolverines. The band was
elated by the reception from the IU crowd, their Gennett release was in the stores, and they had secured work for part of
the summer at the Casino Gardens in Indianapolis. With Gennett engineer Wickemeyer in the control room, the Wolverines' second date at Gennett revealed much about the greatly
improved band, with Beiderbecke again in the forefront, playing clear, confident solos.

The session's play list reflected the band's comradeship
with other area bands, as the Wolverines recorded songs by
Carmichael, Indiana bandleader Charlie Davis, and Indiana
saxophone player Charlie Naset, all of which were pressed and
released by the company. Too often, creative musicians are
thought to operate in a vacuum; in fact, the best musicians
eagerly absorb the inspiration around them. The Wolverines
were no exception. They pulled into Starr Valley for the May
recording date with an honest enthusiasm for the music of their
musical associates in Indiana. Carmichael had not exaggerated
about the Hoosier jazz scene. Because Wiggins and Wickemeyer often dictated which songs a band recorded on Gennett,
the Wolverines were afforded tremendous latitude in opting for
untried songs, such as Carmichael's "Free Wheeling."

Wickemeyer pressed the Wolverines' fourth attempt at
Carmichael's "Free Wheeling," which was retitled "Riverboat
Shuffle" by someone in the band, most likely Beiderbecke. As
Carmichael recalled, "Someone got me out of bed Saturday
morning and there was the record. I felt as flustered as a new

bride. I sobered up and experienced a strange detachment from it, maybe setting the pattern of my emotional experiences to almost all the tunes that followed. Nothing."[6]

For his first stab at composition, Carmichael created with "Riverboat Shuffle" a clever, melodic tune, with three distinct sections. Reminiscent of the bouncy, breezy compositions coming out of New Orleans, it was appropriately titled. Beiderbecke complemented his friend's song with a simple, beautifully structured solo, almost a song within Carmichael's song. It included Beiderbecke's first foray into blues phrasing on a recording, as the solo broke into a long, sustained descending slide in pitch without accompaniment. Notoriously self-critical, Beiderbecke later looked back on his early Gennett sessions as somewhat rudimentary. And clearly, his solo on "Riverboat Shuffle" three years later, with the Frank Trumbauer Orchestra on OKeh Records, shows far greater originality and fluidity. Yet, Beiderbecke's conservative, carefully crafted solo on Gennett for this future jazz standard was modeled by white musicians in the mid-1920s.

Also released by Gennett was a Wolverines interpretation of Charlie Davis's "Copenhagen," written in the generic popsong style prevalent in the 1920s. The Wolverines first heard the song when the Charlie Davis Band performed at the Ohio Theatre in Indianapolis. Beiderbecke was struck by its rhythm and sought Davis's permission to record it. The next step was for Davis to give the song a name. "Copenhagen" does not refer to the Danish capital, but to a brand of tobacco snuff used by Davis's sousaphone player. The Wolverines' loose arrangement of "Copenhagen" has saxophonist George Johnson and clarinetist Jimmy Hartwell each playing an ad lib chorus. Gennett issued the recording later in 1924, and soon afterward the Melrose brothers published the song with lyrics as a stock arrangement. The improvised clarinet and saxophone solos on the recording were transcribed straight onto the published music.

"The Wolverines made that tune jump right off the wax,"

Davis said. "George Johnson's tenor sax chorus was a classic—an improvisational gem that might well have been reason enough for 48 different bands to record 'Copenhagen' over the years."[7] It was not the first or last time that an improvised jazz solo on a record became permanently attached to a song. For many years after the original Gennett release, new recorded renditions of "Copenhagen" retained the opening Hartwell and Johnson solos, note-for-note. "Copenhagen" became a regular number in the Wolverines' repertoire. The other two songs pressed from the Wolverines' May session, "Oh Baby" and "Susie (of the Islands)," are standard pop fare. Neither tune has much to do with jazz, though they reflect the cheerful breeze surrounding a band with steady work. Bob Gillette's banjo solo on "Susie" was picked up remarkably well on Gennett's recording horn, but Voynow is barely audible on the Starr piano. Proper balancing of the instruments in the Gennett studio, despite the test pressings, was a constant aggravation. As the red light went on, signaling the approaching three-minute limit for "Susie," the band closed out with an excellent interchange between Beiderbecke and Hartwell.

For all the excitement with this second batch of records, it marked the beginning of the end for the Wolverines, who were relegated to the role of backup band for Beiderbecke's authoritative lead lines and masterful solos. Gone is Beiderbecke's tentative cornet playing from his first morning in Richmond. Wickemeyer positioned Beiderbecke near Gennett's acoustic recording horns to be heard distinctly. The young cornetist developed quickly, while his band mates provided the driving rhythm to keep pace with his seemingly limitless ideas.

Recorded for the ages, the Wolverines' "Copenhagen" was a fitting tribute to Charlie Davis, who had descended on the young band like a guardian angel and helped them find work in central Indiana. The Wolverines returned the favor by promoting the Charlie Davis Band with Wiggins and Wickemeyer as a candidate for the Gennett label. Besides, a Starr Piano executive and his wife had reportedly enjoyed dancing to the Charlie Davis Band at the Casino Gardens, just off the White River in northern Indianapolis.

So a recording date was set up in Richmond. Davis's septet attempted to record the song "There'll Be Some Changes Made." It was a nightmare. "No crowd of dancers, no gushing lovelies with their requests, no shining stars in the moonlight, only that monster horn sticking out from the wall, scaring everyone to death and daring the musicians to play well or else," said Davis. "That horn heard the band play it ['There'll Be Some Changes Made"] and the playback sounded like a mishmash. It was tame, disoriented and godawful. The next try was more of the same only worse; everyone played the lead. Three more takes and the technician gave up." The Gennett engineer told them, "Boys, come back again sometime with some notes on some papers."[8]

While Davis's dance band was a smash success at the Casino Gardens and a failure at the ominous Gennett studio, the Wolverines were just the opposite. Fresh off the highly successful second session at Gennett, the Wolverines opened at the Casino Gardens in the late spring of 1924, in an engagement arranged by Davis. They bombed. The Casino Gardens patrons were middle-aged, not the friendly college students whipped up by Carmichael and anticipating hot jazz. Within three weeks, attendance was down and the Wolverines were fired.

The Wolverines would not tone down their hot, improvisatory style to accommodate the softer tastes of older audiences, and the band appeared to be near the end of the line. But during their limited Indianapolis engagement, the Wolverines secured additional work through a Chicago drummer named Vic Berton. An experienced musician at age 28, Berton heard the Gennett disc of "Jazz Me Blues" in Chicago and was intrigued. He traveled south to Indianapolis to hear the Wolverines in early June and offered to manage them. Using his connections, Berton promised work in the Midwest, and he certainly had the credentials to make believers of the young Wolverines. He was older and had played with the Chicago

Symphony Orchestra and John Philip Sousa. A fast, solid drummer, Berton was among the best of his generation.

When the Wolverines returned to the Gennett studio on June 20, Berton's strong drumming proved to be an asset. Yet on this final session for the Wolverines in Richmond, Beiderbecke's cornet melodies of growing sophistication essentially dominated. Three songs were pressed, the standards "Tiger Rag" and "Royal Garden Blues," and an oddity, "I Need Some Pettin'." The rendition of "Tiger Rag" is a bit hurried, but Beiderbecke's solid, round tone and brilliant phrasing are prominent. His soloing elevated "Tiger Rag" as a jazz number to a level reached by the New Orleans Rhythm Kings on Gennett just the year before.

"Royal Garden Blues" finds the Wolverines playing in an easy-going style. Jazz author and critic James Lincoln Collier has cited Beiderbecke's masterful solo as a classic example of the correlated chorus style of jazz improvisation developed first by Armstrong: Play two measures, play two more related measures, and follow these four bars with four more related bars, and continue in that pattern. Beiderbecke's solo chorus in "Royal Garden Blues" was nothing short of a mini-composition that can stand on its own.

"It opens with a rising and falling, more or less chromatic, line for two bars, which is then recapitulated in the second two bars," Collier writes. "This rather quiet, introspective statement is followed by a gradual increase in intensity, rising to a climax with a starker, more forceful figure, both louder and higher, which in turn descends to a slightly quieter denouement and ends with a little reflective phrase reminiscent of the opening figure."[9]

Perhaps if Fred Gennett had known that his label's jazz releases would later merit such detailed, flowery analysis, he might not have allowed the takes selected for release to be determined by Wickemeyer, Wiggins, Gennett secretaries, salesmen, or whoever was available in the notoriously short-handed company on any given day.

While Beiderbecke's solo on "Royal Garden Blues" epitomizes the correlated chorus style, his lengthy solo on "I Need Some Pettin' " is a powerful dissertation on early jazz rhythm and blues phrasing. It is alarming today to play this extremely rare disc on an old spring-wound phonograph. It was part of Gennett's "personal recording" series and not for public distribution. Through the scratchy, low-fidelity muddle bursts a bright cornet solo light years ahead of its time. The experience is comparable to listening to bebop innovators Charlie Parker or Dizzy Gillespie on their original 78-rpms from the 1940s. Innovative, timeless jazz improvisation always sounds in the wrong context when it has been reproduced on primitive sound recording technology.

By mid-1924, the Wolverines recordings on Gennett, despite a limited distribution network, made inroads for young white musicians. On the heels of Gennett's releases by the New Orleans Rhythm Kings, the Wolverines' discs enabled emerging white musicians, such as the Austin High School Gang, trombonist Tommy Dorsey, saxophonist Jimmy Dorsey, and New York cornetist Red Nichols, to follow Beiderbecke's musical progress. These young musicians, all established players by the 1930s, viewed the Wolverines, on the strength of Beiderbecke's lead horn, as the third great white jazz orchestra, after the Original Dixieland Jazz Band and New Orleans Rhythm Kings.

It was obvious that the Wolverines did not rely heavily on the standard stock arrangements being published for working dance bands. Awakened by Chicago's leading musicians, the Wolverines aspired more to the level of jazz originality established by Oliver, Armstrong, Morton, Roppolo, and Brunies. As an example of Beiderbecke's influence, in 1924 the George Olsen Orchestra recorded "You'll Never Get To Heaven With Those Eyes" for Victor. Red Nichols was lead cornet, and for his solo, the arranger transcribed note-for-note Beiderbecke's solo on "Jazz Me Blues" from his first Gennett session. When Nichols traveled the Midwest with a band that summer, he journeyed down a series of dirt roads in eastern Indiana to see the Wolverines firsthand. The meeting between Beiderbecke and Nichols, both leading jazz cornet players of the late 1920s, at a rural Indiana dance was the beginning of a long relationship.

"Hearing them today on old [Gennett] recordings," Carmichael recalled in 1965, "with all their scratchy faults, no Dixieland group, even of recent years, quite comes near to what the boys had. Even such important figures as Bud Freeman, Pee Wee Russell, and Charlie Teagarden, among many fine combo men when playing as a group, lacked just a little something in all-over sound and beat compared to the Wolverines at their top."[10]

During July 1924, Berton booked the Wolverines in Indianapolis at the Palace Theatre, as the "Vic Berton Wolverine Orchestra, famous recorder for Gennett Records." In August, he booked the band in Gary, Indiana; but his series of bookings had gone dry. Again, the Wolverines' streak of paid engagements was ending, when band member Min Leibrook struck gold. With help from one of his musician contacts in New York, the Wolverines were booked at the new Cinderella Ballroom at 48th and Broadway in New York City.

In September 1924, the band made the long, harrowing drive to New York. With Vic Moore back on drums, they opened almost immediately on arrival. A few days later a recording date was scheduled at the Gennett studio on East 37th Street, by now well known in jazz circles for its numerous releases by Ladd's Black Aces and Bailey's Lucky Seven. On a recommendation from Richmond, in the final months of 1924 the New York studio recorded what proved to be the last records by the Wolverines.

Shaping the Beiderbecke Legend

For their first visit to the Gennett New York studio in September 1924, the Wolverines recruited one of their old heroes from Chicago, trombonist George Brunies, who was in the city playing with the Ted Lewis Orchestra. Former member of the New Orleans Rhythm Kings, Brunies was no stranger to Gennett or to Beiderbecke, who apparently insisted that he sit in with the Wolverines for the recording date. The studio took the conservative route, having the Wolverines record two popular songs from the Original Dixieland Jazz Band play list, "Sensation" and "Lazy Daddy."

In covering the two standards, the Wolverines were well integrated, and yet, looser than ever before in their approach to playing jazz. Behind Beiderbecke's vibrant cornet, the band achieves a fluidity with the songs not evident in the original, more widely circulated, renditions by the Original Dixieland Jazz Band. While keeping up with Beiderbecke's expanding technical skills was increasingly difficult for the other band members, the ensemble's supporting role was commendable. The months of barnstorming the cities and small towns of the Midwest made the Wolverines competitive with just about any traditional jazz band operating in New York.

The September session coincided with encouraging reviews from their live engagements at the Cinderella Ballroom. The local magazines complimented the band for its sense of rhythm and tempo, and described an enthusiastic response from dance fans. *Variety* magazine noted that the Wolverines had already recorded for Gennett, but that other record companies in New York were lining up to do the same.

Nice publicity, but not true. Jazz bands were still a very tough sell with the record labels, and the Wolverines never graduated beyond the small Gennett label. Although Gennett's distribution network could not compete with Columbia or Victor Records, the Wolverines discs managed to reach influential people in the music industry. One of them was Jean Goldkette, a classically trained pianist whose highly successful thirteen-piece band in Detroit included a young Pennsylvania trombonist, Tommy Dorsey, and his saxophonist brother, Jimmy. Beiderbecke's cornet playing on the Gennett records so impressed Goldkette that he took a train to New York to hear Beiderbecke at the Cinderella Ballroom. The live shows further confirmed what Goldkette could decipher on the low-fidelity Gennett discs. He offered Beiderbecke a spot in his Detroit orchestra, which Beiderbecke could not turn down. The Goldkette outfit offered steady work, better pay, the challenge of a larger orchestra with schooled musicians, and far greater record exposure on the Victor label. As always, the pocket change offered by Gennett lost out to the potential of mighty Victor.

After discussing the offer with the Wolverines, Beiderbecke accepted, thus ending an eventful year-long run with his first touring band. As Beiderbecke was serving his notice, the Cinderella Ballroom informed the Wolverines their three-month contract would not be renewed. Carmichael later called the band's failure to succeed in New York one of jazz's great mysteries. It was not the last instance in which creative jazz players were not commercially viable.

Before Beiderbecke joined the Goldkette outfit, he was committed to a final Wolverines session at Gennett's New York studio. In early October 1924, the band recorded the songs "Tia Juana" and "Big Boy," with arrangements spiced with the Charleston dance rhythms sweeping the college crowds in the East.

"Big Boy," which showcased Beiderbecke, was not a run-of-the-mill dance recording for 1924. He opens with a strong lead melody on the cornet and then plays an elegant, contrapuntal, ragtime-style piano solo. He picks up the cornet again for a bright, lyrical solo during the track's finale. Beiderbecke's piano solo is modernly dissonant, supporting Carmichael's assertion that the young cornetist avidly studied the piano works of twentieth-century French modernists Claude Debussy and Maurice Ravel. On "Big Boy," Beiderbecke's musical influences are shown to expand well beyond Armstrong, Oliver, Roppolo, and the other less-schooled jazz musicians. Beiderbecke never lost the admiration for classical music that was instilled in him as a child in Davenport.

Beiderbecke's first recorded piano solo was a revelation to many of his contemporaries. In his later years, Beiderbecke focused more attention on piano technique and composition. But at the "Big Boy" recording session, his piano solo was more of an afterthought, according to Fred Rollison. A cornetist with Curtis Hitch's Happy Harmonists, a popular, Indiana-based dance band, Rollison had chummed with the Wolverines in Bloomington and was invited to New York to audition as Beiderbecke's replacement. He and Beiderbecke had worked out a cornet duet for the "Big Boy" recording, but at the last moment, Beiderbecke opted for the piano solo. Rollison was left on the sidelines, watching the 21-year-old Beiderbecke exhibit, in a three-minute time span, a remarkable level of lyricism on two instruments in a very new musical genre.

The Wolverines set up live engagements in Florida for December, with Beiderbecke's huge shoes to fill. The first choice was Gennett alum Paul Mares from New Orleans, who declined. Next, they tried Rollison, but he could not master the band's vast repertoire, which was now about a hundred songs. Finally, they settled for the seventeen-year-old leader of Chicago's Austin High School Gang, Jimmy McPartland, who had played the northern Indiana resorts when the Wolverines were in Gary. The Austin Gang listened religiously to the Wolverines discs, as they had the New Orleans Rhythm Kings discs. So when McPartland arrived in New York for the audition, he knew from memory many of the Wolverines' favorite tunes from his collection of Gennett records.

When McPartland debuted with the Wolverines at the Gennett studio in December 1924, Beiderbecke's towering presence was sorely missed. For their sad exit from the recording business, the Wolverines opted for the pop number "When My Sugar Walks Down the Street" and Elmer Schoebel's jazz tune "Prince of Wails." The recordings are downright monotonous. Without Beiderbecke's golden-toned cornet playing, the Wolverines lacked a strong lead melody and any sense of musical imagination. Their last releases on Gennett, through studiously arranged, have little to do with jazz. McPartland performed like a promising but timid teenager. By the late 1920s, he was recording in Chicago with the likes of Benny Goodman and Jack Teagarden. One of jazz's most endearing horn players, McPartland enjoyed a successful career that spanned over half a century. But his record debut as a tentative youngster at Gennett's New York studio unfortunately coincides with the last hurrah of a once-great band. Beiderbecke proved to be an impossible act to follow, especially for an inexperienced kid.

Throughout 1924, Gennett's Richmond and New York studios produced more than a dozen releases by the Wolverines. Because they contained lengthy solos by the most original white jazz cornetist in the land, these discs were soon treated like scripture by the growing coterie of hot jazz players. The discs became prized collectors' items after Beiderbecke's death in 1931, bolstered by the mythology that subsequently surrounded his life.

Despite the antiquated fidelity, Gennett's Wolverines sides still hold their luster. These rare discs not only launched Beiderbecke's career but also committed Carmichael to composition after the release of "Riverboat Shuffle." Through the initial record sales by Starr Piano stores and independent record distributors, and later, through reissue recordings, the Wolverines recordings were celebrated in the major cities of America and Europe, where they influenced an entire generation of jazz players. The Wolverines sides, like the King Oliver discs on Gennett, became available over the decades on numerous labels worldwide, from England and France to Japan and Czechoslovakia.

Because Beiderbecke later associated with far more talented musicians, historians too often dismiss the Wolverines; this is a terribly short-sighted perspective. The records find the Wolverines a genuine improvising band, capable of loosening up the rigid, polyphonic textures of Dixieland music. By employing basic riffs on such songs as "Tiger Rag" and "Royal Garden Blues," they wove instrumental lines into a driving, cohesive sound. While most white jazz bands at the time clung to campy novelty gimmicks, the Wolverines, like the New Orleans Rhythm Kings, could swing. The Wolverines recorded an equal mix of Dixieland and pop numbers and depended heavily on the Original Dixieland Jazz Band song book, the standard practice of 1920s white jazz bands. However, with Beiderbecke's cornet and Voynow's arrangements, the Wolverines bore their own signature on these standards.

Fortunately, Gennett's musically untrained sound engineers gave Beiderbecke and George Johnson the freedom to express themselves in the studio with relatively long solos. It was not standard practice in 1924, as many bands, including King Oliver's groups, opted for short, pre-rehearsed solos in the New Orleans tradition. Even on the Wolverines' first recording date, the twenty-year-old cornetist cut loose with a lengthy solo on "Jazz Me Blues." Because of Beiderbecke's distinct improvisations on Gennett, musicologists have long bemoaned the studio's destruction of the band's many rejected outtakes, but that was part of the standard method for doing business. That a struggling territory band from the 1920s was actually recorded for posterity is something of a miracle.

Not only did Fred Gennett deliberately look for musicians offering something different, but his fundamental goal was to produce records with the least overhead (not to mention shellac) possible. This meant giving an enormous body of unknown musicians their first crack at recording. As we have already seen, this enabled the Gennett organization to attract undiscovered musicians of great originality, like the Wolverines or King Oliver, and later, the early country and blues musicians. Many of these relatively obscure Gennett artists were far from the commercial mainstream, and they played in musical genres which reflected and appealed to the grassroots, ethnic pulse of America.

While the demise of the Wolverines concluded the first

phase of Beiderbecke's professional career, his association with Gennett lasted another year. Just days after leaving the band, Beiderbecke was back in the New York studio for an impromptu gathering with three members of Ray Miller's dance orchestra, who had booked recording time in mid-October 1924.

Inviting Beiderbecke to the session were trombonist Miff Mole, a fixture around Gennett's New York studio from his days with Ladd's Black Aces, Frank Trumbauer on C-melody saxophone, and pianist Rube Bloom, one of New York's leading pianists and composers. With Beiderbecke set to leave for Detroit in a couple of days, Trumbauer quickly threw together the band for the Gennett date. To round out the group, the Wolverines' Min Leibrook sat in on bass and Vic Moore played drums.

Under Trumbauer's direction, the group recorded Bloom's bouncy "Flock o' Blues" and Trumbauer's "I'm Glad." For Mole, Trumbauer, and Bloom, all capable improvisors, the session was a break from the limitations of playing in a larger orchestra. Working from formal arrangements, Beiderbecke is loose and fluid, though he is clearly along for the ride and does not stand out from the rest of the band. Trumbauer was one of the best jazz saxophonists in the mid-1920s in terms of technique and tone. The Gennett session marked the beginning of a long association between Trumbauer and Beiderbecke through several bands, including the Jean Goldkette Orchestra and the Paul Whiteman Orchestra. Trumbauer's 1920s recordings inspired several latter-day saxophone giants, such as Lester Young and Benny Carter. "After hearing those old Trumbauer records, I got very excited about the saxophone," said Carter. "Very early on, it became my goal to play like him. I thought he had a marvelous tone."[11]

Perhaps since Ray Miller was under contract with the Brunswick label, the pickup band on the Gennett date remained incognito on the release. Hiding behind pseudonyms, a longtime practice in the recording industry, musicians try to escape the notice of a competing label which previously bound them to an exclusive recording contract.

Beiderbecke apparently suggested the name The Davenport Six for the pickup band, in honor of his Iowa hometown. Trumbauer did get Iowa represented, but the name on the release ended up as The Sioux City Six. While this particular recording session proved a success, Gennett's New York studio was not always so accommodating to the young Beiderbecke and his rowdy friends. Mole recalled one night when he, Berton, Beiderbecke, and Jimmy Dorsey took two quarts of gin into the studio with the drunken desire to produce the greatest jazz record ever. A few drinks and a few muffed songs later, they were ordered out by the Gennett staff.

By late October 1924, Beiderbecke was on the bandstand with Goldkette's band in Detroit. He struggled with the written charts and left the band within a couple of months. He was soon scraping for work around Indianapolis and hanging out with his old friend from IU, Carmichael. During this brief inactive period for Beiderbecke, there was a recording session in Richmond which has been the subject of speculation among Beiderbecke buffs ever since.

In December 1924, Marion McKay and His Orchestra booked recording time in Richmond. A banjoist from the small southwestern Ohio town of Wilmington, McKay headed a popular dance band that played around the Midwest in the 1920s, particularly Dayton and Cincinnati. "I was working a ballroom in Dayton one night when I was contacted by the Gennett people who asked me to pop up and make a recording," said McKay. "That led to a pretty nice arrangement with the fellas in Richmond over a period of years."[12] McKay recorded numerous sides in Richmond, billed as Marion McKay and His Orchestra or as the Lange-McKay Orchestra. He had hired Indiana drummer Jack Tilson, who knew Beiderbecke from engagements around the state, and with the cornetist idle in Indianapolis, Tilson apparently invited him to the Gennett session. Here, the mystery begins.

Beiderbecke was allegedly persuaded to join McKay's band on the recording of "Doo Wacka Doo." Some jazz historians have even claimed that he played the cornet solo on the Gennett release. Speculation was further fueled when the "Doo Wacka Doo" recording appeared on the Italian Raretone label's 1972 album *Bix—To Be or Not to Be,* a collection of 1920s discs that were thought to include Beiderbecke on cornet.

According to McKay, the legendary cornetist played a few choruses with his band in the Richmond studio. But was he recorded on "Doo Wacka Doo"? "You used to do a lot of test pressings [at the Gennett studio] to get the sound just right, and I honestly don't know if Beiderbecke was on the take used to make the record," said McKay in 1991, when he was 93 years old. "It seems I've been asked this question about Beiderbecke at the Gennett studio more than any other. I wish I could have put it to rest, but at the time, it wasn't something I was really thinking about."[13]

Record researchers Warren Plath and Frank Powers, after conducting exhaustive interviews in the 1970s with McKay and his surviving band members, concluded that the debated cornet solo on "Doo Wacka Doo" was actually performed by one Leroy Morris, a talented cornetist who played briefly with the Marion McKay Orchestra.[14] Morris possessed the rich tone and smooth legato style commonly associated with Beiderbecke's playing.

Whether it was Beiderbecke's solo or not, McKay fondly remembers the young cornetist as "just one of the boys with a horn that hung around the Richmond studio in the 1920s."[15] So often, firsthand accounts of an immortal figure are augmented over time as the legend builds and any event surrounding the person becomes significant. In recalling Beiderbecke, McKay has a more down-to-earth perspective.

He remembers Beiderbecke in relation to the vibrant musical environment in which they both worked. "There were tremendous players on those early Gennett records, and

Beiderbecke was one of them. Indiana, in particular, had great players. Back then, a lot of guys didn't stick with it and ended up doing something else for a living so they aren't remembered today. The musicians didn't make a whole lot of money with those [Gennett] records. The whole idea of recording was very new. You didn't let the recording time get in the way of the live bookings, which were far more important. That's where you made the money. Playing at the big hotels in New York or Detroit, that's what you wanted to do back then. The records were more something you did for fun. It was new and everybody got a kick out of it."[16]

McKay said he probably paid Beiderbecke $20 to $30 for the December Gennett session with his band. "I always paid the band members about $20 or so, and I had my own arrangement with Gennett where I took 10 percent royalties for the records sold. That made me a little money, but I sure should have pushed those Gennett records more. It was so different back then. Dance bands were just beginning to make records. We didn't know what it would become."[17]

A month after the McKay recording date, Beiderbecke, still stranded in the Midwest, made his last recording for Gennett, which proved to be one of his greatest recorded performances. He arranged for a reunion of old friends to meet in Richmond on January 26, 1925. Two days before, Beiderbecke headed to Indianapolis to meet Carmichael, who had been visiting his parents for the Christmas holidays. Beiderbecke invited Carmichael to the Richmond date, where he planned to record in a slow-drag style, with Goldkette sidemen Tommy Dorsey on trombone, Don Murray on clarinet and saxophone, Paul Mertz on piano, and Howdy Quicksell on banjo. Tom Gargano from Detroit was on drums.

The plan called for the Goldkette members to drive to Richmond from Detroit and hook up with Beiderbecke at the studio on Monday morning, January 26. An important incentive with this recording date was that Dorsey promised to bring three quarts of booze. Having bought himself a new Ford, Carmichael volunteered to drive Beiderbecke. The night before the session, the two musicians drove to the Ohio Theatre in Indianapolis and banged out choruses to "Royal Garden Blues" on grand pianos in the orchestra pit. At about 3 A.M., they started east on the National Road to Richmond. En route, Beiderbecke suggested that they pull to the side of the highway and blow their cornets out into a snow-covered field. Even today, the stretch of U.S. 40 between Indianapolis and Richmond makes for a stark, lonely ride at night. Carmichael recalled Beiderbecke's playing: "a clean wonderful banner of melody filled the air, carved the countryside. Split the still night. The trees and ground and the sky made the tones so right. I battled along to keep up a rhythmic lead while Bix laid out for the tillers of the soil."[18]

The gang united in Richmond in the morning around Dorsey's bottles and organized an arrangement from a melody Beiderbecke had created. Quicksell did not arrive in time for the start of the session. With little or nothing of a score written out, the group made three masters of Beiderbecke's first composition on record, dubbed "Davenport Blues" by Dorsey. Fortunately, one of the masters was pressed for posterity. The other takes were destroyed because of surface pops on the copper-plated master discs, caused by powdered graphite in the grooves of the wax disc.

After "Davenport Blues," the band tried "Toddlin' Blues," a slow blues written by the Original Dixieland Jazz Band. Again, several copper master takes were discarded because of surface pops before one was finally saved and pressed for posterity. The band tried another number called "Magic Blues," but all three master discs were affected by surface pops and were destroyed. The group also tried another tune, "No One Knows What It's All About," which Paul Mertz later described as appropriate, given the nature of the band's playing at this point. Apparently, the alcohol had taken its toll and the song was never played to anyone's satisfaction.

The Gennett ledgers list the recording date under "Leon B.

Beiderbecke and His Orchestra." But "Davenport Blues" and "Toddlin' Blues" were released back-to-back under "Bix and His Rhythm Jugglers." Despite the technical difficulties in the pressing room and the free-flowing alcohol that morning, the releases create a laid-back, pleasant atmosphere. Beiderbecke's desire to record music in slow drag, though somewhat ragged, was readily accomplished. His swan song on the Gennett label, "Davenport Blues," finds the cornetist dabbling in real improvisatory mastery, in terms of both rhythm and harmony. Musicologists in ensuing years have dissected his improvised solo, praising the exploratory melodies that stretched the established boundaries of jazz during that period.

No question, Beiderbecke had played free of inhibition. Throughout his career, he was more at ease and in a mood to experiment in small, informal groups. "Davenport Blues" is a classic example of the young trumpeter in his most comfortable setting with no limits on his creativity.

The photographs taken that morning basically tell the story. In one picture, the band is crowded around the piano, smiling and looking inebriated, particularly the young, bespectacled Dorsey. In another, Beiderbecke is playing the cornet while leaning against the piano. Dorsey is slumped back against a high chair. Beiderbecke's pickup band captured the easy-going mood associated with the Roaring Twenties. Despite latter-day romanticism, a professional jazz musician working in the Prohibition era was surrounded by illegally brewed alcohol, which posed serious health problems, and was involved in risky business. By 1931, Beiderbecke, Gargano, and Murray were dead. Fortunately for jazz history, Beiderbecke recorded prolifically with small and large groups later in the 1920s, closing out his short, but memorable, career with the enormously popular Paul Whiteman Orchestra.

The Beiderbecke legend was instantly fostered by the many musicians who were dazzled firsthand by his remarkable skills. Musicians loved primarily his originality, as Beiderbecke was largely unknown to the general public during his short life. But unlike, say, Buddy Bolden, the pioneer turn-of-the-century New Orleans cornetist with mythical status in jazz today, he left behind a substantial recorded legacy.

Recording technology, even for Gennett Records, would improve drastically between the acoustic recordings of 1924 and the introduction of electronic recording technology in late 1926. The difference in sound quality is night and day, for example, between the Wolverines' original "Riverboat Shuffle" for Gennett in 1924, and the 1927 rendition for OKeh by Trumbauer's group, with Beiderbecke again soloing on cornet. Still, Beiderbecke's first recordings on Gennett continue to attract serious attention for they detailed an advanced, unique approach to jazz improvisation, supported by a competent cast of supporting players.

The Beiderbecke legend was documented first on Gennett recordings. Even though his marvelous, somewhat notorious, association with the Indiana label concluded one drunken morning in Richmond, his musical legacy in that studio would be felt for years. Beginning in 1925, it was Carmichael's turn in the drab Richmond studio. His early compositions on the Gennett label are a direct tribute to his inspirational association with Beiderbecke.

From Obscurity to Stardust

Hoagy Carmichael was toughing out his last year at law school at Indiana University when he chauffeured Beiderbecke to Richmond for the 1925 Rhythm Jugglers recordings. At the time, he was torn between two potential careers: a promising legal profession or a less-secure future in music, the route chosen by most of his friends. Over the next couple of years, the recording studio in Richmond's Starr Valley would play a substantial role in Carmichael's ultimate decision to cast his law training to the wind.

Gennett Records, however, did not aggressively promote the young composer. The Richmond studio—Wiggins in particular—was indifferent to the sophisticated, eccentric songs that Carmichael composed for his own recording dates. By the late 1920s, Wiggins and the Gennett staff were focusing more attention on producing "old time" country records, which had become a mainstay for the Gennett label. Although Wiggins remained receptive to jazz, many of Carmichael's compositions and arrangements were not considered marketable. Besides, the handful of Carmichael songs that are important now and that debuted on the declining Gennett label between 1925 and 1928, attracted limited interest except with fellow jazz musicians. Yet, these recordings helped to launch the career of one of America's most significant twentieth-century songwriters.

Carmichael's connection with Gennett Records began with the Wolverines' recording of "Riverboat Shuffle" in 1924. Later that year, the band's pianist and arranger, Dick Voynow, played a copy of the Gennett disc for music publisher Irving Mills of New York's highly influential Mills Music Co. Before long, Mills Music mailed a contract to Carmichael in Bloomington. "Hoagland, the lawyer, didn't notice it had no promise to publish, only a line to pay royalties if they did publish," he recalled. "I was too happy to be legal."[19]

But Mills did publish "Riverboat Shuffle" in early 1925 as a ragtime-style piano piece. Credited along with Carmichael as composer was Voynow, and Mills staffer Mitchell Parish was named as lyricist. Voynow's credit is legitimate, even if his appearance on the song did come as a surprise to Carmichael. After all, Carmichael never provided the Wolverines with a written arrangement of "Riverboat Shuffle" for the 1924 recording date in Richmond. Voynow and Beiderbecke basically took Carmichael's song outline and scored it on the spot.

To the young Carmichael, it all seemed so easy. Write a tune, hand it to the Wolverines, they record it for Gennett, then the song is taken to New York and published. A few hun-

dred more songs, and royalties would be pouring in, he figured. Incredibly, his next two compositions, the Wolverines-
inspired "Boneyard Shuffle" and the epic "Washboard Blues,"
followed along the same lucky path as "Riverboat Shuffle."
Only this time, Carmichael's passport into the Gennett studio
was not the Wolverines, but an Indiana band called Curtis
Hitch's Happy Harmonists.

Hitch's brief career as a local bandleader would be completely obscured in the annals of jazz if not for his brief association with Gennett Records, Beiderbecke, and most important,
Carmichael. Because he helped to expose Carmichael's music to
a larger audience, Hitch's bit part in 1920s jazz should not be
overlooked. Born in 1897 on a farm near the village of Princeton in southern Indiana, Hitch was a self-taught pianist who
played by ear. At age 23, he helped organize a band which included a talented local cornetist, Fred Rollison. The name
Hitch's Happy Harmonists was inspired by the nearby historic
village of New Harmony.

In 1923, the band played around Evansville, Indiana, on
the Ohio River, with occasional dates up north on the Bloomington campus. Later that year, the Happy Harmonists recorded "Cruel Women" and "Home Brew Blues" at Gennett,
followed in February 1924 by the songs "Steady Stepping
Papa," "Baptistown Crawl" (inspired by Evansville's black
district), and "Ethiopian Nightmare." The last piece follows
the same chord sequence as "Alexander's Ragtime Band," in
an inventive approach for 1924. (In the 1930s and 1940s, jazz
players, especially bebop players, routinely took the chord
progressions of pop numbers and constructed jazz tunes
around them.)

Hitch and his band became friends with the Wolverines
during the 1924 engagements in Bloomington. The Wolverines' approach to jazz captivated the Happy Harmonists.
Hitch's band members, particularly Rollison, were taken by
Beiderbecke's remarkable lyricism. Late in 1924, Rollison
made an unsuccessful bid for the chair vacated by Beiderbecke

in the Wolverines. He became musical director of Hitch's outfit early the following year for a recording session in Richmond, just one week before Beiderbecke and Carmichael
rolled into Gennett for the historic Rhythm Jugglers date.

For the January 1925 session, the Happy Harmonists had
the same instrumentation as the Wolverines. Wiggins had instructed Hitch to produce songs in the jazz/ragtime style. His
directive may have stemmed from the fact that the Melrose
brothers in Chicago were marketing stock arrangements of
classic rags, and Gennett Records could help promote them.
Hitch's band recorded the classic tunes "Cataract Rag" and
"Nightingale Rag Blues" with all the spirit and interplay of a
Wolverines session. Rollison had a stellar musical role model
in Beiderbecke, whose influence is evident in Rollison's playing on both recordings.

If a band such as the Happy Harmonists played hot jazz in
southern Indiana in the mid-1920s, Carmichael would make
its acquaintance. Hitch, who was not a great pianist, was impressed with Carmichael's creative, eccentric approach to ragtime and jazz music. In the spring of 1925, Carmichael played
for Hitch one of his new compositions, "Washboard Blues."
Hitch asked him to compose another number so that the
Happy Harmonists could record both at a Gennett date in
May. Carmichael responded with a sequel to "Riverboat Shuffle," a likable jazz tune called "Boneyard Shuffle." With these
two numbers, the band loaded up Carmichael's car and
headed to Richmond. But this time, Carmichael wasn't a spec-
tator; Hitch put him on the grand piano. This music required
the composer's touch!

Down along the Whitewater gorge, past the long row of
Starr manufacturing buildings, Hitch's band entered the studio
by the tracks which had been admitting jazz innovators since
1922. The studio's atmosphere afflicted Carmichael as it had
the Charlie Davis Band: "I didn't feel too sure of myself. I was
nervous in anticipation of my first recording. The studio was a
dreary looking Rube Goldberg place with lily-shaped horns

sticking oddly from the walls. It didn't have the effect of sooth-
ing me. The horns sticking from the walls looked spooky and I
was pretty upset by the time we were ready to make test
records."[20]

After Wickemeyer produced test records of the songs offered by Hitch, the engineer settled on "Boneyard Shuffle,"
but not "Washboard Blues," which came out about twenty seconds short of the required duration of just under three minutes. Wickemeyer proposed that they throw out the song.
Carmichael protested. Hitch, wanting both Carmichael compositions recorded, offered a solution: The law student would
fill in the necessary twenty seconds with an unaccompanied
piano solo. Carmichael was terrified. Hitch gave the band a
ten-minute cigarette break by the railroad tracks while Carmichael quickly came up with something to play: "They left
tactfully and I stood staring at the piano. And I tried to think of
a piano solo. I thought of my family, my little sister's funeral,
my mother playing hymns on the old golden oak. Everything
whirled past, but my fingers lay numb on the keys, and time
was running out. Scared, worried, I hit the piano, thumping
out notes. Five minutes later I called the boys back."[21]

The piano solo came toward the close of the song. "My
hands were damp as I hit the keys, getting into the start of it.
The rest was just prolonged nerve reflexes—I wasn't having
any part of it myself. And then it was over. I was entirely un-
conscious of anything I had played. We staggered through the
last chorus. It was finished, done—buried."[22] When the song
was played back, it sounded historic and far away to Carmichael. McKay described playbacks at Gennett in exactly the
same manner. "It never really sounded like what you had just
played," said McKay, echoing Carmichael's thoughts. "Coming back to you through that horn, it was a funny feeling. It
sounded like something you had played ten years before. You
wondered how it could be you."[23]

After the successful recording of "Washboard Blues," the
band members danced around the studio howling like

Apaches. Carmichael had successfully pulled it off. "Washboard Blues" and "Boneyard Shuffle" were mastered and pressed back-to-back on Gennett for Hitch's Happy Harmonists. Three compositions by Carmichael were now saved for posterity on Gennett. He was seeing stars. The studio portrait taken of the Happy Harmonists before the "Washboard Blues" recording shows a nervous Carmichael, clad in a college sweater and bow tie, sitting on the piano bench close to Hitch, who could pass for a proud father even though he was just two years older than Carmichael. Drummer Earl McDowell is confidently smoking a pipe behind a bass drum with "Hitch's Happy Harmonists" painted on the front. The band is arranged around the recording horns in a manner reminiscent of the Wolverines the previous year.

The Gennett recording of "Boneyard Shuffle" could pass for a Wolverines tune, it was so similar in melody and arrangement. Beiderbecke's influence is everywhere. Hitch's band was tight and capable, a reasonably good imitation of the Wolverines. The only glaring fault on the disc was Gennett's typically horrible sound reproduction of cymbal crashes: they sound as though McDowell were hitting garbage can lids with a hammer.

The Gennett "Washboard Blues," saved by Hitch's last-minute suggestion and Carmichael's fast thinking on the piano, is a sketchy instrumental rendition; it was developed into the more-refined, subsequent recording by Paul Whiteman's Orchestra. Although Hitch's version is somewhat tenuous and lacking in clarity, the song's memorable characteristics are all present: dramatic orchestration, shifting tempos and time signatures, unusual modulations and chord progressions.

Carmichael's improvised piano solo resurfaced several years later as the basic framework for his hit tune "Lazybones," which Johnny Mercer put to lyrics in 1933. We will never know if Wickemeyer used the twenty-second discrepancy as a quick excuse for not recording "Washboard Blues." In 1925, few people were writing pop music, and certainly not jazz music, with the level of sophistication and shifting emotions present in this song. Not in New York, Chicago, or anywhere. "Washboard Blues" was as eccentric as its composer. Though musicians and bandleaders quickly recognized its underlying genius, "Washboard Blues" never became a hit with the public.

After Gennett pressed "Washboard Blues," Carmichael's college friend Harry Hostetter wrapped a copy of the disc in an old shirt and took it to a stone cutter named Fred Callahan in the small southern Indiana town of Bedford. After listening to the record a few times, Callahan wrote lyrics about a black woman endlessly scrubbing clothes with a washboard.

Despite Carmichael's success in getting the Wolverines and Hitch's Happy Harmonists to record his compositions, the master promoter had little luck convincing Gennett staffers that his own college band, Carmichael's Collegians, could produce acceptable music. Even by the leader's own admission, the band had a difficult time keeping up with his antics on the piano. Carmichael did not write or play conventionally and often came off like a wild college kid, which, for all practical purposes, he was.

In early 1926, Carmichael was wrapping up law school and preparing for life as an attorney. He was ready to put jazz playing behind him. During a previous trip to West Palm Beach, Florida, Carmichael had met an attorney named M. D. Carmichael (no relation), who offered him a job in his law practice. On the eve of his departure that February, Carmichael made what he thought would be his last drive to the Gennett studio. As a farewell gift to his Collegians, he arranged with Wiggins to record two songs with his Bloomington outfit: "Watch Your Hornin' " and "Bridal Waltz."

The studio playbacks were not particularly clear, but nobody in the band minded. Some of the fellows, caught up in the sentiment of one of their last performances together, even got a little teary-eyed. "I know each one of us put his heart into that record and it must have been good and true," Carmichael wrote. "That record plays itself in my memory and I can hear it clearly. Then fate put her big foot in, and before we could get a single pressing, the master record was destroyed in some technical mix-up. Three years of musical sweat and friendship melted away into a blob of twisted copper."[24] At least, that is the story Carmichael was given by the Gennett staff.

Before heading to Florida, Carmichael went to New York and proposed to Irving Mills that "Washboard Blues" be published. In 1926, Mills Music published piano sheet music of the song, with Callahan and Irving Mills listed as collaborators. Carmichael was working aimlessly in the Florida law firm until a shocking discovery changed the course of his life. He heard "Washboard Blues" playing on a phonograph from the music shop across the street. And it was not the Gennett release.

Red Nichols was well aware of the Gennett record by Hitch's Happy Harmonists. Nichols and His Five Pennies, with Jimmy Dorsey on clarinet and alto saxophone, had recorded the same tune in December 1926 on the Brunswick label. On the flip side was Carmichael's "Boneyard Shuffle." Carmichael was flabbergasted. Again, a seemingly obscure Gennett disc managed to fall into the right hands where it could have a major impact. It was not long before Carmichael grew homesick for Indiana and jazz. He quit the law practice and returned home.

During 1927–28, Carmichael laid the groundwork for a memorable career in music. Not only was he composing more, but he began working with musicians such as Don Redman, a brilliant black saxophonist and arranger, as well as with members of Jean Goldkette's organization. While traveling with Goldkette's band, Carmichael finally learned to read music properly. Under the guidance of Goldkette's saxophonist, Pink Porter, he dabbled in orchestration.

Carmichael was well respected by the Goldkette crowd. These young musicians—including Beiderbecke, Trumbauer, Leibrook, and Jimmy and Tommy Dorsey—would soon join the Whiteman Orchestra, the best-paying dance band in the land in the late 1920s. Carmichael's coterie of young jazz friends had advanced beyond Gennett Records and were inching into popular music's upper echelon. Whiteman, an exclusive artist for Victor Records, played the best venues in America. Carmichael was now associating with people who could open the right doors for him.

In the fall of 1927, as Carmichael was hanging out backstage with the Whiteman band at the Indiana Theatre in Indianapolis, Whiteman commended him for the Gennett recording of "Washboard Blues." Carmichael told the bandleader about the new lyrics created by an Indiana stone cutter, and Whiteman asked to hear them. With Beiderbecke, Whiteman, and the Dorsey brothers around the piano, Carmichael reluctantly sang through a chorus. Whiteman responded by buying a ticket for him to join the orchestra for a recording date in Chicago.

In October 1927, the Paul Whiteman Orchestra recorded "Washboard Blues" with Carmichael timidly providing the vocals. From a musical and technical standpoint, the Victor Records version is a vast improvement over the rough take by Hitch's band in Richmond. But Carmichael's piano solo was basically unchanged. The experience with Whiteman was the high point to date in Carmichael's musical odyssey.

Later that month, Carmichael rounded up six members of Whiteman's group in Indianapolis, including the Dorsey brothers and Indiana cornetist Andy Secrest, and headed to Richmond. In the early morning, the band recorded "One Night in Havana," a rhythmically bizarre number that Carmichael composed during a ten-day cruise in Florida. (In New York in late 1930, at Beiderbecke's last recording session before his death in 1931, a Carmichael-led band again recorded "One Night in Havana," but it does not capture the spontaneity and energy of the original madcap Gennett session.)

Around this time, Carmichael was wrestling with a new melody, which, he said came to him on the Indiana University campus while recalling an old romance. As he did with previous melodies, Carmichael refined it on the piano at the Book

Nook, organizing the tune in a ragtime style. A student on campus dubbed the melody "Star Dust."

Carmichael never really understood the rationale behind the title, which may explain why he liked it. "Star Dust," originally a two-word song title, stuck. With local Bloomington bands, Carmichael began playing the basic outline of "Star Dust" at various campus functions. By late 1927, he developed the song's chorus, then a verse, a piano solo, and a clarinet passage. For a Gennett recording date, Carmichael searched for a suitable band. He found one of the best ensembles in downtown Indianapolis in Emil Seidel and His Orchestra.

Seidel grew up in the music business. His family operated a chain of music stores in Indianapolis, where, in the 1920s, they sold piano rolls, records, sheet music, and instruments. In the early 1920s, Seidel worked in New York City, making piano rolls and playing in orchestra-pit bands. He returned to Indianapolis and joined the house band at the Apollo Theatre on Illinois Street. By 1925, Seidel was the band's leader. The Emil Seidel Apollo Theatre Orchestra was one of the city's most respected orchestras. A brilliant musical director, Seidel was regularly sought out by fledgling composers.

Carmichael approached Seidel at the Apollo with a lead sheet of his new dance stomp, "Star Dust." Carmichael was either unable, or simply too impatient, at this time to provide Seidel with an arranged score. In Duncan Schiedt's book *The Jazz State of Indiana*, a remarkable account of the state's early jazz scene, former Seidel saxophonist Dick Kent described Carmichael's method for prepping the band on the song's nuances: He took aside reed players Kent and Gene Woods, and trumpeter Byron Smart, and hummed their parts while walking down an Indianapolis back alley. (Decades later, the same method worked for the Beatles' John Lennon and Paul McCartney, who would hum instrumental lines to record producer George Martin, who scored them for such giant hits as "Penny Lane," "For No One," and "Strawberry Fields Forever.")

On October 31, 1927, Carmichael, Seidel, and seven members of his band headed for Richmond for the first recording of "Star Dust," arranged as an instrumental stomp. Harold Soule, a classically trained musician, was Gennett's chief engineer for the session. Soule had replaced Wickemeyer, who had been hired away in early 1927 by one of Gennett's larger competitors. Soule recalled the debut recording session for "Star Dust" as more of a major inconvenience than some special moment in music history. "They called me at 3 A.M. and told me, 'We've got a band over here for you to record.' So I got out of bed and went down to record them. "I got the first take [of 'Star Dust'] at 5 o'clock in the morning. Old Hoagy fell backwards off his piano stool and says, 'My masterpiece,' and it was."[25]

Well, almost. Carmichael later accurately assessed this recording, admitting that the band had not performed wonders. Identified on the Gennett release as "Hoagy Carmichael and His Pals," it would have benefited greatly from a little more rehearsal, more formally arranged scores, and perhaps, some rest before making the 70-mile drive to Richmond. The solo instrumental lines are lacking in confidence, and guitarist Don Kimmell never quite timed the complex chord progressions of "Star Dust" with the solo lines. One saving grace from a performance standpoint is Carmichael's meandering, but beautiful, piano solo.

To hear Carmichael's original "Star Dust" on Gennett at its original up tempo, with performance and recording warts and all, is absolutely fascinating today. The hundreds of later recordings benefit from Mitchell Parish's lyrics, the brilliant vocals of an Ella Fitzgerald or a Frank Sinatra, gorgeous orchestral refinements, and pristine recording technology. But the rough Gennett version, thrown together by Carmichael and his friends down at the piano factory, is true to the composer's original conception and inspiration.

Carmichael never quite understood the actual inspiration behind "Star Dust." The verse is reminiscent of Beiderbecke's melodic style. A phrase from Louis Armstrong's "Potato Head Blues" was evidently lifted. "I got a queer sensation as we recorded," Carmichael wrote of the Gennett session. "This melody was bigger than I was. It wasn't a part of me. Maybe I hadn't even written it. It didn't sound familiar in the playback, and I lost the recollection of how, when, and where it all happened. Back there in the old ratty recording studio, I was vague in mood as the strains hung in the rafters of the place. I wanted to shout, 'Maybe I didn't write you, but I found you.' But I couldn't say anything."[26]

"Star Dust" was released with "A Night in Havana" on the flip side on Gennett's new black-labeled "Electrobeam" series, which began in 1927 after the studio installed electronic recording equipment. Wiggins agreed to pay Carmichael the standard one cent per side in royalties. But from the extreme rarity of this disc (only a few dozen original copies appear to remain today), it is clear that he could not have paid the rent from this venture. At the October 31 session, Carmichael and Seidel's band also recorded "Friday Night," an aggressively orchestrated number, released under "Emil Seidel and His Orchestra." Carmichael apparently played piano and cornet on the recording. The Gennett log also listed "When Baby Sleeps," a number rejected by Wiggins.

Seidel returned to Richmond many times over the next several months, recording more than twelve songs for Gennett. The sides are crisp and highly professional, though they are hampered by a schmaltzy repertoire and forgettable vocals. Among Seidel's better recordings were "The Best Things in Life Are Free," a standard 1920s pop tune, and "We Together," both recorded in November 1927. Today, Seidel's rare discs still show up in antique stores around Indiana.

Carmichael made his last stop at the Richmond studio on May 2, 1928. By now, the 28-year-old elder statesman among Bloomington-area jazz players had noteworthy credentials: confidant of Beiderbecke and the Dorsey brothers, published composer, one-time singer with Paul Whiteman's highly popu-

lar orchestra, and a Gennett recording artist. So when Carmichael needed to round up a pickup band for what turned out
to be his final Gennett session, he was able to lure the best
players in central Indiana.

The eight-piece Carmichael's Collegians for the May recording date was a powerhouse. A key player in organizing the
unit was trumpeter and arranger Bud Dant, a mere freshman
music student at Indiana University, who recruited a nineteen-
year-old classmate named Chauncey Goodwin, an alto saxophonist. Others included banjoist Arnold Habbe, who played
with Carmichael on Curtis Hitch's 1925 Gennett date, and a
foot-stomping fiddle player named Eddie Wolfe. Sparing no
one's ears, Carmichael brought along his dented cornet. "We
really dug Hoagy," Dant recalled. "He was older and the most
talented among us, but we still considered him just one of us.
He was always trying to round up guys to play jazz, and he had
his own style of playing that we all enjoyed."[27]

When Carmichael rounded up the band to go to Richmond, Dant and his classmates had never heard of Gennett
Records. "We never really thought much about cutting a record," he said. "Jazz was so new in those days and we just
thought going over to Richmond with Hoagy would be a kick.
Hoagy was easy to work with. He would write out basic head
arrangements, but you had to transpose it for your instrument.
Mostly, you went on Hoagy's explanations and we were pretty
used to doing that."[28]

When the band entered the Gennett studio, Dant and the
boys were impressed, even by 1928 standards, with the technical equipment in the engineer's room. It was all new to
them. "I remember seeing those large single-sided platters of
beeswax that were used for recording," Dant said. "We knew
that if you made a mistake, a new platter had to be used. It was
a fun night, but we were pretty serious about what we were
doing. We weren't nervous; we were prepared."[29]

The band was also ambitious, attempting six songs during
the late-night session. But Wiggins pressed only two of the

numbers, released back-to-back on the Electrobeam Gennett series: Carmichael's "March of the Hoodlums" and Shelton Brooks's "Walkin' the Dog." So Carmichael's last hurrah at Gennett is intriguing for the takes saved for posterity as well as for those that Wiggins unmercifully tossed out.

The brilliant Gennett recording of "March of the Hoodlums" was nothing short of well-orchestrated bedlam, in which Carmichael's simple melody line quickly clears the way for brief, hypersonic solos by Dant, Carmichael, Wolfe, and Goodwin. The effect is fantastic. In laying down a solid rhythmic base, Habbe strums the banjo like there's no tomorrow. The hoedown fiddle solo by Wolfe, whom Dant described as a "fun crazy nut," just adds to the frenzy. Goodwin's bold alto saxophone solo is rhythmically brilliant and actually prefigures the bebop phrasing popularized by Charlie Parker in the 1940s.

The recording closes with all the soloists driving the march home in reckless abandon, spared only by a very short and odd Carmichael piano solo. As Habbe later recalled, "I don't know if we had ever played that number before, or how many times if we did, but it didn't matter—we didn't use music. Everyone just took off."[30]

"Walkin' the Dog" is slightly more restrained, but no less effective, thanks to Dant and Carmichael's clever arrangement. The tremendous improvement in sound reproduction in the Richmond studio, brought about by the new electronic recording system, enabled bassist Jack Drummond's walking solo to be heard distinctly. Carmichael's cornet solo reveals his ear for lyrical jazz improvisation. He tried to emulate Beiderbecke on the cornet, but as he later admitted, his cornet solo was fine unless one appreciated good tone. Dant said Carmichael was never a good cornet player, but that "he really got up for that recording."[31] Overall, Carmichael's pickup ensemble really grooves on the Brooks tune, particularly the young Goodwin. "Walkin' the Dog" never sounded better.

The Gennett disc of "March of the Hoodlums" and

"Walkin' the Dog" represents some of the era's hottest jazz. And yet, Dant and his friends never bothered to pick up a copy of the record after it was released. Dant said he did not hear the recording until many years later.

Unfortunately, "March of the Hoodlums" is seldom included in jazz record anthologies compiled to represent the era's best recordings. But that is not inconsistent with the arbitrary omission by many jazz historians of Carmichael as an important voice in jazz. His records and the views of his music contemporaries show that Carmichael's unique approach to jazz was highly influential. The problem with his original Gennett recordings, such as "March of the Hoodlums" (a tune later re-recorded by Duke Ellington and Eddie Lang), is that they were recorded several years too late to be considered on the forefront of jazz.

For all of its originality, "March of the Hoodlums" pays tribute to the smaller jazz ensembles of the early 1920s, such as the Wolverines. By Carmichael's last Gennett date in 1928, the trend in jazz was away from small hot ensembles and toward more full-blown jazz orchestras. The most popular of these orchestras was the Paul Whiteman Orchestra; the most innovative included the ensembles headed by Duke Ellington and Fletcher Henderson. Still, Carmichael's "March of the Hoodlums" and "Walkin' the Dog" capture the Jazz Age at its wildest and most eccentric. In recent years, both recordings have resurfaced on digitally remastered compact discs on small independent jazz labels from the United States to Australia.

In fact, the musical energy and polish on the Carmichael's Collegians 1928 date leaves jazz history wondering what Wiggins destroyed when he failed to release the takes of "Smile," "Shimmy Shawobble," and "One Night in Havana." Decades later, Carmichael recalled attempting a calypso rendition of "One Night in Havana" at the Gennett studio, which may have occurred at this session.

Far more tragic is the loss of the second recorded attempt

of "Star Dust," for which Carmichael produced lyrics and vocals. Dant wrote down and saved the composer's original
lyrics from the 1928 recording session in Richmond:

> Star dust melody, you hold a charm
> Through the lonely years;
> Star dust strain, beautiful refrain
> I hear you ringing in my ears,
> But the world goes by, paying no attention to you;
> To me you're everything in life and in love
> I know, indeed it's so,
> [ad lib scat singing for eight bars]
> Oh, star dust strain, in my heart you will remain,
> Star dust melody, I love you heart and soul I do.

Carmichael's failed effort at recording "Star Dust" was
also remembered by Joseph Geier, a young technician in the
Gennett studio for the 1928 session. "The normal recording
time for a song was two and three-fourths minutes to three
minutes. He [Carmichael] had something like two minutes [for
'Star Dust']. So he sat down and wrote out another chorus and
on it went. Words and all."[32]

But when Wiggins later reviewed the Carmichael takes, he
killed off "Star Dust" with the infamous note on one of Gennett's recording information cards, "Reject. Already on Gennett. Poor seller." This single decision, just after releasing the
original instrumental of "Star Dust" with Seidel's outfit, was
remembered by people around Richmond for decades. Florence Gennett, wife of former Richmond studio technician
Harry Gennett, Jr., recalled Wiggins as the man who "threw
out" the American song classic: "Harry always said Wiggins
was a little on the temperamental side, and you couldn't
change his mind."[33]

Wiggins had been successful in the early 1920s in securing
legendary jazz talent. But his ability to identify music trends
had slipped over the next few years, and the competing labels
already controlled the lion's share of America's jazz output.

Besides, Clayton Jackson, assistant to Wiggins, pointed out that Gennett Records never had a great reputation for the overall accommodation of its recording artists. "Hoagy [and his band] came down to the studio at their own expense," Jackson said. "They bought their own meals. Hell, we didn't even buy them a sandwich."[34]

Carmichael never showed any animosity, however. Instead, he offered nothing but sentimental praise for Gennett Records for the remainder of his life, dubbing the Richmond studio the birthplace of jazz recording. In fact, at the 1928 recording date, the Richmond studio apparently provided Carmichael with a souvenir single-sided pressing of the never-released recording of "Star Dust." When Dant visited Carmichael many years later at the composer's Los Angeles estate, the two would enjoy playing it for old time's sake. But after Carmichael's death, the disc was not found among his belongings. "Hoagy used to look back fondly on those early days in Indiana," Dant said. "He knew those first few songs on Gennett were the beginning of something."[35]

Certainly, Carmichael owed much to Gennett Records. Even though the original "Star Dust" release on Gennett never sold to the company's satisfaction, the disc gave the struggling composer something to use in promoting the tune. "As a boy, I just happened to be in the studio when Hoagy was there," said Richard Gennett, son of Fred Gennett. "You have to remember, back then he was considered some kid from Indiana University and nobody paid any attention to him [at Starr Piano]. But they recorded him because that's the way Gennett Records worked. They recorded anybody who would ask and that meant Hoagy got to make a few records, and 'Star Dust' happened to be one of them."[36] Through Carmichael's persistence, that little-known song on the obscure black-labeled Gennett disc changed his life.

After Carmichael left Indiana in 1928, he was unable to find work as a songwriter in Hollywood and ended up plugging songs for Mills Music in New York. Around this time, Irving

Mills hired lyricist Mitchell Parish to provide lyrics for "Stardust," which became a one-word title. Almost two years after the Gennett recording date, "Stardust" was finally published and became part of the repertoire at the Cotton Club in Harlem.

Journalist Walter Winchell tirelessly promoted the song. In 1930, during the time Carmichael was leading a studio jazz ensemble for RCA Records, Isham Jones and His Orchestra made a hit with a slower, ballad rendition of "Stardust." The flood gates opened. The song would be recorded more than a thousand times over the decades by major American singers and instrumentalists, including recent renditions by country star Willie Nelson and jazz trumpeter Wynton Marsalis.

With Carmichael's prolific songwriting activities in the 1930s, his first Gennett recordings soon represented a tiny fraction of his overall recorded output as performer and composer. But they did not diminish in importance. These extremely rare releases preserve Carmichael's first inspirations in jazz, as well as his aspirations to become a bandleader. In the 1930s and 1940s, when he had become America's great songwriter, the public soon forgot, or never knew, that Carmichael started out as an improvising jazz musician. Ellington once called him America's greatest tunesmith, which he attributed to the fact that Carmichael started out playing jazz. His songs always contained a strain of jazz, but nowhere is this foundation of Carmichael's musical experience more evident than in the gorgeous passages in "Stardust."

It is appropriate that Carmichael would be haunted by the song's origins in the early morning of October 31, 1927, during the first recorded playbacks down at the old piano factory. The elegant melody and the rhythmic sophistication, rare attributes in a pop hit of any generation, were inspired by such seminal jazz artists as Beiderbecke and Armstrong, who also made their first mark in music playing in the drab, wood-paneled recording studio by the railroad tracks.

Rural Recordings in the Electronic Era

T he innovative music released on Gennett Records did not stave off the financial challenges facing the label in the mid-1920s. The foremost threat was the rise of radio, which had begun to change American leisure just as phonographs and records had in the previous decade. Radio was no longer a curiosity embraced by amateur operators. The proliferation of inexpensive sets and of commercial stations offered a new evening diversion for millions of Americans. They could relax with hour-long programs instead of jumping up every three minutes to change a phonograph record; and by 1924, the sound quality of radio receivers was often superior to that of records.

The entire record industry soon felt the pinch. After reaching a peak of about 100 million records annually in 1921, record revenues declined steadily over the next several years, while radio sales skyrocketed. In 1922, the year Henry Gennett died and his Starr Piano and record division were at a financial high, nationwide radio sales hit $60 million. By 1929, that figure rose to an astounding $850 million.

In addition to home radio, Gennett Records had its own special problems. The higher-quality Victor, Columbia, and Brunswick discs continued to dominate the sales for classical and pop music, the leading market segments. The search for new record buyers had led Fred Gennett to produce the seminal jazz discs of 1922–24, which contributed to the growing popularity of jazz. But leading jazz musicians, including former

Gennett artists Louis Armstrong, King Oliver, and Jelly Roll Morton, soon migrated to the higher-paying New York and Chicago studios of the larger labels.

The small Indiana label also faced problems of quality, in addition to the usual poor fidelity. To save on production costs, in the early 1920s the Richmond plant began to substitute less-expensive materials for some of the shellac in Gennett discs. The hardness of the shellac enabled discs to withstand the wear and tear caused by the heavy tone arms and steel needles of the early phonographs, such as the ubiquitous Victrola. By the mid-1920s, Gennett discs were wearing out faster than those issued by many competing labels.

Facing this array of troubles, Fred Gennett developed a strategy to shore up the record division. For starters, in 1925 he initiated a series of popular song and dance releases on a special red-label Gennett disc at a reduced price of 50 cents. *Talking Machine World* lauded the move, noting that "there has been a considerable demand for a cheaper record and the company (Starr Piano) expects to do a considerable business with this new series. Dealers' advertising material, including folders and window streamers, will be issued on this series the same as on the higher priced stock."[1] The new series coincided with the issuance of Gennett records in Italian, Spanish, and German for the export market. Gennett aggressively marketed the 50-cent record through 1926, boasting in the industry's leading trade magazine that the new discs were "strongly entrenched in popular favor and many dealers report that these records have been an important factor in renewing their interest in records."[2]

In a more significant move, Fred Gennett applied his late father's philosophy for selling pianos to the record business. Under Henry Gennett, Starr Piano had become both a piano retailer and a wholesale supplier. Starr pianos were sold in company-owned stores, but the company also manufactured pianos with stencil brand names for chain stores outside the Starr retail network. In the same manner, Fred Gennett sought additional retail outlets for the growing body of Gennett master discs accumulating in Richmond. With the budget records, fidelity and quality were not a major concern. Gennett Records became a primary supplier in this market by leasing its master recordings to other small labels. In addition, Gennett Records recorded and pressed discs for independent labels and budget mail-order catalogs. In 1925, Fred Gennett created his own in-house, budget record label for chain stores, called Champion Records, which duplicated the masters previously issued on the established Gennett label.

By the late 1920s, railroad cars in Starr Valley were hauling away thousands of records for more than 25 different record labels worldwide, including budget discs for the Sears, Roebuck mail-order catalogs. The appearance of Gennett masters on numerous "stencil" budget labels has fascinated and baffled vintage record collectors for decades.

From a historical standpoint, Gennett's role as a supplier to budget labels was important because it influenced the music styles the company recorded. Budget records were a big draw with rural consumers, so Gennett began recording rural music traditions, which had been neglected by the record industry and isolated from mainstream America. Between 1925 and 1934, the Richmond studio produced an enormous body of Appalachian vocal and string-band music, the precursor to modern country music. In the 1920s, the genre was marketed as "old-time" music. Among the hundreds of old-time musicians recorded by Gennett were Bradley Kincaid, Vernon Dalhart, Ernest Stoneman, Doc Roberts, and Gene Autry.

At the same time, Gennett became an important supplier to the "race" record market, recording such seminal country blues artists as Sam Collins, Blind Lemon Jefferson, Charley Patton, and Bill Broonzy, who passed virtually unnoticed through the small Quaker town of Richmond as they were being recorded for posterity. Following its historic jazz recordings of the early 1920s, Gennett Records was now a pioneer in recording blues and old-time music from rural America.

While Gennett's later output in jazz never rivaled the landmark discs of 1922–24 and the Carmichael sessions of 1925–28, in the late 1920s the company recorded significant regional jazz and commercial dance bandleaders, including Alphonse Trent, Jimmy Blythe, and Lawrence Welk. In 1927, using portable recording equipment, Gennett produced some early field recordings of jazz and blues music in Birmingham, Alabama.

The business dynamics of the second half of the 1920s, which affected the recording industry in general, also changed the focus of the Indiana label. The emergence of budget record labels and electronic recording technology steered Gennett Records in a new direction, and it ultimately produced some of the finest early rural music on record.

From Electrobeam to Budget Labels

One morning in late 1924, in the Chicago office of Sears, Roebuck & Co., competing record companies were bidding on a sizeable one-year contract to supply discs for the Sears mail-order record catalog. For years, Sears had been contracting out the recording and pressing of its budget discs. Bids were being taken on this particular day on a contract to supply the company's Silvertone record label. Sears record buyer J. J. Shay laid out the company's quantity and price specifications, and officials from the record companies calculated their offers.

Representing Starr Piano was Clayton Jackson, a brash young assistant sales manager working under Fred Wiggins at Gennett Records in Richmond. After half an hour, Jackson laid down his pencil, figuring the record pressing plant in Starr Valley could never meet Sears's basic requirements. "So I sat there," Jackson said. "Finally, old J. J. Shay came back and asked me what was the matter." When Jackson replied that he could not meet Sears's price range, Shay responded, "Well, I guess that's your privilege."[3] Since his train did not leave until later that afternoon, Jackson hung around while his competitors drafted their offers. As the meeting closed, Shay notified everyone that he was buying lunch for the small-town kid from Gennett in order to keep him from getting scuffed up in the big city. But Shay had an agenda.

"I told him that I'd been to Chicago before," Jackson said. "Well, there was nothing anybody could say [to Shay]. They had to be agreeable. So we went down to the Knickerbocker Club and had lunch."[4] After light conversation, Shay began to quiz Jackson about a price range in which Gennett Records could produce records for the Silvertone catalog. Gennett Records had already handled several custom-pressing jobs, including discs for the Buddy label, a record distributed by the Southern Aluminum Co. of Chicago as part of a promotion campaign. Jackson offered an assessment on the Sears contract. Shay then took him to the railroad station for the afternoon train to Indianapolis.

Jackson spent the evening in the state capital, where he reviewed the books at the Starr Piano Store, downtown on Monument Circle. The next morning when he arrived in Richmond, a Gennett production manager was waiting for him at the station. He told Jackson that Shay had already toured the Starr Piano facilities that morning. With sawdust still on his shoes, Shay sat in a company office with Wiggins, and when Jackson arrived, Shay immediately shouted, "You could have told me you were making Ku Klux Klan records! After all, you knew you had lunch [in Chicago] in a Catholic club."[5] Jackson responded firmly that he did not think it was any of Shay's business. He then noticed Wiggins's stogie wiggling. Something big was brewing.

Shay then challenged Jackson's figures on the production capacity at the Gennett record pressing facility. Jackson explained that his estimates had taken into account three shifts a day, which the plant currently did not utilize, and a hypothetical production run of a million records. Finally, Shay shocked everyone and offered Gennett Records a one-year contract for a stunning production run of 500,000 discs on the Silvertone label.

"Fred Wiggins sat over there; he didn't know what was going on," Jackson said. "Shay turned to Wiggins and said, 'I understand you're this man's boss. Are you going to let him take the order?' Wig said, 'I guess I am.' " And, with that, one of the Gennett secretaries drew up a contract, and Shay signed it.[6]

This deal marked the beginning of Gennett's five-year stint as a supplier of millions of discs for the Sears Silvertone, Challenge, Conqueror, and Supertone mail-order record labels. Hundreds of titles on the Gennett label were also issued on the Sears labels and were advertised in mailings targeted primarily for rural consumers, who did not have ready access to department stores. The Richmond plant simply pulled the unreleased or released takes from Gennett recording sessions and pressed them for Sears, using shellac-based materials of slightly lower quality than on the Gennett discs.

By the late 1920s, the Richmond facility had supplied Sears with substantial numbers of old-time, jazz, gospel, pop, and blues records, with the Gennett artists hidden behind pseudonyms for obvious financial reasons. Musicians on the budget labels were paid royalties at only half the going rate for the Gennett label, if they were paid at all. Because of the widespread use of pseudonyms on recordings in the 1920s and 1930s, many pioneering artists were not only denied name recognition but received few, if any, royalties for their work.

Besides, with budget records, the musician's identity was often no more of a selling point to consumers than the song title or the retail price listed in the catalog. While mainstream record labels sold discs for $.50 to $1.10 apiece, the Sears budget records sold for $.17 to $.39.

Sears became Fred Gennett's largest custom-pressing account, with production runs for many Sears titles far exceeding those of the same titles bearing the Gennett label. In 1928 alone, it is believed that Gennett supplied the Sears record division with more than a million discs. The problem for Gennett, according to Jackson, was that Sears understood more about the economics of pressing and selling records than did their suppliers. While Gennett's arrangement with Sears was profitable for the first few years, Jackson claimed that the Richmond plant was losing money on the Sears contracts toward the close of the 1920s. With the onset of the Great Depression, which caused a near collapse of the recording industry and steep operational losses at Starr Piano, Gennett and Sears severed their relationship.

The Gennett account with Sears coincided with the creation of the long-running Champion subsidary label. It was the result of a deal struck by Gennett Records with the Kresge variety store chain following several trips by Fred Gennett and Clayton Jackson to Kresge's division headquarters in Detroit. In September 1925, Gennett introduced a Champion catalog of about 40 releases, pressed from Gennett masters, which were test-marketed in about 90 Kresge stores.[7] The Champion discs, priced at three for $1.00, appeared in several department and variety chain stores, particularly in the South, as well as in some Starr Piano stores in the 1930s.

Initially, Fred Gennett avoided the association between Gennett and the less-expensive Champion releases. The red labels on the first Champion releases made no mention of Starr Piano or of Richmond, Indiana; and the original Gennett matrix numbers were printed on the Champion label in reverse. The return address on the first crates of Champion releases to be delivered to the Kresge stores read simply "South First and A Street, Richmond Indiana." The express agent at the local railway station apparently refused to ship crates with an incomplete return address. Jackson recalled Wiggins running down to the express office to scrawl "Starr Piano" reluctantly on the side of the boxes.

Musicians on Champion releases were also hidden behind pseudonyms. For example, Bailey's Lucky Seven, the prolific and popular studio band for the Gennett label, became The

Seven Champions. Guy Lombardo and His Royal Canadians became The Hill Top Inn Orchestra, and the fantastic Fletcher Henderson Orchestra of 1926 appeared on Champion as Jack's Fast Steppin' Bell Hops. In a downward shift from the amusing to the ridiculous, a black Indiana jazz trio known on Gennett as Syd Valentine & His Patent Leather Kids became Skillet Dick & His Frying Pans on Champion. In the blues arena, Gennett artists Thomas A. Dorsey and Jaybird Coleman became on the Champion label Smokehouse Charlie and Rabbit's Foot Williams respectively, though not respectfully.

The Gennett staff conjured up these pseudonyms as they paired up the Champion sides in the factory. The Richmond telephone book and city directory were popular sources for names. On some occasions, Gennett staffers used the names of friends and relatives. "What worried you was duplicating," Jackson said. "Getting too many Howard Williamses, or something like that."[8]

To add insult to injury, musicians often never knew that their Gennett sides were reissued on the Champion label under pseudonyms. For example, Syd Valentine first learned of his 1927 Champion sides from a jazz enthusiast, Jim Lindsay, at an Indianapolis nightclub in the late 1950s. "Syd was on break from a set and sitting at one of the tables," Lindsay recalled. "So I yelled over 'Hey Skillet Dick!' and he turned and looked at me like I was crazy. I felt like an idiot, so I had to explain to him that he was Skillet Dick on the old Champion records. After all of those years, he never knew that. He couldn't wait to see one of those records."[9]

In addition to the Sears and Champion labels, many tiny labels were supplied with pressings from Gennett masters, including the obscure Bell and Buddy labels. The Buddy releases included Gennett-produced sides by Duke Ellington and His Washingtonians, the New Orleans Rhythm Kings, and Jelly Roll Morton's Incomparables. The outer edge of the Buddy label highlighted the Southern Aluminum Company, New Orleans, Louisiana, and Chicago, Illinois; the Aluminum Specialty

Company, Atlanta, Georgia; and the Associated Manufacturing Company, Galveston, Texas, and Oakland, California. These companies were loosely affiliated with each other, but had no direct connection to the phonograph or recording business. The records appear to have been given away with a portable Buddy phonograph, a promotional vehicle for the aluminum companies. The labels on the extremely rare Buddy discs used the same typeface as the Gennett label.

In the mid-1920s, Gennett also supplied Herwin Records, a discount mail-order label specializing in blues and old-time recordings for rural consumers. Herwin, a name derived from HERbert and EdWIN Schiele, was a subsidiary of the Artophone Corporation of St. Louis, which sold musical instruments. Both Gennett Records and Paramount drew from their vaults of masters to press records for Herwin, using a low-quality shellac. Herwin discs, which are also extremely rare today, included titles by blues giant Charley Patton and old-time singers Ernest Stoneman and Chubby Parker.

In 1925, Harry Bernstein, a Starr Piano distributor in Minnesota, dabbled briefly in the record business using Gennett masters. He operated Northwestern Phonograph Supply Company in St. Paul and contracted Gennett Records to press his obscure Herschel Gold Seal label. In the fall of 1927, Bernstein help to organize recording sessions for the Gennett label in a hotel banquet room in St. Paul, where engineers recorded several Scandinavian musicians from the area, as well as a somewhat popular singer named Les Backer.

Gennett Records also leased masters and distributed discs halfway around the world. From the pressing plant in Starr Valley, crates of records were shipped by railroad to San Francisco, where they were packed onto freight vessels headed for Australia. Upon arrival, they were distributed through Suttons Ltd. in Sydney. By 1928, the Suttons record plant was pressing Gennett masters under a special "Australia Gennett" label. In Canada, Gennett masters were pressed by the Compo Company; and in England, Gennett masters appeared on the Winner, Guardsman, and Coliseum labels, among others. At various times, Gennett also recorded and pressed discs for specialty labels, like the James Vaugh Co., a gospel label in Lawrenceburg, Tennessee; and for two ethnic labels in New York, Irish Music House and Maloof Hebrew.

The combined effects of Gennett's 50-cent record marketing scheme, the Champion label, contracts with Sears and other labels, and a general industry upswing in phonograph and record sales led Gennett Records to declare 1926 one of its best sales years. Since Starr Piano stores sold both phonographs and Gennett records, company officials attributed part of the sales increase to the new Gennett Portophone, a portable phonograph model that the Gennett family obtained from a bankrupt Dayton, Ohio, firm and began marketing in early 1926. The nifty Portophone weighed just sixteen pounds and could play two records without rewinding. The winding crank was detachable and fit inside a traveling case, which stored eleven records. In 1926, Starr Piano claimed the Portophone was selling out in its network of stores.

However, the primary factor behind the phonograph and records sales upsurge for Gennett and its competitors in 1926–27 was the emergence of electronic recording, a technology fostered by the development of radio microphones and amplifiers.

Electronic recording offered dramatic improvements in sound reproduction. No longer did musicians have to crowd around acoustic recording horns. Instead, they could assemble in spacious studios, with proper reverberation, and play into electrically amplified microphones which did not rely on the sheer force of sound, as did the old acoustic system. Treble frequencies from electronically produced records were remarkably clearer and brighter than on acoustic records. Bass frequencies, which were largely lost on acoustic discs, added fullness to electronically recorded discs.

In the United States, Bell Telephone Laboratories, a division of the American Telegraph & Telephone Company, began work on electronic recording in 1919. Predictably, the nation's leading phonograph and record company, Victor, balked at a proposal in 1924 from Bell's marketing arm, Western & Electric, to use the new technology under license. A prevailing attitude in the record business then was to avoid any association with radio technology. Yet within a year, Victor and Columbia, separately and quietly, purchased the electronic recording equipment and aggressively promoted their new high-fidelity records in 1926.

In the same year, Brunswick teamed with the General Electric Company and introduced another electronic recording system. Gennett also worked with General Electric and produced its first electronically recorded disc in 1926. For one of these early recording sessions in Richmond, the Gennett staff rounded up a band from the local Test Junior High School. In late 1926, the Gennett studios in both Richmond and New York battled continuous glitches and failures of the electronic equipment on the way to recording the red-label Gennett series.

Gennett made a full transition to electronic recording in January 1927 and announced the creation of the gold-and-black lettered Electrobeam Gennett series, which sold for $.75. With predictable ebullience, Charles Beisel, controller for Gennett Records, stated in the trade press: "We feel that with our Electrobeam Gennett we are producing a record whose approach to perfection is an outstanding achievement of this industry. The most striking characteristics of this new principle of recording are the exceptional volume secured without a trace of blast or harshness and the rich quality of tone, combined with a bell-like resonance. The secret of this lies in a process of tonal modulation, which our engineers have perfected after more than a year's research. We are also using the finest stock that can be secured."[10]

After strong company sales in 1926, and with the new Electrobeam label, Fred Gennett was so bullish on the record industry in early 1927 that he publicly declared: "The man who fails to get business usually will find that the trouble is within himself and not within the public. He is either not offering the proper goods or is offering the proper goods improperly."[11]

He spoke too soon. Sales of the Electrobeam label, a victim of limited distribution from the outset, barely caused a ripple in the recording industry and never approached the market presence of acoustic Gennett discs during the label's heyday. The budget Champion and Sears records pressed in Richmond were more widely circulated than the Electrobeams. Struggling on the industry's fringe, the new label folded in late 1930, a victim of the Great Depression. It left the Gennett family with only the little-known Superior label, a discount record issued in very small quantities only until 1932, and the better-known Champion label, which was discontinued in 1934.

The merit of commercial records is not assessed solely on sales at the time of their original release, however. Rather, they are judged on their originality and impact on music over several decades, which explains the continued fascination with Gennett records. While it provided no consolation for the businessman Fred Gennett, many original Electrobeam Gennett and Champion discs, like the earlier acoustic jazz records on Gennett, were soon prized by collectors, and held in high esteem by historians of American blues and country music.

Scouting the Hills of Appalachia for That Old-Time Music

Dennis Taylor was a backwoods farmer who worked the land along Taylor's Ford Creek near the small town of Richmond, Kentucky. Like most rural Kentuckians in the 1920s, Taylor loved the down-home, old-time gospel and fiddle music that flourished in the bluegrass hills. Taylor couldn't play a lick himself, but he took a hand at managing a string band he called Taylor's Kentucky Boys, which entertained folks at local dances.

By the mid-1920s, a few old-time rural vocalists and string players had begun to make believers of the major record labels, which slowly recognized rural record buyers as a viable market. Victor, OKeh, and other labels hired talent scouts and sound crews with portable equipment to round up and record southern musicians on location. The informal Gennett operation, on the other hand, let the musicians find their own way to the New York and Richmond studios, where chances were always good they would get recorded.

Aware of Gennett's keen interest in old-time music, Taylor struck a deal with Wiggins. Using his connections with musicians in the hills and farms of his native east-central Kentucky, Taylor became a talent scout for Gennett. He signed up old-time singers and string players, both white and black, for recording dates at the piano factory. He even boarded musicians in his home for long stays, while his wife, who understood music fundamentals, organized rehearsals in the living room.[12]

During the late 1920s, Taylor rounded up more than a hundred Appalachian musicians for sessions in Richmond, where their performances were pressed on the Electrobeam Gennett, Champion, and Sears labels. He paid the musicians a flat fee per session and collected their royalties from Gennett. The studio's recording information cards show that the "one penny per side" royalties from dozens of old-time releases went to Taylor, who probably made thousands of dollars over several years from Gennett sales.

Taylor was not alone. Music agents from Tennessee, Virginia, and West Virginia also found gospel and old-time singers and mountain string bands for recording sessions in Richmond. Many enterprising old-time musicians wrote the studio and scheduled their own recording dates as well. Most were moonlighting string players and singers from the Appalachian hills looking for a few extra bucks. Collectively, the thousands of titles issued on Gennett and its affiliated budget labels contributed substantially to the massive body of old-time records issued by a handful of record companies in the late 1920s and early 1930s. They form the bedrock of today's country music record industry.

The sheer output of old-time recording in the Gennett studios was remarkable. In 1971, *Western Folklore*, a University of California publication, established a computerized discography from Gennett ledgers between 1925 and 1934; during that time 10,500 masters were recorded, including 7,500 in Richmond. Of those 10,500 sides, 2,500, or 24 percent, were old-time or white sacred music recordings. In 1928, about 40 percent of all recording activity in Richmond was in old-time or white sacred music.[13] With the Richmond studio among America's most active producers of old-time music, the locals began to refer to the industrial complex in Whitewater gorge as "Banjo Valley" instead of "Starr Valley."

"As a boy, I used to see these hillbillies with instrument cases walking along the bridge over the Whitewater River on their way to the Starr piano factory," said Richard Gennett. "I'd go down to the administration building and tell the girls in the office ahead of time that another group was coming to make a record. It was a pretty common occurrence."[14]

Gennett recordings fascinate folklorists because they are honest, unadulterated examples of early old-time music. Wiggins could influence what tunes the musicians recorded and often encouraged them to play established old-time songs issued on the larger labels. However, the Richmond studio staff simply waxed the performances, leaving rural musicians to express themselves freely. The Gennett family rarely hired music or recording professionals for the Richmond studio, where employees were typically recruited from the piano factory. This proved important because the studio staff did not have the technical know-how to interfere with old-time musicians' arrangements or playing in order to make the records more accessible to mainstream listeners. This hands-off approach contrasted with some major labels, which tried to polish up or soften the rough edges of the down-home sound.

In the late 1920s, the Richmond studio employed a musical director, Harold Little, the music teacher and bandleader at Richmond High School, who concentrated on Gennett's classical releases. When he expressed no interest in the old-time music recording sessions in Richmond, the Gennett brothers had no interest in holding onto him. After he quit Gennett Records in 1928, his position was left vacant.

Wiggins, who generally dictated what old-time master recordings were pressed for the Electrobeam Gennett or affiliated labels, spent long hours in the Starr administration building evaluating stacks of test pressings on his old, spring-wound phonograph, which lacked the proper audio horn. On several occasions during the electronic recording era, Richmond studio engineers presented Wiggins with high-fidelity test recordings of old-time music, only to have them rejected and melted down. That infuriated the sound engineers because the recordings weren't necessarily of poor sound quality; in fact, the test recordings may have sounded too good.

Yet Wiggins was thinking about the customers. Records with maximum high and low pitches, characteristic of a high-fidelity sound reproduction, could cause his old phonograph to vibrate or produce distorted sounds. While the same discs may have reproduced beautifully on the high-quality electronic phonographs available by the late 1920s, Gennett's old-time record buyers, more often than not, were low-income consumers who owned inexpensive, spring-wound phonographs with inferior reproducers.

Wiggins figured that if his primitive phonograph could not handle the fidelity of a recording, neither could his customers' machines. In addition, maximum high and low pitches captured during recording produced deep indentations along the grooves. That was not a problem for all manufacturers, but Gennett recordings were more fragile because of the limited amount of durable shellac used in pressing Electrobeam discs; and even less shellac was used on some Champion and Sears discs. The Gennett discs might not hold up long on a cheap phonograph. Gennett sound engineer Joe Geier said the phonograph used by

Wiggins was "as lousy a piece of equipment as you could ask for. People were turning out good records and I couldn't understand why the recordings had to be played on this old style rig."[15] He eventually understood Wiggins's position, that the low fidelity on some Gennett discs was actually by design.

This special attention to the less-affluent consumer reflected the changing customer base for Gennett records by the late 1920s. "All the Gennetts [Fred and Harry] were interested in was hillbilly music," said Geier. "That's where they made their money because the Gennett discs catered to Sears, and Sears catered to the hillbillies. So they really were catering to old-time music. The Gennetts figured that the hillbilly record business was kind of theirs, and that they had the edge on it. When I first went down there [to Starr Valley], and they talked about hillbilly musicians coming in there, I thought that was kind of insulting for the person. But it wasn't. They called it hillbilly music themselves."[16]

The term "hillbilly music," once the almost universal, though derogatory, expression for country music, was used by rural musicians and fans alike in the 1920s. The radio stations and the record catalogs preferred to label white gospel, folk songs, and mountain string music as "old-time music," while black jazz, blues, and gospel were grouped as "race" recordings.

The expression "old-time music" was appropriate. This rural music had evolved primarily from the vast repertoire of folk ballads and instrumental pieces brought to America by Anglo-Saxon and Celtic immigrants. However, from the beginning of American history, there was an interchange between white and black rural music traditions, which spread into the Appalachian region. The music of the Appalachian territory was very regional and was passed orally from generation to generation. With the emergence of phonograph records and radio, rural musicians learned the popular tunes from urban America, but gave them an old-time flavor in terms of instrumentation, lyrics, and melody.

Victor Records produced the first hillbilly, or old-time, recordings in New York in June 1922, featuring fiddlers Alexander Campbell Robertson and Henry C. Gilliland. Robertson, a
cowboy from Texas, and Gilliland, an ex-Confederate soldier
from Oklahoma, had both attended a Civil War veterans reunion in Virginia. From there, they traveled to New York and
convinced the engineers at the Victor studio to let them record
a few sides. The discs were released with little fanfare, and
Victor continued to ignore old-time music.

Gennett Records was just months behind Victor in pioneering old-time recordings with its release of several sides by
William B. Houchens. Beginning in September 1922, Gennett
recorded this obscure fiddle player from nearby Frankfort,
Kentucky, on such tunes as "Turkey in the Straw," "Arkansas
Traveller," "Hell in Georgia," and "Big-Eared Mule." The
Houchens sides on Gennett's blue-label acoustic discs were
among the select releases highlighted on Gennett's ornate record jackets in 1923, listed right along with the label's classical and popular releases.

While the circumstances leading Houchens to Gennett are
unknown, the company's habit of accommodating competent
players of any musical genre paved the way for these innovative sessions. However, though Houchens was among the first
old-time players recorded, and probably the first rural Kentucky musician on disc, his obscure Gennett recordings have
generally been ignored by folklore historians.[17] Houchens
never recorded after 1924 and spent most of his life in Dayton,
where he ran a conservatory and gave lessons on various string
instruments.

The birth of old-time records is more associated with
OKeh's recordings of Fiddlin' John Carson in Atlanta, in March
1923. OKeh's Ralph Peer was searching for black artists in
Georgia for the label's race catalog when a local record distributor and furniture store operator named Polk Brockman persuaded him to record Carson, a popular local fiddler. Carson's
renditions of "The Old Hen Cackled" and "The Rooster's

Going to Crow" and other old-time tunes sold quite well for OKeh, leading to additional recording dates by Carson and by an Atlanta vocal group called the Jenkins Family. Also in 1923, OKeh released discs by Virginia old-time singer Henry Whitter. The OKeh old-time releases clearly sparked a trend.

Around the same time, high-powered radio stations with programs tailored to country audiences sprouted in the South and Midwest, like WSB in Atlanta, WBAP in Fort Worth, WLS in Chicago, WSM in Nashville, and WLW in Cincinnati. For rural musicians, the stations offered a vehicle for reaching listeners well beyond the isolated locales. And the stations produced, rather cheaply, live shows for rural listeners by tapping into the abundance of eager, inexpensive local talent in their areas. The stations soon called these live shows "barn dances."

In 1924, just as jazz records gained a market foothold, several record labels also jumped onto the old-time music bandwagon in the hopes of boosting lagging record sales. Columbia Records produced a long series of recordings by blind singers Riley Puckett and Ernest Thompson, and fiddler Gid Tanner. Vocalion began recording the legendary Uncle Dave Macon.

The same year, Gennett recorded the Tweedy Brothers, a seasoned duet from West Virginia. Sons of a country doctor, they grew up just north of Wheeling, West Virginia. Charles played the piano, Harry the fiddle. By 1922, they were performing in area medicine shows, at county fairs, and on riverboats. They debuted on radio at Cincinnati's WLW, a new station created by industrialist Powel Crosley, Jr., which eventually became a national broadcasting powerhouse. The Richmond recording ledgers note the first appearance of Charles and Harry Tweedy in June 1924, when they recorded four tunes: "Rickett's Hornpipe," "Wild Horse," "Chicken Reel," and "Cripple Creek." After the Tweedy Brothers began recording for Gennett, Starr Piano provided them with an upright piano. They loaded it onto a flatbed truck and toured the mountain towns, performing from the truck, which bore a large sign promoting Starr Piano. It was an unusual advertising ploy for the resourceful Gennett organization, as the Tweedy Brothers were among the few old-time groups to record and perform using a piano.

Over a six-year period, the Tweedy Brothers recorded almost two dozen songs in Richmond. The titles of old-time tunes were fashioned to attract rural consumers, and the Tweedy titles were pure mountain vernacular: "Short'nin' Bread," "Dance All Night with a Bottle in Your Hand," "Sugar in the Gourd," "Buckwheat Batter," "Home Brew Rag," "Dixie," "Birdie," "Ida Red," and "Down Yonder." From all indications, the releases sold relatively well in West Virginia. Several Tweedy Brothers sides were also released on the Champion, Silvertone, and Supertone labels.

By late 1924, Gennett began recording another West Virginian singer, David Miller, at a studio established for a short period above the Starr Piano store in downtown Cincinnati. Over the next few years, Miller had a series of records issued on Gennett, including a remake of "Lonesome Valley," the black ballad "The Bad Man Stacklee," "Sweet Floetta," and "A Little Child Shall Lead Them."

As with many old-time and blues artists, blindness forced Miller to scratch out a living as a singer. He was born along the Ohio River and lived in the West Virginia hills before joining the Army during World War I. In the service, he developed granulated eyelids, which caused his blindness. The Richmond studio got great mileage from Miller's pleasing tenor voice on many mountain ballads, which were also issued on Champion under the name Oran Campbell and on the Sears labels under the name Frank Wilkins.

Dennis Taylor, the Gennett talent scout in central Kentucky, began organizing old-time players for Richmond recording sessions in 1925 with the appearance of a long-forgotten singer named Welby Toomey. To accompany Toomey, Taylor recruited his 28-year-old farmer neighbor, the popular "Fiddlin' " Doc Roberts, along with guitarist Edgar Boaz, from nearby Bourbon County. Gennett released a couple of forgettable Toomey solos, "Roving Gambler" and "Little Brown Jug," but these recording sessions were significant for starting a prolific relationship between Doc Roberts and the Richmond studio.

Roberts was born in east-central Kentucky and, as was typical of rural string players, picked up the fiddle as a young child. Folklorist Charles Wolfe, who interviewed Roberts in the 1960s, learned that Owen Walker, an elderly black fiddler, had been his early musical mentor and taught him "Old Buzzard," "Brickyard Joe," and other regional tunes. Roberts' fiddle style was distinguished by clean legato phrases, which are captured on dozens of Gennett sides.

Wiggins considered Roberts the best artist that Taylor brought to Gennett. He even mailed Roberts the lists of popular and old-time records requested by the Sears labels, along with recorded versions of the titles just in case Roberts had never heard them. After all, Roberts did not travel much, and his farm was isolated from the outside world. For all his influence on fiddle players many years later, Roberts remained a parochial musician who preferred the traditional songs from his rural area, such as "Deer Walk" and "Waynesburgh."

Over several years, Roberts appeared on the Gennett acoustic discs as well as on the Electrobeam series. In his correspondence with Roberts, Wiggins described the headaches incurred by Gennett's New York and Richmond studios in switching from acoustic to electronic recording. In October 1926, he wrote to Roberts: "I have just returned from New York where I hoped to find things in such condition that I could advise you immediately in regard to further recordings. I wish that some way could be arranged whereby you could go to our New York laboratory at once. I have wondered if Mr. Taylor or any of your boys own a car and would like to take a sort of vacation and drive through. You might talk this over and let me know. If this could be arranged, I could make arrangements for this work in New York to be done immediately."[18]

A month later, Wiggins alerted Roberts to another old-time session being organized by Taylor: "We have been put out so many times in regard to the new electrical recordings that we have decided to put back our horn recording apparatus here in Richmond in order that we might make a few numbers. Mr. Wickemeyer will arrive some time this week and I will probably be able to have you come next week. I will take the matter up with Mr. Taylor. I believe if I were you, I would come up for this work as you have previously done."[19]

With the electronic equipment finally operating with reasonable success in early 1927, the Electrobeam Gennett series was launched as Taylor brought several musicians to Starr Valley. Among them were old-time singer Aulton Ray and a Virginia-born guitarist and singer named Byrd Moore, whose Gennett recordings of "Back Water Blues," "Snatch 'Em Back Blues," and "When the Snowflakes Fall Again" are prized by country record collectors. Moore, a barber by trade, also appeared as a sideman on several Gennett sessions organized by Taylor.

On April 26, 1927, the Richmond studio recorded Taylor's Kentucky Boys, which included banjo player Marion Underwood and a black fiddler, Jim Booker, according to the Gennett recording information cards. The 1923 Gennett session by Jelly Roll Morton and the New Orleans Rhythm Kings is generally considered the first interracial recording session in jazz, and the 1927 session with Taylor's Kentucky Boys may well have been the first interracial session in early country music.

During that same visit to Richmond, Underwood recorded "Coal Creek March," a wonderful example of skilled finger-picking on the banjo. Because Gennett's release of this song has been reissued several times on record anthologies, it has become a folk music standard, even covered by such banjo players as Pete Seeger. It maintains a stature in folk music comparable to Carmichael's "Stardust" in popular music.

In May 1927, a versatile string band journeyed up from the southern Virginia mountains to record in Richmond under the name of Da Costa Woltz's Southern Broadcasters. In a prolific two-day session, these players from the small mountain community of Galax, Virginia, bordering North Carolina, produced sixteen sides for Gennett. The ensemble included Ben Jarrell and Frank Jenkins, both seasoned mountain singers and instrumentalists, and twelve-year-old Price Goodson, who sang and played harmonica. The band played locally around southern Virginia and North Carolina, still a breeding ground for fine string playing today. The band's collective versatility ranged from a harmonica solo, "Lost Train Blues," to banjo and fiddle solos on "Home Sweet Home" and "Wandering Boy," to the barn dance calls "Richmond Cotillion" and "John Brown's Dream," to a sacred vocal number, "Are You Washed in the Blood of the Lamb?"

The rare Da Costa Woltz discs captured a distinct regional style called the "Galax Sound" or "Round Peak Sound," a blend of banjo, fiddle, and white gospel vocal harmony that had developed over several decades. The Da Costa Woltz band was soon followed into the Richmond studio by a neighboring string band from Surry County, North Carolina, called the Red Fox Chasers. Consisting of Bob Cranford, A. P. Thompson, J. Paul Miles, and G. D. Brooks, the Red Fox Chasers supplied Gennett with several lively sides for the Electrobeam, Champion, and Sears labels. In total, the Gennett releases by Da Costa Woltz and the Red Fox Chasers represent a truly amazing compilation of America's early string band music.

In 1927, the Richmond studio recorded Holland Puckett, a singer, guitarist, and harmonica player from Hollow, Virginia. Puckett, a bookkeeper for a tobacco warehouse, made several sides for Gennett and its affiliated labels. He died in 1934, and legend has it that he was killed in a knife fight during a poker game.

In 1928, Starr Piano published a twenty-page, illustrated brochure called "New Electrobeam Gennett Records of Old

Time Tunes," which promoted artists such as Roberts, Underwood, Puckett, and Taylor's Kentucky Boys. The primary tool for promoting old-time music in the 1920s was printed material, such as record catalog lists, magazine advertisements, and store displays. Yet, unlike the simple lists of song titles and artists routinely issued to advertise old-time recordings in the magazines, Gennett's glossy "Old Time Tunes" brochure showcased its mountain singers and instrumentalists with photos and flowery descriptions.

It declared that Roberts has "won so many old time fiddlin' contests that he has lost track of them," while blind singer David Miller "says it is not necessary to see to be happy." The Da Costa Woltz's twelve-year-old Price Goodson is described as no less than a "boy wonder." The brochure apparently was an attempt to attract sales from the more upscale customers supporting the Starr Piano stores, which carried the Electrobeam Gennett releases.

With the recording industry enjoying a brief comeback in 1927, Fred Gennett had high hopes for the Electrobeam label, as shown by the creation of the "Old Time Tunes" brochure. It may have done little to improve sales for Electrobeam releases, but it remained one of the most elaborate and creative brochures published in the 1920s to promote the pioneering old-time recordings.

The WLS "National Barn Dance" and Its "Kentucky Mountain Boy"

Though inherently associated with rural Appalachia, old-time music gained national exposure through a giant radio station in the heart of the industrial Great Lakes region. WLS (which stood for "World's Largest Store"), a property of Sears, Roebuck & Co., began broadcasting in 1924 from Chicago's Sherman Hotel to listeners throughout the Midwest. With the Sears retail operations catering heavily to farming communities, the broadcasts included weather updates, crop and livestock reports, and an old-time music show called the "National Barn Dance." It became one of the most-beloved and long-running radio shows in country music history.

The program's musical format in those early years evolved from an eclectic mix of fiddle and banjo players, singers of old-time tunes and maudlin pop songs (called "heart songs"), piano and organ players, sacred quartets, and a popular Irish balladeer. By 1927, WLS was well established, and Gennett Records had yet another means of expanding its roster of old-time recording artists on the new Electrobeam label and the Sears budget labels.

While staying in the Sherman Hotel during much of 1927, Gennett's Clayton Jackson spent his days promoting the label with distributors around Chicago. At night, he assumed the role of talent scout, signing up WLS performers, including singer Grace Wilson, banjo player Chubby Parker, the Maple City Four Quartet, the Arkansas Wood Chopper, WLS staff organist Ralph Waldo Emerson, and Bradley Kincaid. The Gennett connection with WLS, combined with the label's recording activities with Chicago-based blues and jazz artists, led Fred Gennett in 1927 to establish a temporary recording studio at the Starr Piano Store in Chicago.

Chubby Parker, a banjo player and singer from Kentucky, was one of the most popular WLS performers to record for Gennett in the mid-1920s, with such releases as "Old Stern Bachelor." The round-faced Parker, whom Jackson claimed to have tracked down in a downtown Chicago speakeasy, exploited the stereotype of the backward hillbilly, with the forgettable sides "Bib-A-Lollie-Boo," "Froggie Went a-Courtin'," and "Nickety, Nackety, Now, Now, Now."

At the opposite end of the WLS spectrum was Bradley Kincaid, a straitlaced, well-dressed college student in horn-rimmed glasses who strummed the guitar and sang old folk ballads in a warm tenor voice. Kincaid became one of America's first national radio stars during his two-year tenure at WLS. Extremely popular among old-time music listeners through the 1940s, Kincaid debuted on record with Gennett in 1927, ultimately recording dozens of sides over two years for the company's Electrobeam and Champion labels, in addition to the Sears mail-order labels. With Kincaid aboard, Gennett Records had a marquee old-time singing star. Through his numerous recordings, radio broadcasts, live performances, and published song books, Kincaid, billed as the "Kentucky Mountain Boy," became a central force in bringing both listeners and respectability to the genre of traditional folk singing.

Kincaid's upbringing was the stuff of folk songs. He was born the fourth of nine children in 1895 in Garrard County, Kentucky, in the Cumberland Mountains. His father, a farm laborer, sang in the church choir; his mother sang old English ballads in their humble Appalachian house. Through his musical parents and relatives, the young Kincaid absorbed the old folk songs, including several originating in the Anglo-Saxon traditions brought to America centuries before. His father traded a fox hound to a farmer for a small guitar, which the young Kincaid soon began to play.

Before the backdrop of Kentucky's majestic landscape, Kincaid's childhood years were difficult. After his mother died, he was forced to leave school in the fifth grade and work in the fields. His father remarried and moved away, leaving Kincaid with an older sister. Essentially on his own at age thirteen, Kincaid worked long days as a farm laborer, except for a brief job in a wheel factory in Louisville. A friend encouraged the teenage Kincaid to attend a small Christian church in the hills, where he responded to the minister's altar call. The event changed the course of Kincaid's life.[20]

Seeking a life beyond the horse and plow, Kincaid, at age nineteen, entered the sixth grade at nearby Berea College, a small Christian college, which also operated an elementary and high school academy. He earned room and board by working at a school-operated hotel and finished three grades in two years. During World War I, Kincaid served two years in the U.S. Army, including one year in France, before returning to Berea to complete school. At 26, he graduated from high school. He fell in love with his music teacher, Irma Foreman, and they were married.

Kincaid worked for the YMCA in Kentucky for two years, but he grew restless. In 1924, the couple sold their belongings and moved to Chicago, where Kincaid attended the YMCA College. His wife rekindled his childhood interest in music, and he joined Chicago's YMCA Quartet, which performed around the city and appeared on WLS. A somewhat reluctant Kincaid informed the WLS program director of his vast knowledge of traditional folk songs. Accompanied only by his guitar, he debuted as a soloist one Saturday night on the National Barn Dance, singing "Barbara Allen," which was soon to become his signature number, and other folks songs he had known as a child. He earned $15.

His radio performances involved more than singing. Kincaid described with sincerity the venerable songs that recalled a rural life he and many of his WLS listeners had left behind for better-paying jobs in the booming Midwest towns and cities. The emotional connection between Kincaid and his listeners was instant. Hundreds of thousands of letters poured into WLS during the late 1920s, praising Kincaid for his traditional songs and stories. To his own amazement, the YMCA College student had become a singing star.

Kincaid made his first records in December 1927 at Gennett's Chicago studio. Jackson said Kincaid was brought to Gennett's attention through another WLS singing team, the Maple City Four Quartet of La Porte, Indiana. Jackson was immediately struck by Kincaid's cordial nature, handsome features, and the small "hound-dog" guitar. Gennett Records pressed two songs from Kincaid's first session, "The Fatal Wedding" and "Sweet Kitty Wells," both nineteenth-century ballads that he had learned as a child from his father.[21] As was the pattern with Kincaid's recordings for Gennett, the company also released the songs on the Champion, Challenge,

Silvertone, Supertone, and Bell labels. To his surprise, Kincaid became John Carpenter on the obscure Bell label and Dan Hughey on the Champion releases.

During 1928, Kincaid appeared at Gennett's Chicago studio many times, and the company pressed more than a dozen sides, including his popular favorite, "Barbara Allen," an old English tune taught Kincaid by an uncle; the standard old-time tune, "Froggie Went a-Courtin"; and "Sourwood Mountain." Kincaid also appeared on a number of "The [WLS] Showboat" discs, which Gennett recorded and pressed for the Sears Silvertone label.

When Kincaid graduated from college in 1929, he was a relatively wealthy man. He took a singing job on WLW radio in Cincinnati, but continued for several months to perform on WLS on weekends. He also managed several visits to Gennett's Richmond studio, about 70 miles from Cincinnati. Years later, he remembered the studio as nothing more than an open room with a single microphone plunked down in the center. Kincaid recorded several numbers that he had learned during his WLS days, such as "Four Thousand Years Ago," "The Red River Valley," and "When the Work's All Done This Fall." He may have been particularly inspired for his Gennett recording of "The Wreck on the C&O Road," given the constant threat of interruption from the railroad line looming above the studio on top of the Whitewater gorge. Overall, Gennett issued more than two dozen sides from Kincaid's 1929 sessions, which were pressed on various Gennett-affiliated labels.

Gennett continued into the early 1930s releasing Kincaid's recordings on the budget Champion and Superior labels, even though Kincaid was now recording for Brunswick. During the Great Depression, he also recorded dozens of songs for Victor and Decca Records. He eventually teamed up with Grandpa Jones and moved from radio station to radio station during the 1930s, journeying as far north as Boston, while faithfully promoting his song books of Kentucky mountain tunes along the way.

Kincaid's Gennett records do not explain his wide popularity in the 1920s. Though his diction was clear and his voice was warm and pleasant, he was not particularly versatile or dynamic. His guitar playing was purely functional. Rural audiences were attracted by Kincaid's repertoire and his obvious respect for the music. Kincaid despised the expression "hillbilly music," calling it derogatory, and considered mountain folk music to be a worthy tribute to Kentucky's Anglo-Saxon heritage. His reverence for traditional Appalachian music influenced the perceptions of his musical contemporaries as well as those of the listening public.

Unlike most early old-time performers, Kincaid was a savvy businessman. He earned a comfortable living as a musician, and that explains why he never looked kindly on his 1920s and 1930s recordings. Kincaid claimed that Gennett issued his recordings under pseudonyms without his knowledge and that the early record labels, including Victor, never paid him the royalties to which he was entitled. Gennett's few surviving financial records indicate that the company was diligent in meeting its modest contractual obligations with its musicians. However, years later, Jackson claimed that Gennett cheated some old-time and blues musicians out of their royalties. Whether that included Kincaid will never be known.

In the 1940s, Kincaid returned to Cincinnati to perform on the WLW and WKRC radio stations before joining the country music team on the "Grand Ole Opry" in Nashville. He played with them for five years, but he never felt that the public accepted him in the way that it took to the younger stars, like Roy Acuff, Ernest Tubb, or Eddie Arnold. By this time, Kincaid's simple approach to mountain folk singing was out of step with the emerging honky-tonk country sounds. In the 1950s, Kincaid retired from performing. Although he was no longer in the rural public's eye, he lived quite comfortably for decades in Springfield, Ohio, where he purchased a radio station and, later, the Kincaid Music store, now operated by his son, James.

In later years, Kincaid cut an occasional album of old folk songs and made a few live appearances, his final performance occurring at Berea College when he was 90. Yet for the most part, Kincaid steadfastly resisted live engagements, even during the 1960s folk revival, when a publicized comeback would have secured him a more deserving place in country music history. "He simply had no desire to go back," said his son. "My father performed when traveling on the road was tough and he never felt he got a fair shake from the record companies. So when he put that part of his life behind him, that was it. He didn't need to be back in the limelight. It just didn't interest him."[22]

The Golden Era of Old-Time Singing

While Kincaid was singing over the airwaves of WLS and WLW, his Gennett releases were still no match for Victor's Bluebird subsidiary label, which produced an enormous body of influential vocal recordings by the Carter Family and former railroad brakeman Jimmie Rodgers, considered the first superstar of country music. The widely distributed Bluebird releases by these rural performers were among the most influential records from any music genre in the late 1920s, as the popularity of old-time singing made a commercial crescendo.

And yet, from an artistic standpoint, Gennett Records held its own against the larger Bluebird, Vocalion, and OKeh labels by recording many of the era's compelling old-time singers. Rural singers rarely worked exclusively with a single record label. The common practice was to make the rounds of the recording studios. As a result, Gennett was able to churn out hundreds of sides by such prolific singers as Vernon Dalhart, Ernest Stoneman, McGhee and Welling, Gene Autry, and Uncle Dave Macon.

Vernon Dalhart was one of the few singers to make a comfortable living recording old-time music. A Texan by birth, he was an operatic tenor who recognized the commercial potential of rural music. He studied at the Dallas Conservatory of Music and spent several years with the Century Opera Company in New York. Between 1916 and 1924, he recorded popular songs with only limited success. Then, after persuading Victor to allow him to record old-time tunes, Dalhart embarked on a new singing career, recording for several labels. Some of his first old-time records in 1924 were produced at Gennett's New York studio, including the popular "The Prisoner's Song" and "Old Fiddler's Song."

Dalhart's vast assortment of old-time songs was laden with the maudlin themes of death and disaster, such as "Wreck of the Old 97," "The Fatal Wedding," "The Dying Girl's Message," and "The Death of Floyd Collins." For Gennett, he recorded the tear-jerkers "Wreck of the No. 9," "Wreck of the Royal Palm," "The Mississippi Flood," and "Get Away Old Man Get Away." His Gennett sides also appeared on the Champion, Herwin, and Buddy labels and on the short-lived Black Patti label. Dalhart was among the era's most prolific old-time recording artists, inspiring other singers, including the now-forgotten vaudeville performer Carson Robison, who recorded numerous sides for Gennett, both in duets with Dalhart and as a soloist.

Another old-time singing star on Gennett, Ernest Stoneman, enjoyed a career ranging from early acoustic recordings to national television in the 1960s. Born in a Virginia log cabin, he began singing in the early 1920s, convinced he was every bit as good a vocalist as Henry Whitter. His first OKeh records with the Dixie Mountaineers in 1924 included "The Titanic," one of the most popular songs in early country music. Stoneman had already recorded for Victor and OKeh when he first entered Gennett's New York studio in late 1926 with his wife, Hattie, who played fiddle.

Stoneman was reluctant to sign up with Gennett, doubting whether the small label could sell many records.[23] He was probably more uncertain when he arrived at the Gennett studio, which was struggling to make the transition from acoustic to electronic recording. The electronic equipment was not in working order, so Gennett engineer Gordon Soule reconstructed the studio's old acoustic equipment in order to wax Ernest and Hattie Stoneman on six songs, including the popular "May I Sleep in Your Barn Tonight, Mister?" In early 1927, Stoneman recorded four more sides at the New York studio, including "Kenny Wagner's Surrender" and "Round Tom Gals."

Stoneman soon regarded the Gennett company as an asset. His recordings were issued on the Gennett, Champion (under the name Uncle Jim Seany), Silvertone, Supertone, and Herwin labels. He was sent notices detailing which budget labels released his recordings and was paid the royalties owed him. Gennett also mailed Stoneman test pressings of his recordings and let him decide which takes should be released, an unusual policy for the Richmond organization.[24]

In July 1928, Stoneman visited the Richmond studio with his cousins, Willie and George Stoneman, and the Sweet brothers, Earl and Herbert. During a Friday session, the recording equipment broke down (not an uncommon occurrence), and the band stayed the weekend and resumed recording on Monday. During the layover, the Gennett staff gave the musicians a tour of the Starr piano and record-pressing facilities. The five titles issued from the session included "Wake Up in the Morning" and "I Got a Bull Dog." Stoneman's honeymoon with Gennett Records soon ended, however, after all the recorded takes from a 1929 recording date with Eck Dunford and the Ward Brothers were inexplicably rejected by the studio staff.

During the same period, several popular old-time singers from Kentucky visited Richmond. The team of Richard Burnett and fiddler Leonard Rutherford, under contract with Columbia in 1926–27, switched to the smaller Gennett label beginning in 1928, recording such numbers as "Under the Pale Moonlight" and "She Is a Flower from the Fields of Alabama."

With the Richmond studio preferring vocal numbers over purely instrumental music, in 1928 Doc Roberts recruited singer and guitarist Asa Martin, a fellow Kentuckian. They also brought James Roberts, then eleven years old, who harmonized with Martin while Dad played the mandolin. These three performers recorded several mountain ballads for Gennett, including "The Dying Girl's Message," and "The Dingy Miner's Cabin," written by Martin's sister. By the 1930s, Doc Roberts drifted out of the recording business and stuck to farming and playing fiddle locally, while Martin and James Roberts traveled as a singing duet. Like many old-time musicians on Gennett, Roberts was rediscovered by folklorists during the 1960s folk revival. Just before he died in 1978, he performed at Berea College, just as Bradley Kincaid had done.

The Richmond studio also recorded its share of West Virginia singing groups, the most prominent being the white gospel team of John McGhee and Frank Welling, an incredibly prolific recording duet. They had been performing together for about a decade in churches and tent shows around Huntington, West Virginia, when they recorded their first sides in Richmond in late 1927. Gennett issued on the Electrobeam and budget labels numerous McGhee-Welling religious numbers, such as "I've Been Redeemed," "Praise the Lord, It's So," "He Abides," "I'm Free Again," "Beautiful Garden of Prayer," and "Life's Railway to Heaven." Their years of performing together is evident in these poignant, highly polished performances. McGhee and Welling also recorded separately and with other singers, including McGhee's daughter, Alma, and Welling's wife, Thelma.

The team of McGhee and Welling produced more than 300 masters for several labels between 1925 and 1933.[25] Gennett engineer Joe Geier remembered McGhee as a resourceful talent scout, similar to Taylor, who organized recording sessions for different gospel groups, paid them a flat fee, and pocketed the royalties. "He was making a killing on this thing," Geier said. "McGhee would hit there [Richmond] maybe twice a year with a group, a half-dozen or so, put them up at the hotel, pay all their expenses and give them maybe $10 a day, and he would sign for the royalties for the whole bunch."[26]

For example, McGhee once arranged for a black minister and his church choir to record in return for McGhee making a donation to their church. The group arrived at the Richmond studio in the evening and was immediately organized for the session. "As soon as the microphone was put up in front of them, it scared them," Geier said. "So the preacher tried to get them going. Well, he like to never got them going in their singing. So finally, after the preacher had tried to explain the red light [signaling a song should wrap up soon], we just forgot about it. The preacher got them going and we just started cutting records. We let them cut several records until finally we turned on the red light and said that was all we wanted."[27] So for a one-time church donation, the Gennett studio got several recordings, and McGhee was set up to collect the royalties.

While McGhee and Welling's records were circulating in West Virginia, another old-time singer from the state, Billy Cox, signed up with Gennett in mid-1929. A singer, guitarist, and harmonica player, Cox moonlighted on the tiny radio station WOBU in Charleston, West Virginia. In researching Cox, folklorist Ivan Tribe discovered the Gennett dates were actually arranged by the owner of WOBU. Cox was often late for his live shows, and the owner planned to use the records as a backup.

Like many of the era's rural singers, Cox emulated the yodeling style of Jimmie Rodgers. Cox also recorded blues numbers, such as "California Blues" and "Alabama Blues." Yet his brush with regional fame was fleeting. In 1965, long after he had drifted into obscurity, a folklorist discovered Cox living in a converted chicken house in a Charleston ghetto.

While Cox was recording for Gennett, another Jimmie Rodgers clone, Gene Autry, signed on with the small Indiana label, a move which actually helped launch him into superstardom. The Texas-born singer and guitarist was working at a small-time radio station in rural Oklahoma when he wrote to the Richmond studio requesting a recording session. A date was set in 1929, and Autry arrived with a large portfolio of ballads, yodeling songs, blues, and cowboy songs.

Autry's first sides were issued on the Electrobeam label; after the label was discontinued in 1930, more than two dozen Autry sides were released on the Champion label. (It was no coincidence that Autry took the "Champion" name for his famed horse.) Devoted to Rodgers' singing style, Autry recorded several yodeling numbers for Gennett, including "Blue Yodel No. 8," "Cowboy Yodel," and "Anniversary Blue Yodel." In fact, Rodgers' yodel on his Bluebird recordings and Autry's on Champion are almost indistinguishable.

Autry gradually restricted his old-time repertoire in the early 1930s, and focused on the singing cowboy image immortalized in his many films. His meteoric rise in the 1930s, which included a stint on WLS in Chicago and numerous records for several labels, including Victor, would have an enormous impact on the entertainment industry.

Autry's many Gennett and Champion sides, reissued by Decca Records in the mid-1930s, continue to hold some interest because they reveal his diverse musical influences before becoming the singing cinema cowboy. In the 1940s Gennett family members proposed a possible reissue album of his Gennett/Champion recordings, but Autry strongly opposed such a project. (When his input was sought for this book, Autry recalled only being involved in the purchase of the Champion label by the American Decca label in 1935.)

In the years leading up to 1934, there were many more old-time musicians on Gennett and its affiliated labels than are surveyed in this chapter. While many were of little significance, it would be an egregious omission not to mention such creative Gennett performers as Alabama's Allison Harp Singers, Tom Ashley, yodeler Clifford Carlisle, the North Carolina Ramblers, Pie Plant Pete, Joe Ryan, Walter Smith, Kirk McGee and Blythe Poteet, the Smoky Mountain Boys, Jess Hilliard, Gray's Cowboy Band, Jimmy Johnson's String Band, Smith and Woodlieff, Henry Whitter and George B. Grayson, and the Walter Family, a jug band from Richmond, Indiana. After the Gennetts discontinued the Electrobeam label in late 1930, the budget Champion label stayed in operation and pressed a large number of old-time sides that were distributed primarily in the South.

In mid-1934, just before the fading Champion label was discontinued, the Richmond studio received an audition disc from Kirk McGee, a Tennessee fiddler who had recorded for Gennett in the late 1920s. It led to one of the greatest old-time recording sessions in Richmond, with brothers Kirk and Sam McGee and the immortal Uncle Dave Macon from Tennessee.

Born in 1870, Macon grew up singing and playing banjo without the professional outlet of phonograph records and radio. He soon made up for lost time, however. In 1925, the 55-year-old Macon teamed with Tennessee guitarist Sam McGee just as Nashville radio station WSM established its live "Barn Dance" program, which later evolved into "Grand Ole Opry." Macon and McGee were one of the first acts to perform on the historic program. The next year, they began recording for the Vocalion label, in seven separate sessions. They became one of the most popular rural singing acts in the late 1920s. When they split in 1931, Sam teamed up with brother, Kirk, and Macon performed and recorded with his sons.

Finally, in August 1934, the 64-year-old Macon reunited with Sam and Kirk for sessions organized in Richmond for the soon-to-be-defunct Champion label. Even though fourteen sides were waxed in two days, only six were ever released. But these precious few sides captured a most fruitful collaboration. The trio performed four moving gospel numbers, "Thank God for Everything," "When the Train Comes Along," "Don't Get Weary Children," and "He's Up with the Angels Now." The McGee brothers sang together without Macon on "Brown's Ferry Blues," while Sam sang solo and played guitar on "Railroad Blues." The latter reflects the musical synergy in the 1930s between black rural blues and old-time playing, as Sam's falsetto voice and expressive guitar mirror the 1920s recordings of southern blues artists Blind Lemon Jefferson and Robert Johnson. This final hurrah on Champion marked the last recording session of Macon and the McGee brothers. Macon continued to record for other labels, but the Champion sides were the last recordings by the McGee brothers for almost two decades.

The milestone Macon and McGee sides were among dozens of Gennett/Champion old-time discs to be reissued, first by Decca Records in the mid-1930s, and later, on hundreds of full-length album anthologies issued by small folk labels over the past thirty years. The resilience of Gennett old-time music is remarkable, considering that many original Electrobeam releases never sold more than a few hundred copies. As one might expect, Gennett's old-time releases on the Sears labels were widely distributed, particularly in the rural South. The Champion releases generally sold only a few thousand copies each.

Through the networking of folklorists and record collectors, such as County Records owner David Freeman, original Gennett old-time discs have been discovered and reissued for new generations of listeners worldwide. During the folk revival of the 1960s, album compilations by Virginia-based County Records featured dozens of Gennett old-time recordings, thus providing young folk musicians and listeners with a body of work that had been out of circulation for decades. Obtaining Gennett discs from private collectors, Freeman reissued the collected works of string musicians Doc Roberts, the Da Costa Woltz Southern Broadcasters, the Red Fox Chasers, and several others.

Old Homestead Records, owned by John Morris, has reissued Gennett sides by Kincaid, McGhee and Welling, Whitter and Grayson, and others for his small, but loyal, group of mail-order record buyers. Many original metal master recordings from the Champion vaults, first obtained by Decca in the 1930s, are now owned by MCA Records. As the twenty-first century approaches, old-time recordings from the Richmond studio are beginning to emerge on country anthologies issued on digital compact disc—a long journey from the worn-out test phonograph in the Starr administration building.

Country Blues Recordings

It was a typical smoldering summer for Birmingham, Alabama, when, in 1927, a working crew for Gennett Records assembled a portable recording studio in the Starr Piano store on Third Avenue. After months of lobbying, the store's assistant manager had persuaded Fred Gennett, back in Indiana, to finance the record division's only field recording expedition in the Deep South.

Starr Piano logically set up the studio in its successful downtown store in Birmingham, one of the region's most industrialized cities, with mining and steel operations that attracted workers from throughout the rural South. The city's urban expansion fostered a lively music scene. White and black dance bands, vaudeville singers, and boogie-woogie pianists worked the local dance halls. By setting up camp in Birmingham, Gennett Records also had greater access to the black South's country blues tradition, which had its roots in the music of slaves and their descendents.

The *Birmingham News* lauded Starr Piano's makeshift record studio as the city's "latest industrial effort," as, over a two-month period, a string of local musicians headed up to the third floor, where Gennett's recently acquired General Electric electronic recording equipment was set up. "The nation looks to the South for its Dixie melodies, its jazz orchestras, its hot music," Gordon Soule, Gennett's sound engineer, told the local Birmingham newspaper in July 1927. "Our initial reception here in Birmingham has been beyond our expectations."[28]

Actually, the Birmingham project was Fred Gennett's second stab at field recordings. A few months earlier, he and Arizona resort operator Fred Harvey decided to make records of Hopi Indian songs and sell them to tourists at Harvey's El Tovar Hotel at the Grand Canyon. Gennett technicians rigged up a portable recording truck and hired Dr. J. Walter Fewkes, chief of the Bureau of Ethnology of the Smithsonian Institution, to supervise the sessions. They drove out to Arizona in December 1926, and Fewkes organized elders of the Walpi tribe of the Hopi Indians for performances of traditional songs. The dozen recordings, issued in early 1927, were the last acoustically recorded Gennett discs and possibly the first pure ethnic discs ever issued by a commercial record label. From a financial standpoint, however, Starr Piano probably wrote off the Hopi project as one of Fred's harebrained ideas. Such Hopi numbers as "Tacheuktu Katcina" and "Tuwina'Av" were not exactly hits with the general public.

The Gennett organization had higher hopes for Birmingham. During July and August of 1927, Soule recorded a cross section of Alabama culture, from white dance orchestras to black jazz groups like the Black Birds of Paradise from nearby Montgomery. A local Baptist minister, Rev. J. F. Forrest, was recorded preaching to his responsive congregation. Johnny Watson, a country blues singer from Mobile, was recorded under the name Daddy Stove Pipe, along with his partner, Whistlin' Pete.

Then came Jaybird Coleman, an obscure country blues singer from the outskirts of Birmingham. Coleman would holler out a verse and then play a response on the harmonica in a style that hearkened back to the field songs of the black South. Soule recorded Coleman on the songs "Trunk Busted—Suitcase Full of Holes," "Man Trouble Blues," "Mistreatin' Mama," and "Boll Weevil," which Gennett issued on the Electrobeam, Champion, and Sears Conqueror labels. These rare discs preserved one of the most distinctive blues harmonica styles uncovered by the record companies in the 1920s. Cole-

man also had the dubious distinction of creating the most rau-
cous song title ever printed on a Gennett label with his number
"Ah'm Sick and Tired of Tellin' You (To Wiggle That Thing)."

Fortunately for Hazel Gennett, Fred's wife, her friends in
the local chapter of the Daughters of the American Revolution
back in conservative Richmond had little idea of the racy blues
records her enterprising husband was pressing for the segregated race record market. After all, this was the same Gennett
family that recorded symphony orchestras and opera singers,
and visibly patronized Richmond's high-brow cultural activities. Yet, as always with the Gennetts, business came first. And
the economic forces that steered Fred Gennett toward recording white Appalachian music also led him in 1927 to compete
head-on in the race recording field. For a brief period in the
late 1920s it blossomed as a result of the growing output of
country blues and gospel music on several record labels.

Before 1927, Gennett Records built its reputation in race
records on the ground-breaking jazz discs. It recorded a smattering of blues musicians on its acoustic discs, but it did not
follow its competitors, such as OKeh, Paramount, and Columbia, in actively scouting the rural South for country blues players in the mid-1920s. Paramount was the industry leader in
recording country blues singers, the most significant being
Blind Lemon Jefferson of Texas. These black street musicians
sang and accompanied themselves on the guitar, banjo, or harmonica. Their primal, less-structured musical style was a sharp
contrast to the more refined "classic blues" records popularized in the early 1920s by female, vaudeville-style singers,
such as Bessie Smith and Mamie Smith, who worked from
stock arrangements and were backed by jazz musicians.

During 1923–24, Gennett's New York studio recorded
several female singers of minor interest in the classic blues
style, such as Viola McCoy, Josie Miles, and Edna Hicks, the
last accompanied by a creative blues pianist named Lemuel
Fowler. Meanwhile, the Richmond studio recorded the equally
obscure Sammie Lewis and Callie Vasser. In 1923, the Rich-

mond studio also produced several personal recordings with a teenager by the name of Jesse Crump, a virtuoso ragtime and blues pianist from Texas. At the time, Crump was in Indianapolis, where he accompanied black stage singers, including Nina Reeves and Charles Stanfield. Several exceedingly rare Gennett personal recordings have been discovered over the years with Crump playing solo piano or backing either Reeves or Stanfield. One of them, touting Stanfield as "the Caruso of the Colored Race," was issued to promote the singer's regular engagements at the Cedar Springs Hotel in New Paris, Ohio, a resort just five miles from Richmond. Crump's brief association with Gennett Records ended when he was hired in 1925 by Chicago blues singer Ida Cox, his future wife. They performed and recorded together for more than a decade.

As early as 1924, Gennett produced some fabulously obscure country blues music, such as "Sundown Blues" and "Stove Pipe Blues," by Johnny Watson, alias Daddy Stove Pipe. How a middle-aged singer, guitarist, and harmonica player from Mobile, Alabama, ended up in Richmond in May 1924 for a recording date will forever be a mystery. It is possible that the Gennett staff signed up Watson, as they did many black entertainers, as he passed through the Indiana-Ohio region as part of a traveling medicine or minstrel show.

Richmond in the 1920s was not particularly accommodating to the black musicians recording at Gennett. If they did not secure housing with a local black family, they could wind up in a boarding house in a largely black neighborhood, known as "Goose Town," just north of the railroad tracks. It was the closest thing Richmond had to a bootlegging, red light district. Jackson noted that if musicians did not make their appointments at the Gennett studio, chances were good they were still down in Goose Town. In such cases, Jackson would call on the services of Charlie Yeager, a Starr Piano employee. "He knew every house in the north end that sold whiskey, bootleg, mountain dew, or what," Jackson said. "He knew where to look for them [musicians]. He could go there after these people without any trouble. If anybody else went down there, it was pretty dangerous."[29]

An oasis for traveling black musicians in Richmond during that period was the Palm Leaf Cafe on North Fourth Street, which was owned by Henry Duncan, a black entrepreneur, music promoter, and barber. The Palm Leaf Cafe was one of the only restaurants in Richmond established for black patrons, and it had a small bandstand with a drum kit and, appropriately, a player piano made by Starr. Harry Leavell, Duncan's son, and, as a youth, an employee at the Henry Gennett mansion, recalled that black musicians routinely organized rehearsals at the cafe before their recording sessions at the piano factory.[30]

In addition to signing up blues players passing through Richmond, the Gennett staff recruited them from the nearby Ohio River cities of Louisville and Cincinnati. For instance, in 1924, the Richmond studio recorded Cincinnati blues singers Sam Jones, alias Daddy Stove Pipe No. 1, and Ernestine Bomburgero, alias Baby Bonnie.[31] Louisville was a hotbed for rural jug and washboard bands, which performed on street corners, in parks, and at local racetracks. These black musicians had migrated from the Tennessee and Kentucky hills with a spirited music similar to that of the region's white string bands. In 1924 the Richmond studio recorded a lively Louisville group called Whistler & His Jug Band, led by Buford Threlkeld on the long-nose whistle, along with violin, guitar, and mandolin accompaniment. Gennett issued four sides by the Whistler band, one of the first jug bands ever recorded, including "Jailhouse Blues" and "I'm a Jazz Baby." Another Louisville band, Walter Taylor and the Washboard Trio, also recorded several sides for Gennett. Taylor blew into the big jug, supported by guitars, mandolin, and kazoo.

With the introduction in 1927 of the Electrobeam label, Fred Gennett made a more serious bid for the race record market by recording an increasing number of country blues and gospel performers in the Richmond and New York studios, as well as in the temporary studios in Birmingham and Chicago. Record sales in 1926 had rebounded to a healthy $128 million, and 1927 promised to be another boom year. Radio did not present severe competition for race records, as radio stations in the late 1920s rarely programmed black blues and gospel.

Race records probably accounted for less than ten percent of total record industry sales. However, it could be a profitable segment, as many black musicians, such as blues singers performing on urban street corners, eagerly entered recording studios for the most paltry sums. Gennett's payments to black blues players were notoriously low. The studio would pay them a flat $5–$15 per recording session or the standard royalty payment of one penny for each copy sold.

Also, Gennett Records was attracted to race records because of its contractual obligations to supply discs for the Sears record catalogs, which served as major retail agents for race records. Possibly because Gennett cleverly pressed the same blues and jazz recordings on the Gennett Electrobeam, Champion, and Sears labels, the Gennett organization never issued its own separate race record series to the public, as did the competing companies. However, Electrobeam may have been the only record label in the late 1920s to have the words "Race Record" printed on it.

Fred Gennett did not limit his 1927 race record activities to the Electrobeam, Champion, and Sears labels. Never afraid of a new recording gimmick or scheme, Fred and Edward Barrett—an executive with Wisconsin Chair Company (which owned Paramount Records)—became silent partners in a short-lived record company which attempted to emulate Paramount, the leading race record label. Gennett and Barrett each contributed $10,000 to establish the Chicago Record Company, which issued the Black Patti label. The name was inspired by the nineteenth-century black opera singer Sissieretta Jones, who was nicknamed Black Patti because her vocal gifts resembled those of a leading white singer of the day, Adelina

Patti. The gorgeous label was printed in purple, setting off a gold peacock with tail feathers fully extended.

To operate the enterprise, the two investors recruited J. Mayo Williams of Chicago, a successful black talent scout and promoter who had signed up several of Paramount's leading black recording artists. His role was to attract black performers and act as front man for the Black Patti label. Williams arranged with Fred Gennett to have Black Patti musicians record primarily at Gennett's Richmond studio or at the company's portable studio in Chicago. Coincidentally, Gennett's portable studio on South Wabash Avenue in Chicago, in the spirit of the Richmond studio, was constantly interrupted by the noise of the elevated trains that sped right past the studio. So the Gennett staff soon moved the studio to a quieter location at the corner of Wabash and Adams.

Finding obscure black artists eager to record for the Black Patti label was easy for Williams. "By that time, so many had come up here from the South and other parts of the country because Chicago was a music center," Williams said. "They'd bum rides, and hop trains to get up here, any way they could get somebody to make a record."[32] The Chicago Record Company paid the Gennett organization $30 for each side recorded for the Black Patti label. Fred Gennett also double-dipped by issuing several Black Patti sides on the Gennett and Champion labels, with the artists hidden behind pseudonyms. Few of the Black Patti artists were noteworthy; among the long-forgotten performers were Liz Washington, Blind Richard Yates, Lil and Will Brown, Mozelle Anderson, Blind James Beck, and Long Cleeve Reed. The Black Patti label also reissued masters recorded for the Electrobeam series, including numbers by old-time singer Vernon Dalhart, WLS staff organist Ralph Waldo Emerson, and Jaybird Coleman.

With amusing bravado, Williams unveiled Black Patti's stable of little-known performers to the black record market in May 1927, proclaiming: "All the world knows Black Patti—our own beloved Sissieretta Jones. The biggest and brightest star in the firmament of song, her lustrous career is a great chapter in the history of music. The crowned heads of Europe applauded her; people crowded to hear her. Her name means everything that is best in the musical art. Knowing that these new, wonderful records are the best that art can produce or money can buy, she not only says they are good, but puts her name on them to prove it. When Black Patti, with her lifetime of experience in what will bring joy at the heart, says a record is fine, you know what that means. Look for Black Patti's name on each one. It is your guarantee."[33]

Unfortunately for the Chicago Record Company, the beloved Sissieretta Jones did not record on the label that bore her name. Williams managed to get Black Patti records distributed in several Chicago stores and in the South. And at least one of the Black Patti releases is held in high esteem by music historians today, jazz cornetist Willie Hightower's "Boar Hog Blues." However, in September 1927, with just 55 sides issued on the purple Black Patti label, Fred Gennett pulled the plug on the operation. Considering the extreme rarity of the discs today, it is apparent that not even the name Black Patti could drum up excitement for an obscure group of entertainers. The label was apparently losing money in its bid to become another Paramount. Gennett sent Clayton Jackson to Chicago to deliver the bad news to Williams, who returned to talent scouting for the record companies. But not all was lost. Fred Gennett quickly shifted his assets from the Chicago Record Company into Chicago real estate in order to salvage his investment.

The Black Patti failure had no bearing on Gennett's steady output of blues and gospel recordings for the Electrobeam, Champion, and Sears labels. The parade of black performers recorded in Starr Valley included Thomas Dorsey, Charles Davenport, Sam Collins, Big Bill Broonzy, Jelly Roll Anderson, Big Boy Cleveland, Lottie Kimbrough ("The Kansas City Butter Ball"), Willie Baker, Katharine Baker, Tommie Bradley, Teddy Moss, Alura Black, Horace Smith, Ivy Smith, Henry Johnson, and Mae Glover. While Gennett never rivaled Paramount,

OKeh, or Columbia in the blues recording field, some of these blues recordings were relatively significant.

In early 1927, the Richmond studio recorded "Cryin'" Sam Collins, a high-pitched singer and guitarist from southern Mississippi. Gennett issued thirteen sides by Collins that year on the Electrobeam, Champion, Black Patti, Sears, and Bell labels. Collins' percussive, bottleneck guitar playing and expressive falsetto singing style on these surviving recordings captured a well-defined grassroots music. The Gennett staff gave Collins the name Jim Foster on the Sears Silvertone label and Big Boy Wood on the Bell label.

In addition to Collins, Gennett recorded a blues guitarist and singer named William Harris from the fabled Mississippi Delta, a pocket of rural black America which exerted an amazing influence on blues music and, later, on rock music. The spontaneous vocal style of the Delta blues, rooted in the oral traditions of isolated black farming communities, was created primarily by illiterate field hands working on the plantations. These blues singers and guitarists earned tips and free drinks at social gatherings in the small black towns of western Mississippi. Hundreds of Delta blues players collectively gave the region its distinct musical style, though only a handful of these musicians were recorded in the 1920s. Harris was among the first.

Harris was allegedly performing at a Sunday picnic when he was recruited for one of Gennett's recording dates in Birmingham in mid-1927. Only one side by Harris was issued from that session, but the following year, Harris visited the Richmond studio and recorded more than a dozen sides, which were issued on the Electrobeam label. Beyond the Gennett recordings, which are extremely rare today, very little is known about Harris. He apparently left the music scene shortly after his brief association with Gennett.[34]

Chicago's black music scene in the 1920s attracted black pianists from the South, who brought with them the influential blues piano technique later dubbed "boogie-woogie." Gennett's Richmond studio recorded several of these innovative pianists, most notably Thomas Dorsey and Charles "Cow Cow" Davenport. Dorsey, who took the stage name "Georgia Tom," migrated from Georgia to the Chicago area during World War I. He worked as a day laborer at a local automotive factory, but supplemented his income with various music jobs, from playing clubs in Gary, Indiana, to plugging his sheet music in black music stores along Chicago's State Street. His composition "Riverside Blues" was recorded by King Oliver. Dorsey also led jazz bands and recorded with blues giant Ma Rainey and slide guitarist Tampa Red.

During Dorsey's first visit to Richmond in 1927, he sang and played piano on eight blues songs for the Electrobeam, Champion, and Supertone labels. He became Smokehouse Charley on Supertone. In late 1930, Dorsey returned to Richmond to record with Scrapper Blackwell, a former bootlegger and blues guitarist from Indianapolis. In the early 1930s, he also recorded on the Champion label in Richmond with Big Bill Broonzy. A former tenant farmer from the Delta region, Broonzy was based in Chicago for several decades and ultimately gained a national audience before his death in 1958.

"Cow Cow" Davenport moved to Chicago in the mid-1920s after working the clubs in Birmingham, Atlanta, and New Orleans. During 1927–28, he recorded for the OKeh, Paramount, and Vocalion labels while also working as a songwriter and arranger. In 1929, the Richmond studio recorded Davenport playing a handful of piano rags and blues, including "Slow Drag Blues" and "Atlanta Rag," for the Electrobeam label. Davenport's piano style was marked by a walking bass in the left hand to complement rich melodies in the right hand. The survival of his rare 1920s discs on several labels has secured Davenport a well-deserved place in the evolution of American rhythm and blues music. By the 1930s, however, he had left the music recording business to operate a store in Cleveland.

Gennett Records made its greatest contribution to blues

history in 1929 by recording, for the Paramount label, the era's most celebrated country blues singers, Charley Patton and Blind Lemon Jefferson. In the 1920s, Paramount recorded numerous black artists at the Marsh Recording Laboratories in Chicago. In 1929, the label ceased recording in Chicago and constructed its own facility in the Grafton, Wisconsin, headquarters of Wisconsin Chair Company. While waiting several months for the completion of this new facility, Paramount contracted with Gennett's Richmond studio, at $40 per side, to record and produce master discs by Paramount musicians. So by happenstance, on June 14, 1929, the Richmond studio produced the first recordings by Patton, the giant among Delta blues players.

Patton's life reads like a blues song: born dirt poor in rural Mississippi in 1891, one of twelve siblings, seven of whom died as children, whipped by his lay preacher father for singing the blues, married eight times, heavy drinker, nearly killed by a jealous husband, preoccupied with death during his life, died in his forties in 1934 under mysterious circumstances. By the turn of the century, Patton's father had moved the family to the Dockery cotton plantation in the Mississippi Delta near the small town of Drew. The plantation, which employed large numbers of black migrant workers, became a meeting place for Delta blues singers. The diminutive Patton, who was light-skinned and had curly hair, became a popular and influential performer on the plantation. He was a raspy-voiced, charismatic singer and a flamboyant guitarist.

After being signed up by Paramount, Patton recorded 50 sides during his career, beginning with the Richmond session in 1929 and ending with a final recording date in New York in 1934. The Richmond studio produced fourteen sides by Patton for Paramount, consisting of spirituals and original blues songs, including "Pony Blues," Patton's signature number and his first release for Paramount. These songs often focused on death and the afterlife, such as "I'm Going Home," "Prayer of Death" (which Paramount issued under the pseudonym Elder

J. J. Hadley), and "Down the Dirt Road Blues." Patton did not play the guitar so much as he attacked it, and his lyrics are at times incomprehensible, though through no fault of the studio engineer. Regardless, Patton's recordings were consistently original and powerful. Today, all of Patton's sides, including those made in Richmond, are available on blues anthologies on both vinyl and compact disc.

Whereas Gennett waxed Patton's first recordings for Paramount, on September 24, 1929, the Richmond studio produced the last records by Blind Lemon Jefferson. Born blind in Texas in 1880, Jefferson scraped by as a blues singer and guitarist, playing for tips at street corners, local picnics, and dances. In the mid-1920s, a Paramount executive found him playing on a Dallas street with a cup on his guitar. Between 1926 and 1929, Jefferson regularly visited Paramount's Chicago studio and became one of the era's best-selling country blues singers. His high-pitched voice, eccentric and competent guitar playing, and amusing lyrics made him a favorite with black record buyers, especially in the South.

At his recording date in Richmond, Jefferson's brief, distinctive guitar solos were cleanly captured on Gennett's electronic equipment. Like Patton, Jefferson had a play list that consisted of spirituals and original blues, which were commentaries on poverty, oppression, and prison life. Women take the traditional blues rap on the songs recorded in Richmond: "Pneumonia Blues" (which tells how Jefferson contracted pneumonia from a woman), "The Cheater's Spell," and "Southern Woman Blues." Less than four months after Gennett waxed a dozen Jefferson sides for Paramount, he died of an apparent heart attack on a Chicago street one wintery night. As with Patton, the circumstances of Jefferson's death are unclear—a situation which fuels the mythology and fascination for the hard-living, down-on-their-luck, pioneer blues players.

The Great Depression of the 1930s decimated the race records market. After the Electrobeam label was discontinued in late 1930, Gennett's budget Champion and Superior labels did issue some blues recordings, though many had been issued previously on Electrobeam. In 1931, the Indianapolis duet of Leroy Carr and Slapper Blackwell recorded several sides in Richmond for Champion. In 1932, Broonzy recorded a handful of songs on Champion, including "Big Bill Blues"; and Roosevelt Sykes, a Chicago-based singer and pianist, recorded on Champion his famous "Highway 61 Blues," which became something of a blues standard in the 1930s.

The production runs in Richmond for some of the Champion releases were amazingly small in the final days. One of the rarest recordings in the history of blues music was issued on Champion just before its demise in December 1934. The disc featured a pianist named Frank James on the numbers "Mistreated Blues" and "Forsaken Blues." Only nineteen copies of the disc were shipped out of the Starr Valley plant.[35] It isn't known whether all the copies sold, and if so, whether James ever received the royalty payments of $.19!

Gennett's Last Hurrah in Jazz

Despite a shrinking presence in the industry, in its final years Gennett Records still managed to produce some fascinating, albeit obscure, jazz records. Gone were the glory days of the early 1920s, when Fred Wiggins and Fred Gennett happened to be in the right place to leap-frog the competition and issue ground-breaking jazz recordings. By the late 1920s, the audience for jazz had grown sizably, and the record companies based in New York held exclusive rights to most of its established players.

As always, however, the door to the Indiana recording studio remained wide open to lesser-known Midwestern jazz players and touring bands eager to experience the novelty of making a record. And, invariably, some major talents ended up at the piano factory. While the young Hoagy Carmichael was the most celebrated beneficiary of the company's liberal recording policy in the late 1920s, other lesser-known musicians on the struggling Electrobeam and Champion labels contribute to our overall understanding of early jazz.

Gennett's continued association with the Melrose brothers, the Chicago jazz music publishers, led to several recordings by the State Street Ramblers. This studio band, organized by Lester Melrose for recording dates, consisted of a small group of Chicago-based, black jazz musicians led by pianist Jimmy Blythe. Between 1927 and 1931, the Electrobeam and Champion labels issued more than two dozen sides by the State Street Ramblers, which were recorded at Gennett's Chicago studio and in Richmond.

In 1915 Blythe moved from his native Kentucky to Chicago, where he was influenced by Clarence Jones, a ragtime pianist, bandleader, and composer. Like Jones, Blythe produced hundreds of piano rolls, a steady source of income for accomplished ragtime and jazz pianists in the 1920s. In 1927, Melrose arranged for Blythe to record piano solos and piano duets with W. E. Burton for the Gennett label. It was the same year that the State Street Ramblers were organized by Lester Melrose, who collected the band's record royalties. With the exception of Blythe, its personnel changed over the course of the seven recording sessions for Gennett. The band included, among others, Burton, cornetist Natty Dominique, clarinetist Johnny Dodds, and drummer Baby Dodds. (The Dodds brothers, of course, were members of King Oliver's historic 1923 band.) The group's last recording session was in Richmond in March 1931, with sides issued on the Champion label as Blythe's Blues Boys. Three months later, the 30-year-old Blythe was brutally stabbed to death.

The State Street Ramblers recorded primarily blues and stomps, such as "Endurance Stomp," "Barrel House Stomp," and "Brown-Skin Mama," in the traditional jazz style that was especially prominent in Chicago. The recordings did not break new ground in jazz and, thus, are largely ignored by historians today. But because of the excellent musicianship and improvisation on these hard-to-find discs, they are prized by collectors of traditional jazz records. The fidelity of these electronically recorded discs is quite good.

For a different reason, collectors actively seek the 1928 Electrobeam recordings of "Spiked Beer" and "Shanghai Honeymoon," done by none other than Lawrence Welk and His Orchestra. Did the affable Welk actually record a dance number about a blatantly illegal beverage? (Decades later, he did, after all, open his TV show with champagne bubbles!) His debut recordings, which contained a touch of jazz rhythm, so excited the young bandleader that he allegedly painted "Gennett Recording Artist" on the side of his touring bus in 1928, even though his association with the company amounted to only a couple of visits to the Richmond studio.

One of the era's great white Dixieland cornetists, the one-armed Joseph "Wingy" Mannone, twice recorded in Richmond in the last days of the Electrobeam label in 1930. A New Orleans native, Mannone had settled in Chicago in the late 1920s. For his Gennett recording date, he organized a five-piece jazz group and recorded six sides under the name Barbeque Joe and His Hot Dogs. In a fitting tribute to Gennett's influential New Orleans Rhythm Kings discs, Mannone recorded "Weary Blues" and "Tin Roof Blues."

By the late 1920s, though, jazz bands were evolving into full-blown dance orchestras, emulating the commercial success of Paul Whiteman's huge ensemble. The industrial cities of the Midwest supported their own established white and black jazz orchestras, many of which recorded for Gennett.

Cincinnati-based Zack Whyte and His Chocolate Beau Brummels was one of the region's better jazz orchestras to visit Richmond. In 1929, Whyte's band recorded six entertaining sides for the Electrobeam label, including the Oliver classic "West End Blues" and Thomas Dorsey's "Tight Like That." These obscure recordings remain favorites with collectors because they feature a nineteen-year-old Melvin "Sy" Oliver, soon to become one of jazz's great cornetists and arrangers.

Arguably, the Electrobeam label's most significant contribution to jazz was in providing the world with the only recordings by the Alphonse Trent Orchestra, the decade's great jazz band from the Southwest. Trent was a well-educated, black pianist from Arkansas, who made his big break in the mid-1920s leading a band at the Adolphus Hotel in Dallas. During its unprecedented eighteen-month stay at the hotel, Trent's ten-piece band played to elaborate musical scores, wore impressive uniforms, and caused a local sensation.

In 1927, the 22-year-old Trent took his orchestra, billed as the 12 Brown-Skinned Marvels, on a tour of the Midwest. They settled for a long stint in downtown Cincinnati at the lavish Greystone Ballroom, the code name assigned to Music Hall's popular Topper Club ballroom when black bands were booked. While based in Cincinnati, Trent's orchestra performed live on the powerful WLW (called "the nation's station") and also took the 70-mile bus trip north to the Richmond studio. On October 11, 1928, the Trent orchestra recorded four brilliant sides for the Electrobeam label, including "Black & Blue Rhapsody" and "Nightmare." The band was loaded with virtuoso soloists, including A. G. Godley, one of the first jazz drum soloists, violinist and singer Stuff Smith, trombonist Snub Mosely, and trumpeter Peanuts Holland. Trent's arrangements could be wildly complex, including rapid modulations. A good example is his very original introduction to the 1930 Gennett recording of the Turner Layton standard "After You've Gone," which has Smith as the lead vocalist. Another recording from Trent's 1930 session in Richmond, "St. James Infirmary," includes lively solos by Smith, Holland, and Mosely.

Several musicians, including Fletcher Henderson, encouraged Trent to set his sights on the more-lucrative New York hotels and ballrooms. Instead, he stayed with the Midwestern cities, apparently fearing that too much exposure would cause his prized soloists to jump ship and sign up with more-recognized, better-paid orchestras. Largely because of this self-imposed exile from New York and Chicago, the band's only records were for Gennett.

Disaster struck in 1930, while Trent's orchestra was playing at the Plantation Club in Cleveland. The club burned down, destroying the orchestra's instruments and arrangements. Over the next three years, Trent's celebrated band slowly dismantled, suffering from poor business management and fewer bookings during the Great Depression. In early 1933, just before the orchestra disbanded, the Trent bus pulled into Starr Valley and recorded "Clementine" and "I Found a New Baby" for the budget Champion label. "Clementine" finds the Trent orchestra still swinging with its typical precision.

In later years, several big bandleaders, such as Jimmie Lunceford, openly praised the Trent orchestra for its impact on the emerging swing era. While Trent's recording career amounted to only a few Gennett sides, the orchestra was a favorite among musicians who heard the live engagements and radio broadcasts. Word within the jazz community has always traveled quickly. Only because the Richmond studio remained accessible to territory bands, however, has the sound of the Trent orchestra been permanently documented. These extremely rare discs by the famous Trent orchestra still surface from time to time on record anthologies of the early jazz bands.

5

Yet the Music Lives On

The Great Depression, sparked by the October 1929 stock market crash, clobbered the record manufacturers, forcing company closings and a rapid restructuring of the survivors. The consolidation within the industry had already begun in the late 1920s, when Columbia Records purchased the OKeh label and Radio Corporation of America (RCA) acquired historic Victor Records. However, the early 1930s brought economic catastrophe, as annual sales of records dropped from 104 million in 1927 to just six million copies in 1932.

The industry ran for cover. Weeks after the stock market crash, an aging Thomas Edison announced that his company would halt the production of Edison phonographs and records in order to give full attention to radios and dictating machines. In 1931, Consolidated Film Industries purchased and streamlined the embattled Brunswick, Vocalion, and Melotone labels. A year later, Wisconsin Chair Company discontinued its Paramount Records subsidiary, the leading race label. During part of the 1930s, Columbia-owned OKeh, once a leading jazz label, was out of circulation. Several obscure discount labels, such as Herwin, simply dropped out of sight.

Gennett Records, at best a marginally profitable venture before the Depression, was swept up in the chaos. In addition to piano manufacturing, Starr Piano had diversified by 1930 into Starr-Freeze refrigerators and industrial refrigeration supplies. Harry Gennett, Starr Piano president, felt that the company should concentrate on these product lines and discontinued the failing Electrobeam record label in December 1930.

Starr Piano's spring-wound phonographs went out of production about the same time, with a little income still derived from the repair of existing machines. In 1932, Starr Piano discontinued Superior records, a short-lived, discount label of no consequence that was pressed from Gennett and Champion masters. The more-established Champion label, a mainstay discount record in the 1920s, hung on by a thread before its demise in December 1934. During its last days, the paper labels on Champion discs changed colors, from red to orange to black to green. The assumption is that the Gennett staff used up the ink remaining in inventory from the defunct Gennett and Sears labels. By the mid-1930s, Gennett's recording studio on Long Island was shut down, and the only new recordings being produced in the Richmond studio were sound effects records, a small sideline business managed by Harry Gennett, Jr.

Recording opportunities dried up in the early 1930s for scores of musicians. In the classical music field, American record labels occasionally pressed records of symphony orchestras from master discs purchased or leased from European record companies. For the American labels, this approach was less expensive than financing their own studio sessions with American orchestras. Hundreds of pop, jazz, blues, and old-time musicians who recorded in the 1920s on a variety of mainstream and discount labels would never enter a recording studio again. As a consequence, certain regional music trends, such as country blues, were much better documented in the 1920s than in the succeeding decade.

The historic music preserved on the Gennett label in the 1920s easily outlived the company. By the early 1930s, hard-to-find Gennett discs of musical importance, especially the acoustic jazz recordings, were hoarded by enthusiastic collectors in the United States and Europe. "If a Yale man and a Princeton man entered a junk shop, there was no danger of collision," wrote music reviewer Stephen Smith in 1939. "The Yale man would almost invariably collect Ellingtonia and a smattering of Fletcher Henderson, and the Princetonian would burrow through the dust for the Red Heads, Bix, especially Bix, and Roppolo on Gennett Records. One of the Princeton gang felt that the Wolverine Gennetts were so rare and valuable that he kept each one packed in a box of cotton batting."[1]

In 1935, hundreds of original metal masters from the Electrobeam and Champion era, which were gathering dust in a warehouse in Starr Valley, were reissued on a new Champion label, now operated by American Decca Records. American Decca Records was the brainchild of Jack Kapp, a colorful entrepreneur who started in the record business in 1913 as a fourteen-year-old shipping clerk in Columbia's Chicago office. He soon moved up the industry ladder, as a talent scout, salesman, distributor, and, finally, as an executive with Brunswick. By 1934, the American record industry was primarily under the control of two giant holding companies, RCA and Consolidated Film Industries, with the average retail price for a record at $.75. Despite the difficult economic environment, Kapp was convinced that record buyers would welcome a new discount record label as long as it featured established performers.

When Brunswick did not embrace his proposal for a new label, Kapp left the company in 1934 and negotiated with Decca Record Company Ltd. of England. The result was a new Decca subsidiary in America under Kapp's leadership. His new $.35 Decca record was hardly a novel idea, but Kapp used his connections from the years at Brunswick to sign up many of the era's most popular entertainers on radio and records, such as Bing Crosby, Ted Lewis, the Dorsey Brothers, Ethel Waters, and the Mills Brothers. (The Mills Brothers, as regulars on WLW radio in Cincinnati in the late 1920s, had tried unsuccessfully to land a record contract with Gennett Records.)

Since Kapp was starting from scratch, he needed to expand his record line as quickly as possible. He accomplished this objective by acquiring, at bargain rates, the rights to old master discs of failed record companies. Kapp sent his treasurer, Milt Rackmil, to Indiana to negotiate a lease on one of the Starr buildings and equipment, as well as the rights to both the Champion label name and the master discs in the Starr Piano warehouse. Decca officials picked through the stacks of masters pressed on the Gennett Electrobeam and Champion labels, uncovering sides by Gene Autry, Windy Mannone, Doc Roberts, Asa Martin, Bradley Kincaid, Uncle Dave Macon, and others. In late 1935, Decca unveiled its new subsidiary Champion label, drawing from hundreds of old masters in Starr Valley, as well as masters from other defunct companies, and issued popular (on the 40,000 series), old-time (45,000 series) and race (50,000 series) recordings.

Kapp also arranged to have Starr masters issued on budget labels produced by Compo Company Ltd. in Canada. When the Montgomery Ward discount record catalog contracted with Decca to supply recordings in 1936, numerous Electrobeam and Champion masters were again reissued, including several sides by Autry, who was skyrocketing to stardom.

By the mid-1930s, the hot, small-group jazz of the early 1920s had become enormously popular in England. In 1936, Kapp assisted the Brunswick organization by producing English Brunswick's *Classic Swing Album,* which contained some of Gennett's historic 1922–24 recordings by King Oliver, the Wolverines, and the New Orleans Rhythm Kings. The Gennett sides in the Brunswick album were of poor fidelity, having been dubbed from worn, scratched, and even cracked Gennett shellac discs. It is not clear why Kapp did not have access to the original metal masters of these Gennett jazz discs, which were still stored in Starr Valley at the time and would have produced a higher-quality reissued product.

Also, it is uncertain whether Starr Piano was properly compensated for the many reissue recordings that were pressed by Decca and others from the Gennett masters and Gennett shellac discs. In the 1940s the Gennett family made Decca stop reissuing original Gennett and Champion recordings, alleging that Starr Piano had been short-changed on the deal for years. By then, however, the dubbing of original 78-rpm jazz discs for inclusion in new record anthologies was fairly widespread, as traditional jazz underwent a major revival in the United States and Europe.

For example, in 1939, the Commodore Music Shop in New York used shellac copies of Gennett's King Oliver sides for its reissue series on the United Hot Clubs of America label. Other labels continued to reissue new discs by dubbing from the old Gennett jazz recordings. The practice contributed significantly to the growing stature of these historic discs, while the Gennett family was no richer for it.

The Gennetts, however, always knew one sure way to earn cold cash from the metal plates stored in Starr Valley. At one point in the 1930s, Fred Wiggins had thousands of them pulled from a storage building and loaded into railroad cars along Starr Piano's secondary railroad line, where they were hauled away and sold for scrap.

"You have to remember, times were hard at Starr Piano, and the company may have needed cash to meet payroll," said Ryland Jones, an employee on the work detail that day. "We spent most of the day hauling out these metal discs. They were sold for the copper they contained. The talk has always been that those metal parts would be worth a million bucks today, though I couldn't tell you what recordings were there. I remember Fred Wiggins being there, because he was Fred Gennett's man in charge of Gennett Records. After that day, I don't think he ever looked back on the recording end of things again."[2]

The Noisemaker: Harry Gennett, Jr., and His Sound Effects Records

The men of the Gennett family had distinct personalities. The patriarch, Henry Gennett, was the demanding, hard-driving deal maker behind the rise of Starr Piano. Harry, his eldest son, who succeeded his father as company president in 1922, was full of charm, a favorite of his mother, and popular with the German craftsmen in the piano factory. Clarence, the company treasurer, was a polished socialite, the family's walking coat of arms. Fred, the youngest son and the company secretary, was the dreamer, an eternal optimist, and the creative force behind Gennett Records.

Yet in a family of colorful men, the short, chain-smoking Harry Gennett, Jr., was the most eccentric Gennett in the family record company. During the 1930s, with activity in the Richmond studio dwindling, Harry, Jr., found a way to keep producing new releases. He loaded up the Gennett recording truck and roamed the country, recording bullfrogs, rare birds, hog-calling contests, machine guns, crashing cars, people walking on ice, and airplanes. Even though Starr Piano formally dropped out of the music recording business in 1934, Harry, Jr., and his band of noisemakers had a blast during the Depression years by creating sound effects records on special Gennett and Speedy Q labels.

The market for sound effects records developed in the 1920s when movie theatre operators synchronized these specialized discs with silent films. Later, radio stations used them to produce live dramas and commercials. By the early 1930s, however, the motion picture industry recorded sound straight onto film. This development, combined with the general business downturn from the Depression, forced many record labels to abandon sound effects recording. Yet Harry Gennett, Sr., allowed his son to keep Starr Piano in this business in the 1930s and beyond, with a large catalog of recorded sounds that were sold by mail to radio stations and film companies.

Gennett's sound effects business was actually inspired in 1928 by the trains thundering along the rim of the Whitewater gorge, which disturbed many a session down in the recording shed. Gennett staffers hauled microphones and electric cable up the steep side of the gorge and placed the microphones at various distances along the railroad tracks. As the trains passed, the sound engineer faded from one microphone into another, producing the continuous sound of locomotives. The trains heard on some of the early radio programs were derived from one of Gennett's first sound effects records.

The Gennett sound effects catalog grew substantially in the early 1930s after Harry, Jr., became actively involved. During and immediately after his high school years, he took various odd jobs around Starr Piano, as his father insisted that he learn the family business from the bottom up. But like his uncle Fred, Harry, Jr., was fascinated with recording technology and soon gravitated to the recording studio. At night, he completed correspondence courses in radio, engineering, and electronics.

After electronic equipment was installed at the Richmond studio in 1927, Harry, Jr., now 21, became one of the staff engineers and built a large amplifier for use in recording sessions. Two years later, he headed for Hollywood and worked for a brief period as a record and sound mixer for several movie productions, including Paul Whiteman's *The King of Jazz*. For reasons unknown, Harry, Jr., was back in Indiana by 1930, working in Starr Piano's Richmond retail store at 10th and Main streets. It was a huge change from Hollywood, and selling pianos and freezers was not exactly his calling. He returned to the struggling Gennett studio. With the Electrobeam label closed and the budget Champion label barely breathing, Harry, Jr., concentrated on Gennett's sound effects records, which had a small but established customer base.

In the early 1930s, he formed a team of hand-picked Starr Piano employees, including Joe Geier, Robert Conner, and Ryland Jones, to assist in the endless search for marketable noises for a sound effects catalog that ultimately listed 375 different recordings. When Jones worked as a young man in Starr Piano's lumber yard, he was dazzled by the 1929 Gennett sound truck that Harry, Jr., and Geier used to record sound effects on location. Jones made a point to get acquainted with them, and he soon joined the sound crew.

"I was just a dumb kid when I started at Starr Piano, and Harry would tell me he was going to Africa and would take me with him," Jones said. "They were pulling my leg, but as time went on, I really learned some tricks about recording from those guys. Harry was a real prince and everybody loved him. He was a real character. I think he probably drove his father crazy. We'd go out on the road and have a pretty good time at the company's expense while coming up with these sound effects records. There was always a lot you could do on the road, you know. I didn't make any money working for the Gennetts, but I sure had a ball when Harry was around."[3]

Most Gennett sound effects records originated from authentic sources. The record of a traffic jam, for example, was produced in Los Angeles before the age of eight-lane highways. Several animal sounds were recorded at the Cincinnati Zoo, where officials demanded that Harry, Jr., and Conner sleep in the recording truck to avoid being accidentally shot by zoo guards. The zoo also warned that giraffes might mistake the electrical wires for snakes and have a conniption.[4] Harry, Jr., recorded a noisy rooster on a relative's farm near Richmond and billed him as "The World's Best-Known Rooster." He spent several muggy nights on Lake Wehi, near East Germantown, Indiana, recording croaking frogs. His recording of a low-pitched voice declaring "Beeeeee Ooooooo!" [B.O.], used for a Lifebuoy Soap commercial on the radio, was produced in the Los Angeles harbor with a fog horn. He staged a car crash for a recording by driving a beat-up old automobile with loose fenders into a heavy truck.

Harry, Jr., recorded steamboats along the Ohio River in Cincinnati. He also drove to Arizona to record the Hopi Indians, in a repeat of the unusual recording session organized by his uncle Fred back in 1926. He played sirens and rang bells in Starr Valley to create more recorded sounds, incurring the wrath of the factory's piano tuners. Jones, a volunteer deputy sheriff, borrowed a machine gun for use on a record. The most popular Gennett sound effects record was possibly No.

1008–B, "Automobile Continuously Running." Jones remembered orders for that recording arriving almost daily.

Young Harry occasionally invited his wife, Florence, to help in the search for unusual sounds. In 1936, she joined him on a cross-country trek to record passenger trains. In Central City, Nebraska, they attracted the town marshal. "We set our alarm clock to get up at the right times to record these trains and tried to get a little shut-eye in between," recalled Florence Gennett. "We'd go to this little beanery during the night to get lemonade. The town marshal followed us around the entire evening. He followed us back to the motel. He got the motel manager up, because he thought we were very suspicious characters. The manager told him what we were doing, and he left. The manager told us about it the next day and said that, if he hadn't told the marshal about it, we would probably have been arrested. We laughed about that one."[5]

The Gennett noisemakers also created sound effects through trickery or by accident. The recording of an alley cat was actually a human voice. Several uninhibited Starr Piano employees helped create the sound of a medieval battle. Recording gun blasts at slow speed made convincing thunderstorms, while combining a human whistle with a gun blast at slow speed produced the sound of a bomb.

One night when young Harry and Conner were recording crickets and other outdoor noises on a country road near Richmond, a sheriff's deputy drove by and fired a shot in the air. They figured that the deputy recognized the Gennett sound truck and was trying to pull a prank. But just the opposite resulted: the blast of the deputy's revolver was recorded and pressed into a record. Harry, Jr., and Conner tried to record a controlled fire in an old building next to the Richmond studio. The flames were nearly out of control when Conner pulled a water hose into the building before a wall came down.

In late 1935, young Harry and his wife moved to Los Angeles. He worked in the accounting department of Starr Piano's Pacific Division and occasionally produced special sound effects for the radio networks. He also sent master recordings of sound effects back to Richmond for inclusion in the sound effects catalog, now sold on the Speedy Q label. At Starr Piano in the early 1940s, Jones continued to send supplements of the company's latest sound effects records to a long list of radio stations.

Harry, Jr., and Florence returned to Richmond in the mid-1940s. He was vice president of Starr Piano when it was sold in 1952. He then became a sales engineer for a Richmond furniture plant. Demand for sound effects records had evaporated, but occasional mail orders would trickle in, and he would fill them from his home. He died in 1957 at age 51, and even after that date his wife received a few requests for the old recordings.

In 1961, the British Broadcasting Company contacted Florence Gennett, requesting sounds of certain birds. The story in the local newspaper included a campy photo of Florence and her two daughters holding a sound effects catalog.[6] Florence kindly taped her late husband's original discs for the BBC. Harry, Jr., had recorded the birds thirty years earlier, during one of his notorious recording expeditions into the Indiana countryside.

The Final Accounting

A bitter business breakup within the Gennett family came on the heels of the demise of Gennett Records. Like other durable goods manufacturers, Starr Piano was dealt a severe blow by the Depression. The company had aggressively distributed pianos on consignment to dealers, who asked very small down payments from their customers. When unemployment rates rose in the early 1930s, many consumers stopped paying the installments on their pianos. Starr Piano was stuck with enormous quantities of unpaid merchandise all over the country and no way to recoup its losses. The steep business slide fueled the tension that had been building between the five owners: Henry Gennett's widow, Alice; her sons, Harry, Clarence, and Fred; and her daughter, Rose Gennett Martin.

The three sons managed the company's day-to-day operations after Henry Gennett's death, but they discussed major decisions with Alice, who was a board director. As losses mounted in the early 1930s, daughter Rose became more immersed in the troubled family business. Also a company director, Rose had been largely inactive in Starr Piano before 1930. Now, she and her husband, Robert Martin, were concerned that her assets in Starr Piano might be in jeopardy.

In the mid-1930s, the Martins and Alice Gennett moved to Los Angeles and assumed control of Starr Piano's Pacific Division, headquarters for the company's distribution network in the West. With the participation of her nephew Harry, Jr., Rose hired an accounting firm to explore the Pacific Division's books. Florence Gennett recalled the alarming audit of the division's sales accounts with the stores in the Pacific Northwest: "We found instances of them having shipped carload after carload of pianos up there on consignment," she said. "Some of those dealers had sold baby grand pianos to farmers with $10 down. We tried to check the collateral on some of those accounts, and naturally there wasn't any. The losses in the Pacific Northwest alone were just tremendous."[7]

Meanwhile, back in Starr Valley, disagreements among the three Gennett brothers intensified. Ryland Jones witnessed several embarrassing shouting matches between Harry and Fred in front of employees in the Starr administration building.[8] Feuds between the Gennetts made employees fearful of showing more loyalty to one brother than another. "It was actually a close family at one time," said Henry Martin, son of Rose Gennett Martin. "But with the Depression, as the family fortune was being lost, everyone started pointing fingers. Things were not the same after that."[9]

In 1937, with no agreement on the future direction of Starr Piano, the five tense owners sat down with a lawyer in

Richmond and split up the company's diversified holdings by breaking Henry Gennett's will. It was not a congenial gathering. "My dad [Fred] asked me to join the meeting," said Richard Gennett. "After everyone sat down, it was suggested that grandmother [Alice] should have the first pick of what she wanted. So she took a building down in Nashville, Tennessee. I was sitting there keeping my mouth shut for once, until my aunt Rose asked Grandmother to put the building in her name. Well, I said 'Whoops!' and laughed like hell. The lawyer stopped the proceedings and told my dad that I had to leave. My dad refused. They were all individualists in that room."[10]

When the dust settled, Harry, Alice, and Rose controlled the piano operations and the Pacific Division. Harry continued to run the Richmond factory; Alice and the Martins operated the Pacific Division. Fred and Clarence shared one-third of the piano company between them, but they were removed from daily management. The company's remaining assets were divided between the owners and their children; Clarence assumed large real estate holdings, and Fred acquired refrigeration supply assets. Soon after, with Alice and Rose living in California, the splendid family mansion that Henry Gennett had built on Main Street was sold, and some of the proceeds were used to pay off a business debt.

Fred's departure from Starr Piano's daily operations was only one of several personal setbacks during the Depression. In 1933, he and his wife, Hazel, lost their first child, seventeen-year-old Fred, Jr., in an automobile accident. Four years later, Fred, at age 51, was no longer an integral part of Starr Piano. For years, he had been the vision behind Gennett Records, an unlikely pioneering label that contributed significantly to American recorded music. However, to the Gennett family, the record division was strictly a sideline of the piano company and was judged solely on its commercial viability. The Depression finally killed it. "Dad never really got over being out of the piano business," said Richard Gennett. "Grandmother [Alice] and Rose were smart cookies, and they could make money like the old man [Henry Gennett]. But Dad felt they teamed against him."[11]

Fred, however, was far from destitute and never short on ideas. With guidance from his son Richard, Fred established a small company on Main Street, a short walk up the hill from Starr Valley. The company started producing metal meat cases, ice cabinets, and other stainless steel products. Fred Wiggins, the old operations manager at Gennett Records, joined his life-long friend in the new company, which was eventually named Gennett & Sons. For decades, the company produced and sold stainless steel hospital equipment, plumbing and heating supplies, and paints.

In the 1940s, Starr Piano, under Harry's control, produced low-budget pianos, radio cabinets, and caskets. Piano manufacturing was always Harry's first love. By now, however, the company's stature in the piano industry, as well as its place in the Richmond business community, had faded substantially.

During the decade, Starr Piano continued to lease record-pressing and shipping facilities in Starr Valley to Decca Records. Another Gennett record label actually reappeared briefly during World War II, under the ownership of New York promoter and producer Joe Davis. In 1944, he produced records on the Gennett, Beacon, and Joe Davis labels, many of which were pressed in Starr Valley. These recordings were primarily forgettable dance and pop releases, in addition to party songs with raunchy lyrics.

In August 1948, Fred Wiggins, who lived alone on Richmond's west side, was visiting friends at the Elks City Club downtown when he died of a heart attack. He was 67. The obituary in the local newspaper noted his long service to Starr Piano, including his term as manager of the Chicago store, but made no reference to his role at Gennett Records. "He knew a lot of people in the music business, but he never talked much about the recordings in Richmond after it all ended," said Richard Gennett. "He was kind of funny that way. He was sure loyal to my dad."[12]

A few months later, on January 20, 1949, the temporary layoff of some Starr Piano employees hit the local newspaper. Despite its reputation for meager salaries, Starr Piano rarely fired anyone. The company had been profitable in the 1940s, but trouble was clearly ahead. For one, the quality of Starr keyboards was now a far cry from the durable upright pianos produced in Starr Valley decades before. "Harry [Gennett, Sr.] hired me as a piano tuner around then," said Sam Meier. "Since I was under the legal working age, he took me down to the courthouse to get a special work permit. One of the first things Harry told me was, if I could tune a Starr piano, I could tune anything. Harry was great, but I can't say that about the pianos we were putting out."[13] Piano manufacturing was a labor-intensive business, and labor costs were rising in the late 1940s. Finally, Harry, Sr., the family member most committed to piano manufacturing and most hesitant to diversify the company into other areas, was in his 70s and in failing health.

The early 1950s were tumultuous years for the Gennetts. In 1951, rumors about Starr Piano's future circulated in the press. Clarence Gennett, who returned to Starr Piano in his older brother's absence, quietly negotiated a sale. In early 1952, just weeks after Alice Gennett, 92, died of pneumonia in California, one of Richmond's oldest companies was sold to the J. Solotkin Co. of Indianapolis, which dealt in scrap metals and paper salvage. At the time, Starr Piano had owned 450,000 square feet of floor space in Starr Valley, with 165,000 square feet leased to Decca Records.

The new owners intimated that piano manufacturing might resume one day in Starr Valley, but it was already too late. Several months passed as the sprawling industrial complex stood silent, except for the buildings operated by Decca. In July 1952, the Solotkin Co. announced that Starr Piano assets would be sold at auction.

On a warm summer afternoon, some retired Starr Piano employees gathered in Starr Valley to watch the auctioneer, standing on a push-truck, sell off lumber, office supplies and furniture, and large pieces of machinery. Among the crowd was a German craftsman named William Kaeuper. He and his brother, Fred, between them, had a combined 100 years of employment at Starr Piano. "Kind of a funny feeling to watch it go," Kaeuper told a local reporter as equipment was being hauled off.[14]

A month after the auction, an ailing Harry Gennett made a rare public appearance at a birthday party for a veteran Starr Piano employee. Old stories abounded as it was revealed that the years of service by Starr workers at the celebration totaled 605. On November 5, 1952, Harry died at age 75. A few months later, Harry, Jr., sued his sisters, claiming that his father was of unsound mind when he signed his will. After the suit was tossed out of court, Harry, Jr., then joined his sisters in contesting the attorney's fees for settling their father's estate. This time, he was on the winning side.

On the other hand, as the elder Harry Gennett was near death, brothers Clarence and Fred never abandoned the idea of manufacturing pianos. They established the Richmond Piano Company with a couple of employees in late 1952, with plans to assemble pianos from pre-fabricated parts in the back rooms of the former Starr retail store. On January 14, 1953, however, Clarence, now 73, suffered a heart attack while walking to his office at Gennett Realty. He managed to reach the office and call for help, but he died later that day in the hospital. Richmond Piano Company never got off the ground.

When Starr Piano facilities were being cleared out in late 1952, the Solotkin Co. asked Harry, Jr., to assist. As part of the deal, they gave him the recording ledgers of Gennett Records, which provide a detailed account of the daily recording activity in the Richmond and New York studios during the 1920s and early 1930s. In addition, he obtained stacks of metal masters, mothers, and stampers that had somehow escaped the scrap pile over the years, and were tucked away in one of the old buildings. Harry, Jr., stored these metal plates in his basement, along with the metal plates from his many sound effects records. Because he and his family planned to move again to California, he put the whole collection up for sale.

In early 1953, John Steiner, a Milwaukee chemist and record entrepreneur, and Bill Grauer, operator of Riverside Records in New York, traveled to Richmond to bid separately on the large assemblage of metal plates. "Harry really didn't know what all was there, though most of the metal parts were sound effects," said Steiner. "He did comb through and show me a mother disc of one of the famous King Oliver recordings. There may have been other prized metal parts, I don't know."[15]

However, Grauer outbid Steiner and purchased the collection for about $2,000. In May 1953, Harry, Jr., shipped him 24 crates of metal plates, four cartons of filing cards, and two cartons of original Gennett phonograph records. "We had the masters of what were left of these old Gennett jazz things," said Florence Gennett. "Nobody had any interest in them, then. We were going to California. We didn't know what to do with it all."[16] Two weeks after Harry, Jr., sold the collection, a U.S. Navy officer in Chicago offered him $10,000. "Harry was just sick," Florence said. "And from then on in, until we left for California, we had long distance calls from all over the country. But we just couldn't take them [the metal plates] with us because we didn't know what to do with them. They'd been dormant for so many years."[17]

Grauer sold the metal plates for scrap and reaped a nice profit. Soon afterward, his Riverside Records reissued the classic Gennett recordings by King Oliver, the Wolverines, Jelly Roll Morton, and the New Orleans Rhythm Kings. As with the earlier Brunswick reissues, the sources for the Riverside reissued classics were copies of the Gennett shellac discs, not the original metal plates.

Ever since 1953, fastidious jazz record sleuths have wondered just what Gennett gems may have been in the collection that Harry, Jr., owned, for Gennett's metal plates from the historic jazz sessions of 1922–24 have never been discovered.

Were they sold for scrap in the 1930s? Did Harry, Jr., sell them to Grauer? Were they misplaced or stolen? Henry Gennett Martin remembered seeing Gennett metal plates, including several of the early 1920s jazz classics, locked up in the 1940s in Henry Gennett's old abandoned office in Starr Valley. Others besides the King Oliver metal plate apparently belonged to Grauer. He is alleged to have owned a couple of Wolverines metal plates.

Over the years, vinyl test recordings of Gennett jazz classics by the New Orleans Rhythm Kings and the Wolverines have surfaced; they were obviously pressed in the 1940s straight from original metal plates. Yet the fate of those metal plates may always remain a mystery. Collectors love to fantasize about cleaner reissues of King Oliver, the Wolverines, Jelly Roll Morton, and the New Orleans Rhythm Kings pressed from the lost Gennett metal plates.

That is not likely to happen. Fortunately, though, the Gennett Records ledgers and a Gennett metal master by Cow Cow Davenport were donated to the Rutgers University Institute of Jazz Studies in New Jersey. In addition, MCA Records has possession of numerous metal plates of jazz and old-time music from Electrobeam and Champion sides of the late 1920s and early 1930s.

By the late 1940s, the Gennett family had developed a reputation among the record magazines and collectors for being less than cooperative when questioned about the glory days of Gennett Records. The first comprehensive article about Gennett Records appeared in *The Record Changer* in June 1953. The author, George Kay, managed to interview Fred Gennett and Harry, Jr., who died four years later. Kay doggedly pursued Fred for years with hopes of uncovering minute details about Gennett Records and its subsidiary labels. The Gennett family's view of its own record label never matched the fascination held by the scholars, buffs, and record researchers, however.

From his office at Gennett & Sons in 1960, the 75-year-

old Fred responded to Kay's written requests for more information: "You're asking me for very much more than I would be
willing to undertake. A recollection is a good thing, when it is
understood when you are speaking in that manner, but to give
you actual facts would require access to books and records
which have not been preserved intact, and frankly I lack the
interest to do so."[18] Two years later, Fred again brushed off
Kay, responding in a pointed letter: "I am exhausted trying to
recollect things I do not remember. It is 25 years now since I
left the record business and most of the people are dead who
worked for the company in executive positions."[19]

Fred spent his final years in a quaint country home outside
Richmond. His wife of 51 years, Hazel, had died in 1959. In
early 1964, the local newspaper printed a photograph of Fred,
holding one of the World War I airplane propellers produced
by Starr Piano, for a story about the company's government
contracts. That same year, Fred died at age 79. He never really
retired. At the time of his death, he was president of Gennett
Investment Company, Gennett & Sons, and the Richmond
Travel Bureau. The local obituary characteristically made no
mention of Gennett Records. Most Richmond citizens, even
today, are surprised to learn that old music recordings produced in their city are still valued around the world.

In the 25 years after Starr Piano was shut down, several
buildings in the Starr Valley industrial complex were leased to
various companies, from moving and storage firms to small
manufacturers, as well as to record pressing operations for the
Mercury and Phillips labels. Over time, the Starr Valley industrial park deteriorated, with vandals preying on the abandoned
buildings. The old shed that housed Gennett's historic recording studio stood boarded up for decades, until it gradually col-
lapsed, and was cleared away.

In 1976, the Starr Valley property was bought for $84,000
by Frank Robinson, a local real estate investor. For years,
Richmond had failed to obtain government grants for preservation projects in Starr Valley. But in 1978, Robinson, thinking

that the city might prevail in developing a park or a community center on the property, began demolishing the old buildings. By 1983, only a couple of abandoned structures remained, including a mammoth piano assembly building with a large, fading Gennett Records sign painted on an outside wall, just high enough to avoid the graffiti accumulating below it.

Out in California, Starr Piano's Pacific Division never really died. Over the decades, Rose Gennett Martin and her son, Henry Gennett Martin, developed the division into a successful refrigeration supply distribution company. In 1978 the Martin family renamed the company RSD. It sells refrigeration supplies in several branch stores in California. In 1991, Rose Martin celebrated her 100th birthday. She had driven her own car to work until she was 85 years old.

While Starr Valley was being cleared out in the early 1980s, a local insurance executive, Wayne Vincent, spearheaded a federally funded project to preserve Henry Gennett's mansion on Main Street. For decades, it had been a deteriorating apartment complex, but by the mid-1980s, the mansion was fully restored, placed on the National Register, and converted into office units. In recent years, Richmond citizens have held fund raisers for Starr Piano/Gennett Records preservation projects. So far, none has materialized. However, a Starr Piano and Gennett Records exhibit is prominently displayed in the Wayne County Historical Museum on North A Street.

As for the closed-off, decimated industrial complex in Starr Valley, which Robinson recently sold to the city, music enthusiasts from all over the continent still make pilgrimages to Richmond. They rummage for a souvenir brick near the site of the Gennett studio and have their pictures taken by the fading Gennett Records sign on the condemned piano assembly building, which nearly burned to the ground in 1993.

Over the years, Robinson received requests for bricks and other debris from Starr Valley from music historians as far away as Japan. "One guy came down asking for a window frame from one of the buildings,'' said Robinson. ''When I met him down in the valley, he was playing a cassette tape of some very old jazz in his pickup truck. He said the music had been recorded right there in the valley at the Gennett studio. Imagine that. I'm told they recorded some pretty good jazz down there.''[20]

Appendix: Gennett on Reissue Anthologies

Despite the passing of six decades, a large number of Gennett jazz, blues, and old-time country discs from 1922–34 can be heard on reissue anthologies on compact disc and vinyl long-playing record albums. Because of their significance and rarity, Gennett records have long been a favorite of small specialty labels that hunt down surviving 78-rpm discs and dub them onto CD and LP collections. These reissue compilations attract an enthusiastic, though limited, audience and tend to go in and out of print. Therefore, their availability can be unpredictable.

Gennett's jazz classics from 1922–24 by the New Orleans Rhythm Kings, King Oliver's Creole Jazz Band, the Wolverines, Jelly Roll Morton, and the Red Onion Jazz Babies have been reissued numerous times since the 1950s on such record labels as Riverside, Jazz Classics, Fountain, Herwin, Olympic, Smithsonian, and Milestone, which reissued more than 80 sides of Gennett jazz on several LPs in the 1970s.

In 1992, Milestone repackaged its Gennett jazz classics on CD. Thanks to the noise-reduction technology used in transferring the records onto CD, the sound quality is surprisingly good, considering the poor fidelity inherent in Gennett's acoustic 78-rpm discs and the scarcity of clean original copies. The new Milestone CD reissue series includes the following collections:

The New Orleans Rhythm Kings & Jell Roll Morton (MCD–47020–2). Totaling 28 takes, this CD contains the band's Gennett releases from three recording dates during 1922–23 in Richmond, Indiana, including a July 1923 session with Morton joining the band on piano, considered the first racially mixed recording date in jazz history. From a fidelity standpoint, this collection of landmark recordings has never sounded better.

Louis Armstrong and King Oliver (MCD–47017–2). Though Armstrong gets top billing, the CD contains all thirteen Gennett recordings by King Oliver's Creole Jazz Band made in 1923 in Richmond. The documentation of pure jazz mastery began with these releases, including Armstrong's first recorded cornet solos on "Chimes Blues" and "Froggie Moore." The CD also contains seven sides by the Red Onion Jazz Babies, a pickup band fronted by Armstrong which recorded in 1924 at Gennett's New York studio.

Jelly Roll Morton 1923/24 (MCD–47018–2). Gennett's acoustic recording equipment was cruel to solo pianists. Still, the Richmond studio produced the first significant body of solo jazz piano music with the sixteen Morton releases included here. Among the small group recordings in this collection is the 1926 Gennett release "Mr. Jelly Lord," performed by Jelly Roll Morton's Incomparables.

Bix Beiderbecke and the Chicago Cornets (MCD–47019–2). Drawing exclusively from Gennett sides from 1924–25, this CD contains fifteen sides with Beiderbecke leading the Wolverines in sessions in Gennett's Richmond and New York studios, two sides with Beiderbecke and the Sioux City Six, and two cuts by Bix and His Rhythm Jugglers. Also included are two Wolverines sides, with Jimmy McPartland replacing Beiderbecke, and seven sides by the Bucktown Five, with Muggsy Spanier on cornet.

Gennett jazz recordings by Ladd's Black Aces, Hoagy Carmichael, Lois Deppe with Earl "Fatha" Hines, Doc Cook's Dreamland Orchestra with Freddie Keppard, the Alphonse Trent Orchestra, Zack Whyte, and other, lesser-known artists have appeared on any number of reissue collections.

England's Fountain Records label, for example, once issued an LP called *Indiana Summer,* a compilation of Gennett releases by Indiana bands, such as Hitch's Happy Harmonists, Carmichael's Collegians, and the Emile Seidel Orchestra. Finding these reissue anthologies of 1920s jazz can be a hit-or-miss proposition. A reliable retail outlet is the Jazz Record Mart, 11 W. Grand, Chicago, Illinois 60610, which stocks one of the nation's largest assortments of hard-to-find 1920s jazz anthologies on LP and CD, including many with Gennett tracks.

The blues and old time discs of 1927–34 from Gennett and its subsidiary Champion label appear randomly on reissue collections of rural music. Some of the specialty LP and CD labels in this field include the following:

County Records. Since the 1960s, label owner David Freeman has reissued old-time singing and string music from Gennett and Champion 78-rpm discs, including sides by the Red Fox Chasers and the Da Costa Woltz Southern Broadcasters. Though many County LP reissue compilations are out of print, the company is repackaging many of them on CD. For a free catalog, write to County Records, P. O. Box 191, Floyd, Virginia 24091.

Old Homestead Records. Operated by John Morris, a pharmacist-cum-record-label owner, Old Homestead has issued LP collections of old-time singing from such Gennett artists as Bradley Kincaid, Vernon Dalhart, Frank Welling and John McGhee, Carson Robison, and others. For a free catalog, write to Old Homestead Records, P. O. Box 100, Brighton, Michigan 48116.

Yazoo Records. This label, operated by Rich Nevins, has issued dozens of blues anthologies. Nevins estimates that

twenty percent of Yazoo's classic sides feature Gennett/
Champion artists, including Jaybird Coleman, William
Harris, Bill Broonzy, and Cryin' Sam Collins. The Blind
Lemon Jefferson and Charley Patton compilations include
several sides recorded in Gennett's Richmond studio for
Paramount Records. For a free catalog, write to Yazoo Re-
cords, 37 E. Clinton St., Newton, New Jersey 07860.

Notes

1. A Music Dynasty in Victorian Indiana

1. *History of Wayne County* (Chicago: Inter-State Publishing Co., 1884), p. 69.

2. Henry Clay Fox, *Memoirs of Wayne County and the City of Richmond, Indiana* (Madison, Wis.: Western Historical Association, 1912), p. 158.

3. John MacKenzie Collection, Indiana Historical Society Library, Indianapolis.

4. Craig H. Roell, *The Piano in America* (Chapel Hill: University of North Carolina Press, 1989), p. 32.

5. Interview with Wilson Taggart, 1970, John MacKenzie Collection, Indiana Historical Society Library.

6. Ibid.

7. Personal interview with Henry Gennett Martin, 1991.

8. "Rose Gennett Celebrates 100 Years," Richmond *Palladium-Item,* July 13, 1991.

9. "Starr Piano Company Has an Interesting History," Richmond *Palladium,* September 12, 1913.

10. Starr Piano Company, Amended Articles of Incorporation, 1915, John MacKenzie Collection, Indiana Historical Society Library.

11. Roland Gelatt, *The Fabulous Phonograph* (Philadelphia and New York: J. B. Lippincott Co., 1954), p. 189.

12. *The Federal Reporter,* vol. 263 (St. Paul, Minn.: West Publishing Co., 1920), p. 189.

13. *Federal Reporter,* vol. 281 (1922), p. 60.

14. Ibid.

15. George W. Kay, "Those Fabulous Gennetts! The Life Story of a Remarkable Label," *The Record Changer,* June 1953, p. 8.

16. Personal interview with Marion McKay, 1990.

17. In 1957, jazz researcher Phil Pospychala visited the abandoned Gennett recording studio building in Richmond. He found the old Mohawk rug still hanging on the wall, where it had been since the early 1920s. Florence Gennett told Pospychala the rug came from the home of her father-in-law, Harry Gennett.

18. Interview with Rena Clark, 1970, John MacKenzie Collection, Indiana Historical Society Library.

19. Personal interview with Marion McKay, 1991.

20. Ibid.

21. Personal interview with Bud Dant, 1992.

22. Interview with Wilson Taggart, 1970, Indiana Historial Society Library.

23. According to Richard Gennett, in later years, his father (Fred) knew that many Gennett jazz discs had become historically important. But with no personal interest in jazz, Fred expressed far greater satisfaction from the label's association with Bryan.

24. Interview with Clayton Jackson, 1970, John MacKenzie Collection, Indiana Historical Society Library.

25. Ibid.

26. Interview with Wilson Taggart, 1970, Indiana Historial Society Library.

27. Personal interview with Richard Gennett, 1991.

28. Interview with Clayton Jackson, 1970, Indiana Historical Society Library.

29. Interview with Wilson Taggart, 1970, Indiana Historical Society Library.

30. Ibid.

31. Interview with Harold Soule, 1964, John MacKenzie Collection, Indiana Historical Society Library.

32. Interview with Florence Gennett, 1961, John Mac-Kenzie Collection, Indiana Historical Society Library.

33. Personal interview with Richard Gennett, 1992.

34. Interview with Wilson Taggart, 1970, Indiana Historical Society Library.

35. Roell, *The Piano in America,* p. 200.

2. A New Wind Is Blowing through Chicago

1. Personal interview with Richard Gennett, 1991.

2. Interview with Harold Soule, 1964, Indiana Historical Society Library.

3. Nat Hentoff and Nat Shapiro, *Hear Me Talking to Ya* (New York: Rinehart, 1955), p. 123.

4. Ibid., p. 119.

5. Ibid., p. 121.

6. George W. Kay, "Those Fabulous Gennetts! The Life Story of a Remarkable Label," *The Record Changer,* June 1953, p. 10.

7. Larry Gara, *The Baby Dodds Story* (Los Angeles: Contemporary Press, 1959), p. 69.

8. John Chilton and Max Jones, *The Louis Armstrong Story* (Boston: Little, Brown and Company, 1971), p. 71.

9. Ralph J. Gleason, from his liner notes to the album *Louis Armstrong and King Oliver,* Milestone Records, 1974.

10. Gara, *The Baby Dodds Story,* p. 70.

11. Ibid., p. 48.

12. Alan Lomax, *Mister Jelly Roll: The Fortunes of Jelly Roll Morton, New Orleans Creole and Inventor of Jazz* (New York: Grove Press, 1950), p. 285.

13. Personal interview with James Dapogny, 1983.

3. Jazz Hysteria in the Hoosier State

1. Richard M. Sudhalter and Philip Evans, *Bix: Man and Legend* (London: Quartet Books, 1974), p. 101.

2. Hoagland Carmichael, *Sometimes I Wonder* (New York: Farrar, Straus and Giroux, 1965), p. 112.

3. Hoagland Carmichael, *The Stardust Road* (1946; reprint, Bloomington: Indiana University Press, 1983), p. 25.

4. Carmichael, *Sometimes I Wonder,* p. 46.

5. Carmichael, *The Stardust Road,* p. 46.

6. Carmichael, *Sometimes I Wonder,* p. 134.

7. Charlie Davis, *That Band from Indiana* (Oswego, N.Y.: Mathom Publishing Co., 1982), p. 29.

8. Ibid., p. 30.

9. James Lincoln Collier, *The Making of Jazz* (Boston: Houghton Mifflin, 1978), p. 171.

10. Carmichael, *Sometimes I Wonder,* p. 112.

11. Personal interview with Benny Carter, 1987.

12. Personal interview with Marion McKay, 1991.

13. Ibid.

14. Warren K. Plath, "Is It Bix on Those McKay Gennetts?" *International Association of Jazz Record Collectors Journal,* vol. 8, no. 2 (1975), p. 7.

15. Personal interview with Marion McKay, 1991.

16. Ibid.

17. Ibid.

18. Carmichael, *The Stardust Road,* p. 94.

19. Carmichael, *Sometimes I Wonder,* p. 135.

20. Ibid., p. 140.

21. Ibid., p. 141.

22. Ibid., p. 142.

23. Personal interview with Marion McKay, 1991.

24. Carmichael, *Sometimes I Wonder,* p. 158.

25. Interview with Harold Soule, 1964, Indiana Historical Society Library.

26. Carmichael, *Sometimes I Wonder,* p. 188.

27. Personal interview with Bud Dant, 1992.

28. Ibid.

29. Ibid.

30. Duncan Schiedt, *The Jazz State of Indiana* (Pillsborough, Ind.: published by the author, 1977), p. 85.

31. Personal interview with Bud Dant, 1992.

32. Interview with Joseph Geier, 1970, John MacKenzie Collection, Indiana Historical Society Library.

33. Interview with Florence Gennett, 1961, Indiana Historical Society Library.

34. Interview with Clayton Jackson, 1970, Indiana Historical Society Library.

35. Personal interview with Bud Dant, 1992.

36. Personal interview with Richard Gennett, 1992.

4. Rural Recordings in the Electronic Era

1. "Special Gennett Records to Retail at Fifty Cents," *Talking Machine World,* June 6, 1925.

2. "Gennett Record Sales Take Decided Upward Trend," *Talking Machine World,* December 25, 1925.

3. Interview with Clayton Jackson, 1970, Indiana Historical Society Library.

4. Ibid.

5. Ibid.

6. Ibid.

7. Ibid.

8. Ibid.

9. Personal interview with Jim Lindsay, 1992.

10. "Starr Piano Announces the Electrobeam Gennett Recording Process," *Talking Machine World,* January 15, 1927.

11. "Fred Gennett Believes 1927 Will Bring Vital Changes," *Talking Machine World,* February 15, 1927.

12. Charles K. Wolfe, *Kentucky Country: Folk and Country*

Music of Kentucky (Lexington: University Press of Kentucky, 1984), p. 27.

13. "Gennett Hillbilly Records," *Western Folklore*, July 1971, p. 182.

14. Personal interview with Richard Gennett, 1991.

15. Interview with Joseph Geier, 1970, Indiana Historical Society Library.

16. Ibid.

17. Wolfe's *Kentucky Country: Folk and Country Music of Kentucky*, p. 25, provides a brief biographical sketch of Houchens, based on information from interviews with the Houchens family by folklorist Gus Meade.

18. Letter from Fred Wiggins to Doc Roberts, October 23, 1926. Courtesy of Charles Wolfe.

19. Letter from Wiggins to Roberts, November 22, 1926. Courtesy of Charles Wolfe.

20. Loyal Jones, *Radio's "Kentucky Mountain Boy" Bradley Kincaid* (Berea, Kentucky: Berea College Appalachian Center, 1980), p. 15.

21. Ibid., p. 150. A complete discography of Kincaid's recordings was prepared by Norm Cohen of the John Edwards Memorial Foundation in 1976 and has been reprinted here.

22. Personal interview with James Kincaid, 1992.

23. "Ernest Stoneman," *John Edwards Memorial Foundation Newsletter*, no. 7, University of California, Los Angeles, September 1967.

24. Ibid.

25. Ivan Tribe, *Mountain Jamboree: Country Music in West Virginia* (Lexington: University Press of Kentucky, 1984), p. 29.

26. Interview with Joseph Geier, 1970, Indiana Historical Society Library.

27. Ibid.

28. "Southern Artists to Make Records," *Birmingham News*, July 12, 1927.

29. Interview with Clayton Jackson, 1970, Indiana Historical Society Library.

30. Personal interview with Harry Leavell, 1992.

31. Tom Tsotsi, "Gennett Champion Blues Part 2," *78 Quarterly,* vol. 1 no. 4 (1989), p. 78. Tsotsi, a record collector, surveyed the extremely rare Gennett/Champion blues recordings in a four-part series for the magazine (nos. 3–6).

32. Interview with Mayo Williams, 1970, John MacKenzie Collection, Indiana Historical Society, Library.

33. Advertisement, *Chicago Defender,* May 21, 1927.

34. Gayle Dean Wardlow, "Big Foot William Harris," *78 Quarterly,* vol. 1, no. 3 (1988), p. 47.

35. Kay, "Those Fabulous Gennetts! The Life Story of a Remarkable Label," p. 12. Using Gennett ledgers and other company records, Kay disclosed the production runs for specific Champion and Superior recordings.

5. Yet the Music Lives On

1. Stephen W. Smith, "Hot Collecting," in *Jazzmen,* edited by Frederick Ramsey, Jr., and Charles Edward Smith (New York: Harcourt Brace Jovanovich, 1939), p. 289.

2. Personal interview with Ryland Jones, 1992.

3. Ibid.

4. Bob Corya, "Gennett Recalls a Trip to Zoo to Make Animal Noise Records," Richmond *Palladium-Item,* November 12, 1956.

5. Interview with Florence Gennett, 1961, Indiana Historical Society Library.

6. Eloise Beach, "British Seeking Sound Recordings Made over 30 Years Ago by Gennett Brothers," Richmond *Palladium-Item,* August 10, 1961.

7. Interview with Florence Gennett, 1961, Indiana Historical Society Library.

8. Personal interview with Ryland Jones, 1992.

9. Personal interview with Henry Gennett Martin, 1992.

10. Personal interview with Richard Gennett, 1992.

11. Ibid.

12. Ibid.

13. Personal interview with Sam Meier, 1992.

14. "Starr Piano Auction Draws Mixed Feelings," Richmond *Palladium-Item,* July 31, 1952.

15. Personal interview with John Steiner, 1992.

16. Interview with Florence Gennett, 1961, Indiana Historical Society Library.

17. Ibid.

18. Letter from Fred Gennett to George Kay, May 19, 1960. John MacKenzie Collection, Indiana Historical Society Library.

19. Letter from Gennett to Kay, July 19, 1962. John MacKenzie Collection, Indiana Historical Society Library.

20. Personal interview with Frank Robinson, 1992.

Selected Bibliography

Allen, Walter, and Rust, Brian A. *King Joe Oliver*. London: Sidgwick & Jackson, 1958.

Barlow, William. *Looking up at Down: The Emergence of the Blues Culture*. Philadelphia: Temple University Press, 1989.

Biographical and Genealogical History of Wayne, Fayette, Union, and Franklin Counties, Indiana. Chicago: The Lewis Publishing Company, 1899.

Burton, Thomas G., ed. *Tom Ashley, Sam McGee, Bukka White*. Knoxville: University of Tennessee Press, 1981.

Carmichael, Hoagland. *Sometimes I Wonder*. New York: Farrar, Straus, and Giroux, 1965.

———. *The Stardust Road (1946)*. Reissue, Bloomington: Indiana University Press, 1983.

Chilton, John, and Jones, Max. *The Louis Armstrong Story*. Boston: Little, Brown and Company, 1971.

Collier, James Lincoln. *Louis Armstrong, An American Genius*. New York: Oxford University Press, 1983.

———. *The Making of Jazz*. Boston: Houghton Mifflin, 1978.

Dance, Stanley. *The World of Earl Hines*. New York: Charles Scribner & Sons, 1977.

Dapogny, James. *Jelly Roll Morton: The Collected Piano Music*. Washington: Smithsonian Institution Press, 1982.

Davis, Charlie. *That Band from Indiana*. Oswego, N.Y.: Mathom Publishing Co., 1982.

Dixon, R. M. W., and Godrich, J. *Recording the Blues*. London: Hatch, 1970.

Docks, L. R. *Record Guide.* 3d ed. Florence, Ala.: Books Americana, 1986.

Driggs, Frank, and Lewine, Harris. *Black Beauty, White Heat: A Pictorial History of Classic Jazz 1920–50.* New York: William Morris & Co., 1982.

Ewen, David. *American Songwriters.* New York: H. W. Wilson Co., 1987.

The Federal Reporter. St. Paul, Minn.: West Publishing Co., vol. 263, 1920, and vol. 281, 1922.

Fox, Henry Clay. *Memoirs of Wayne County and the City of Richmond, Indiana.* Madison, Wis.: Western Historical Association, 1912.

Gara, Larry. *The Baby Dodds Story.* Los Angeles: Contemporary Press, 1959.

Gelatt, Roland. *The Fabulous Phonograph.* Philadelphia and New York: J. B. Lippincott Co., 1954.

Godrich, J., and Dixon, R. M. W. *Blues & Gospel Records, 1902–1942.* London: Hatch, 1964.

Harrison, Max; Fox, Charles; and Hacker, Eric. *The Essential Jazz Records, Ragtime to Swing.* London: Mansell Publishing, 1984.

History of Wayne County, Indiana. Chicago: Inter-State Publishing Co., 1884.

Jones, Loyal. *Radio's "Kentucky Mountain Boy" Bradley Kincaid.* Berea, Ky.: Berea College Appalachian Center, 1980.

Kernfeld, Barry, ed. *The New Grove Dictionary of Jazz.* London: Macmillan Press Ltd., 1988.

Lomax, Alan. *Mister Jelly: The Fortunes of Jelly Roll Morton, New Orleans Creole and Inventor of Jazz.* New York: Grove Press, 1950.

Lombardo, Guy, and Altshul, Jack. *Auld Acquaintance.* Garden City, N.Y.: Doubleday & Company, 1975.

Lornell, Kip. *Virginia Blues, Country, and Gospel Records, 1902–1943.* Lexington: University Press of Kentucky, 1989.

Malone, Bill C. *Country Music U.S.A.* Austin: University of Texas Press, 1985.

Malone, Bill C., and McCulloh, Judith, eds. *Stars of Country Music*. Urbana: University of Illinois Press, 1975.

Oliver, Paul. *Blues off the Record*. Tunbridge Wells, England: Baton Press, 1984.

———. *The Story of the Blues*. London: Barrie & Rockcliff, 1969.

Oliver, Paul; Harrison, Max; and Bolcom, William. *The New Grove Gospel, Blues & Jazz*. New York: W. W. Norton & Co., 1986.

Priestley, Brian. *Jazz on Record*. New York: Billboard Books, 1991.

Ramsey, Frederick, Jr., and Smith, Charles Edward, eds. *Jazzmen*. New York: Harcourt Brace Jovanovich, 1939.

Read, Oliver, and Welch, Walter. *From Tin Foil to Stereo*. Indianapolis: H. W. Sams, 1976.

Roell, Craig. *The Piano in America, 1890–1940*. Chapel Hill: University of North Carolina Press, 1989.

Rust, B. A. L. *American Record Label Book*. New Rochelle, N.Y.: Arlington House, 1978.

———. *Jazz Records 1897–1942*. 4th ed. New Rochelle, N.Y.: Arlington House, 1978.

Schiedt, Duncan. *The Jazz State of Indiana*. Pillsborough, Ind.: Published by the author, 1977.

Schuller, Gunther. *Early Jazz*. New York: Oxford University Press, 1968.

Shapiro, Nat, and Hentoff, Nat. *Hear Me Talking to Ya*. New York: Rinehart, 1955.

Sudhalter, Richard M., and Evans, Philip. *Bix: Man and Legend*. London: Quartet Books, 1974.

Tribe, Ivan. *Mountaineer Jamboree*. Lexington: University Press of Kentucky, 1984.

Williams, Martin. *Jazz Masters of New Orleans*. New York: Macmillan Press, 1967.

Wolfe, Charles K. *Kentucky Country: Folk and Country Music of Kentucky*. Lexington: University of Kentucky Press, 1982.

Topical Index

Smith, Bessie, 51, 62, 86, 87, 177
Smith, Clara, 51
Smith, Mamie, 50–51, 177
Smith, Stuff, 190
Smithsonian Institution, 68, 176
Snyder, Frank, 57, 73
Soule, Harold, 41, 46, 131
Spanier, Muggsy, 48, 84
Springfield, Ohio, 1, 166
Starr, Benjamin, 4, 6–7
Starr, Charles, 3
Starr, James, 3–4, 6–7
Starr phonograph, 19–22
Starr Piano: formation of, 3–4; early
    growth, 5–6; acquired by Lumsden
    and Gennett, 6–7; expansion 8–9;
    distribution network, 9; Pacific
    Division, 10; factory in 1915,
    10–11; employee loyalty, 11; local
    presence, 12–13; creates
    phonograph and record division,
    13, 19–22; court battle vs. Victor,
    13–14, 23–27; wartime
    production, 22; peak years, 27,
    43–44; diversification of, 192–193;
    decline of, 201–205; demise of,
    205–206
Starr record label, 20–22
Starr Valley, 4, 5, 7, 152, 206–211
State Street Ramblers, 188
Stitzel, Mel, 57, 84
Stockton Club, 94–95
Stoneman, Ernest, 141, 147,
    167–168
Superior label, 193
Supertone label, 144
Sykes, Roosevelt, 187
Sweatman, Wilbur, 86

Taggart, Wilson, 9–10, 35, 38–40, 43
Taylor, Dennis, 150–151, 157–159

Taylor's Kentucky Boys, 151, 159, 161
Teagarden, Jack, 57, 113
Teschemacher, Frank, 57
Toomey, Welby, 157–158
Trayser, George M., 2
Trayser Piano Company, 3
Trent, Alphonse, 142, 190–191
Trumbauer, Frank, 104, 115, 121,
    128
Tweedy Brothers, 156–157

Underwood, Marion, 159

Valentine, Syd, 146
Vassar, Callie, 51
Victor Talking Machine Company,
    13–14, 17–21, 35, 49, 139, 149,
    151, 192
Voynow, Dick, 95, 122

Wagner, Sol, 78
Welk, Lawrence, 142
Whiteman, Paul, 115, 120, 126,
    128–129
Whitewater River, 2, 4, 7, 8, 28
Whyte, Zack, 189
Wickemeyer, Ezra, 31, 33, 37–38,
    55, 125, 131
Wiggins, Fred, 45–48, 59, 90,
    122–123, 132, 142–144, 152–154,
    158–159, 196, 204
Williams, Clarence, 86–89
Williams, Mayo, 181–182
WLS radio (Chicago), 156, 161–165
Wolfe, Charles 158
Wolfe, Eddie, 133–134
Wolverine Orchestra (Wolverines),
    84, 91–92, 94–99, 101–114,
    122–124, 213–214

Yazoo Records, 215–216

Index of Music

Rick Kennedy

is a media relations manager with the
General Electric Company in Cincinnati. He has
worked as a reporter for the
Richmond Palladium-Item and the *Cincinnati Post*
and is a jazz pianist.